The Theology *of* Paul *in* Three Dimensions

The Theology *of* Paul *in* Three Dimensions

Dogmatics, Experience, Relevance

RICHARD H. BELL

CASCADE *Books* · Eugene, Oregon

THE THEOLOGY OF PAUL IN THREE DIMENSIONS
Dogmatics, Experience, Relevance

Cascade Books
An Imprint of Wipf and Stock Publishers
199 W. 8th Ave., Suite 3
Eugene, OR 97401

www.wipfandstock.com

PAPERBACK ISBN: 978-1-6667-0147-0
HARDCOVER ISBN: 978-1-6667-0148-7
EBOOK ISBN: 978-1-6667-0149-4

Cataloguing-in-Publication data:

Names: Bell, Richard H. [author]

Title: The theology of Paul in three dimensions : dogmatics, experience, relevance / Richard H. Bell.

Description: Eugene, OR: Cascade Books, 2022 | Includes bibliographical references.

Identifiers: ISBN 978-1-6667-0147-0 (paperback) | ISBN 978-1-6667-0148-7 (hardcover) | ISBN 978-1-6667-0149-4 (ebook)

Subjects: LCSH: Paul, the Apostle, Saint | Bible.—Epistles of Paul—Theology | Bible.—Epistles of Paul—Criticism, interpretation, etc. | Bible.—Theology

Classification: BS2651 B45 2022 (paperback) | BS2651 (ebook)

VERSION NUMBER 092722

To my students at the University of Nottingham
who have taken the Theology of Paul

Contents

Preface

FOR OVER THIRTY YEARS I have taught the Theology of Paul at the University of Nottingham. Usually the pattern was to teach this course every other year to a group of second and third year students, looking at themes in Paul's theology and specific texts related to those themes. Every year the course was slightly revised but the pandemic necessitated quite a substantial revision when I taught the course in 2020. The lectures were pre-recorded and I held seminars every week, three face-to-face and one online, where among other things we discussed a text from Paul's letters that related to the lecture theme that week. The pre-recorded lectures turned out to be much denser than live lectures where one would break up the lecture by answering questions and including discussion. In order to go beyond the cerebral dimension of the pre-recorded lectures I included at the end of each lecture a piece of music to give some emotional insight into what we had been studying.[1] This then gave me the idea of publishing a book alongside a website that provides the music and adds what I hope is an extra dimension to the study of the theology of Paul.

My concern in this work is, as the subtitle suggests, to look at Paul in terms of three dimensions: dogmatics, experience, and relevance. In teaching the Theology of Paul course I was at the same time giving my students an overview of "Christian dogmatics," covering themes such as sin, salvation, atonement, Christology, and eschatology, and relating these themes to debates in systematic theology. But I also related all this to Christian experience and to the relevance of Paul's theology not only for the church but also for wider society. Further, at certain points I considered it my social

---

1. In pre-covid times I often played some music just before the lecture started; I felt I was doing my bit to compensate for the lack classical music teaching in schools in the UK.

responsibility to ask whether Paul was right on certain issues and to view
the module not simply as a descriptive exercise but one of truth-seeking.[2]

In relating Paul's theology to issues facing churches, many of my examples come from the evangelical tradition. This is simply so because that is
the tradition with which I am most familiar. It may appear at some points as
though I am "getting at evangelicals." If I had come from the Catholic or Orthodox tradition I am sure what I would have written would look as though
I was "getting at Catholic/Orthodox Christians." Although I am at times
critical of the evangelical tradition, my roots from the age of twenty (when
I was converted to the Christian faith) go back to the Christian Union at
University College London and All Souls Langham Place, London. I am
indebted to the many fine members of the Christian Union for introducing
me to the Christian faith and to the ministry I received at All Souls and
later from St. Aldates and St. Ebbe's in Oxford. Although I would not call
myself an "evangelical" now I am indebted to what I have learned from that
tradition in terms of knowing and understanding the Bible. And as one of
my teachers in Tübingen put it, evangelicalism is not a bad place to start!

In the lectures on Paul I made it clear (as I do in all my lectures) where
I stand, for only by doing so can my utterances be fully understood. So for
the benefit of my readers I can say that I am a theologian and not primarily a
New Testament scholar (although I am that also). I am Protestant, Anglican
(and ordained), and very much influenced by the Lutheran tradition. So if
I were to use a label I would now call myself "Lutheran."[3] I have experience
of the Charismatic movement and this has helped give me some insight
into how the earliest Christians were overwhelmed by the reality of Christ
through the Holy Spirit.

One characteristic of this book is that I do appeal to many theologians from the German-speaking world.[4] One reason I am so attracted to
this tradition is because of the time I spent in Germany from 1986 to 1990.
There I deepened my knowledge of Luther and the teaching demonstrated
time and again that theology at it best is both confessional and "scientific"
("wissenschaftlich"). Most of my teachers in Tübingen had not only studied for a long time but also had experience of working in a church at least
as a "curate" ("Vikar"); their work of preaching and pastoral care clearly

2. Any of my former students reading this book will discover a number of addi-
tions to what they heard in the lectures. In particular, I have a greater freedom in this
published book to be more outspoken on church and political matters.

3. Using the German terms I am "Evangelisch" ("Protestant") rather than "Evange-
likal" ("evangelical").

4. I do not assume a knowledge of the German language. I have, however, referenced some German works for those who may have German.

enriched their teaching and research. I hope that my own pastoral experience, working as a curate in Edware Parish Church before my move to Germany, has also enriched my theological understanding.

As mentioned above, every lecture in the course came with a seminar, which included discussing a text from Paul's letters. These texts are given as "further reading" at the end of each chapter. Also at the very end of the book I have included some secondary literature that I have found helpful and that I recommend.

Also as noted above, this book is accompanied by a website (richardhbell.co.uk) that includes the music illustrating the various themes of the book and is meant to enhance the dimension of "experience." Just as it may be noticed that the book gets slightly more demanding as the work progresses, so roughly speaking the music begins with an easy piece (from Johann Strauss, *Die Fledermaus* [*The Bat*]) to works that may require a little more concentration. A range of composers are included, some of whom are not Christian or may be considered to have a somewhat unorthodox faith. Nevertheless, I think the more profound works included all disclose something of the things of God and add an "experiential" dimension in coming to understand the Christian faith. Schleiermacher's *Celebration of Christmas* rightly emphasizes the need for both theological arguments about the incarnation and the need for music, celebration, and child-like spontaneity. As Gerrish summarizes it: "theological reflection, however necessary, makes sense only if it is framed with a life of spontaneous piety, since, when all is said and done, theology is nothing other than honest, persistent, critical reflection upon piety."[5]

5. Gerrish, *Prince of the Church*, 18.

Acknowledgments

THIS BOOK IS DEDICATED to my students over the last thirty years who have taken the Theology of Paul course. I thank them for their enthusiasm for Paul's theology, their questioning of my views, and their sense of fun. I also want to make a special mention of those taking Theology of Paul in the 2020–21 academic year, that year when the course had to be adapted to the conditions of the pandemic. They were model students and when we did meet in person they wore masks, kept to physical distancing, wiped down surfaces, and said "thank you" after every single seminar. If all young people were like these students the world's future would be in safe and capable hands.

I am also especially grateful to those who read through the whole of the earlier version of the book: Robert Morgan, Chiara Bertoglio, and Hannah Maton. I also thank those who gave advice on particular matters: Edward van d'Slot, David Bagchi, Sara Parks, and Trevor Burnard.

Finally I thank the staff of Wipf & Stock, especially Robin Parry, for their customary efficiency in bringing the book to publication.

Abbreviations

ALL TRANSLATIONS, UNLESS INDICATED, are from the New Revised Standard Version (NRSV).

AA   *Kant's gesammelte Werke (Akademie-Ausgabe).* 29 vols. Berlin: Reimer (later de Gruyter), 1900–1997.

ANF   A. Roberts, J. Donaldson and A. C. Coxe, eds., *Ante-Nicene Fathers.* 10 vols. Reprint, Peabody, MA: Hendrickson, 1994.

BSELK   *Die Bekenntnisschriften der evangelisch-lutherischen Kirche.* 10th ed. Göttingen: Vandenhoeck & Ruprecht, 1986.

DJBP   Jacob Neusner and William Scott Green, eds., *Dictionary of Judaism in the Biblical Period.* 2 vols. London: Simon & Schuster, 1996.

EKL   Erwin Fahlbusch et al., eds., *Evangelisches Kirchenlexikon: Internationale theologische Enzyklopädie.* 5 vols. Göttingen: Vandenhoeck & Ruprecht, 1986–97.

FSSW   Gerhard Fricke and Herbert G. Göpfert, eds., *Friedrich Schiller: Sämtliche Werke.* 5 vols. Darmstadt: Wissenschaftliche Buchgesellschaft, 1980.

HchE   Anselm Hertz, Wilhelm Korff, Trutz Rendtorff, and Hermann Ringeling, eds., *Handbuch der christlichen Ethik.* 3 vols. Freiburg/Basel/Wien, 1993.

LW   J. Pelikan and H. T. Lehmann, eds., *Luther's Works.* 55 vols. Philadelphia: Fortress, 1943–86.

NIDNTT   C. Brown, ed., *The New International Dictionary of New Testament Theology.* 3 vols. Exeter, UK: Paternoster, 1975–78

NPNF1   P. Schaff, ed., *Nicene and Post-Nicene Fathers: First Series.* 14 vols. Reprint, Peabody, MA: Hendrickson, 1994.

NPNF2   P. Schaff and H. Wace, eds., *Nicene and Post-Nicene Fathers: Second Series*. 14 vols. Reprint, Peabody, MA: Hendrickson, 1994.

NRSV   *The Holy Bible: New Revised Standard Version*. Oxford: Oxford University Press, 1995.

OCD³   Hornblower, Simon, and Antony Spawforth, eds., *The Oxford Classical Dictionary*. 3rd ed. Oxford: Oxford University Press, 1996.

OTP   James H. Charlesworth, ed., *The Old Testament Pseudepigrapha*. 2 vols. London: Darton, Longman & Todd, 1983–85

RGG³   K. Galling, ed., *Die Religion in Geschichte und Gegenwart: Handwörterbuch für Theologie und Religionswissenschaft*. 7 vols. 3rd ed. Tübingen: J.C.B. Mohr (Paul Siebeck), 1959.

SWNA   Petersen, Julius, et al., eds., *Schillers Werke: Nationalausgabe*. 43 vols. Weimar: Böhlaus, 1943ff.

THAT   E. Jenni and C. Westermann, eds., *Theologisches Handwörterbuch zum Alten Testament*. 2 vols. Munich: Kaiser Verlag/ Zürich: Theologischer Verlag, 1971–76.

ThWNT   G. Kittel and G. Friedrich, eds., *Theologisches Wörterbuch zum Neuen Testament*. 10 vols. Stuttgart: Kohlhammer, 1933–78.

TRE   G. Krause and G. Müller, eds., *Theologische Realenzyklopädie*. 36 vols. Berlin: de Gruyter 1977–2004.

WA   *D. Martin Luthers Werke, kritische Gesamtausgabe*. Weimar: Böhlaus, 1883–.

1

Introduction

PAUL THE CONTROVERSIALIST

ADOLF DEISSMANN WROTE: "THERE has probably seldom been anyone at the same time hated with such fiery hatred and loved with such strong passion as Paul."[1] Deissmann was right. First, Paul has certainly been hated. He has been named the greatest misogynist in the New Testament In 1 Cor 14:34 we read: "The women should keep silence in the churches." He has been hated as the man who did not have the guts to condemn the institution of slavery. In the letter of Paul to the Philemon, a Colossian Christian, Paul actually sends Onesimus, the escaped slave back to his master. Paul, it is claimed, is also the man who has given our western civilization guilt about sex. See 1 Cor 7.1: "It is good for a man not to touch a woman."

On a more theological level, Paul has been named as the one who distorted the teaching of Jesus. Jesus' emphasis on the kingdom of God has been replaced by a butcher's shop theology, Christ as the bloody sacrifice for our sins. Whether these criticism are fair is another question. But these are some reasons why Paul has been hated with such fiery hated.

But at the same time he has been loved. He has been hailed as the apostle who given us the finest gospel we have. So Martin Luther wrote on the epistle to the Romans: "This epistle is really the chief part of the New

---

1. Deissmann, *Paul*, 68. This book, originally published in 1912 (second German edition 1925) captures much of the personality, life, and spirit of Paul as well as discussing his theological ideas.

Testament, and is truly the purest gospel. It is worthy that every Christian should know it word for word, by heart, but also that he should occupy himself with it every day, as the daily bread of the soul. We can never read it or ponder over it too much; for the more we deal with it, the more precious it becomes and the better it tastes."[2]

Not only has Paul been hated and loved; he has also been frequently misunderstood. He was misunderstood in his own lifetime. His gospel of salvation by grace was taken by some to mean that you can sin as much as you wish so that grace may abound (Rom 6:1). He is misunderstood today also. If you like scholarly controversy, you will certainly find it in the literature on Paul. New Testament scholars have accused each other of not understanding Paul and I have witnessed not a few bad-tempered exchanges on Paul at New Testament conferences.

In this book I will present my own understanding of Paul's theology from the perspectives of dogmatics, experience, and relevance. My focus will be on Paul's ideas, not on his life as such, although this will come into focus in chapter 2 (concerning his pre-Christian life and conversion). Discussion of scholarly disputes on Paul (of which there are many) will be kept to a minimum. Most important of all will be a search for ultimate truth (a matter that some New Testament scholars seem to have little interest in),[3] such a search being part of the social responsibility of a university teacher.

The texts of Paul address key issues that face us. The truth of these texts may be the simple message to love our neighbor as ourselves (Rom 13:9), words that go back to the Old Testament (Lev 19:18) and that were quoted by Jesus (Mark 12:31). But it may be also a message concerning our limitations as human beings, our fallenness, and our need for redemption; and it may concern acute existential issues such as fear of death.

WHICH LETTERS DID PAUL ACTUALLY WRITE?

In the Greek New Testament thirteen letters are ascribed to Paul. The scholarly consensus is that seven are authentic. There are the four so-called "main letters" ("Hauptbriefe"): Romans, 1 Corinthians, 2 Corinthians, and Galatians. These were the only ones considered to be genuine by F. C. Baur

---

2. Luther, "Prefaces to the New Testament," *LW* 35:365 (German in Bornkamm, *Vorreden*, 177).

3. In the index of Sanders, *Paul and Palestinian Judaism*, there is an entry: "Truth, ultimate." The pages referenced are 30, 32, 430 . . . and they are all blank. This suggests that although the author has a good sense of humor he either has nothing to say about ultimate truth or perhaps he does not even think there is such a thing as ultimate truth.

(1792–1860). Then in addition most scholars today consider 1 Thessalonians, Philippians, and Philemon to be written by Paul,[4] hence giving seven authentic letters.

The other six can be divided into two categories. First we have Ephesians, Colossians, and 2 Thessalonians. The majority of contemporary scholars consider these to be written by someone other than Paul. The second category of letters is the pastoral Epistles, 1 Timothy, 2 Timothy, and Titus. The vast majority of scholars consider these letters to be written by someone other than Paul. In fact, very few serious scholars consider them to be written by Paul. But it is important that one does not automatically follow the scholarly consensus; anyone engaging in serious study of Paul must make up their own mind.

One problem arises however when we say certain letters are pseudonymous, that is not written by the purported author. If the letter says it is by Paul are we not saying the pseudonymous author was deceptive in writing in Paul's name? In all these letters it is not only the title that claims the letter is from Paul (these titles are later) but also the letter itself says this. To some extent this problem can be answered by saying it was quite customary in this time to write works in the name of someone else.[5] They are called pseudonymous works from the Greek *pseudos* (lie, falsehood) and *onoma* (name). Much of the Jewish literature written at the time of Jesus was pseudonymous. For example 1 Enoch was clearly not written by the Enoch of the Old Testament (Gen 5:21–24);[6] and 4 Ezra was clearly not written by Ezra the scribe (Ezra 7:1–10).[7] There were also many works of the early church that we know to be pseudonymous. The Infancy Gospel of Thomas was clearly not written by the disciple Thomas;[8] the book of James

4. The order in which they were written is probably this: 1 Thessalonians, Galatians, 1 Corinthians, 2 Corinthians, Philippians and Philemon, Romans. Some will no doubt question this ordering, especially my placing Philippians early in an Ephesian rather than in a Roman imprisonment.

5. Indeed this was happening for some centuries before the New Testament era. A good example is the book of Isaiah, now seen as a work not only of Isaiah of Jerusalem in the eighth century BC but also a "second Isaiah" (Isa 40–55) and a "third Isaiah (Isa 56–66) who saw themselves standing in the tradition of Isaiah of Jerusalem. The same principle applies to wisdom and apocalyptic literature. Meade, *Canon*, 105, concludes that "in the prophetic, wisdom, and apocalyptic traditions, literary attribution is primarily an assertion of authoritative tradition, not literary origins." Hence this applies not only to prophetic books like Isaiah, but also to Proverbs (wisdom literature) and Daniel (apocalyptic literature, now widely seen as being composed in the second century BC, not the sixth).

6. For 1 Enoch, see *OTP* 1:5–89.

7. 4 Ezra can be found in the Apocrypha of an English Bible.

8. See Hennecke and Schneemelcher, *Apocrypha*, 1:388–99. In addition there is

was clearly not written by James the brother of Jesus.[9] There were though relatively few pseudonymous letters outside the New Testament.[10]

Returning to the issue of deception, there may be cases where pseudonymous works were written and promoted as "transparent friction."[11] So if the six letters of Paul (2 Thessalonians, Ephesians, Colossians, 1 and 2 Timothy, Titus) came into being in a school then "*within the school* the work would most likely have been openly known and acknowledged to be pseudonymous (though no less authoritative)."[12] However, outside the school it is difficult to avoid the conclusion that some degree of deception was involved. But many of our worries can be allayed if one focusses not on who wrote the letters but on *what the letters contain*.[13] For Luther, as we shall see, the authorship of the works of the New Testament is somewhat irrelevant. The key issues is whether they "urge Christ"; and on this basis they are to be judged.[14]

JOHANN STRAUSS THE YOUNGER:
DIE FLEDERMAUS

To consider further this issue of deception in pseudonymous letters I have chosen music Paul would probably not approve of. Johann Strauss's *Die Fledermaus* (*The Bat*) is an operetta full of great humor.[15] I get the impression that Paul had little sense of humor and so this is one reason he would not approve. But more importantly he would say that much of the humor revolves around the fact that someone wishes to cheat on his wife and is eventually found out (his wife also has certain weaknesses concerning her extra-marital admirer).

---

a gnostic Gospel of Thomas, again not written by the disciple (Valantasis, *Gospel of Thomas*).

9. This book of James is to be distinguished from the letter of James in the New Testament which may well have been written by James the brother of Jesus. The book of James otherwise known as the Protoevangelium of James, tells of the Virgin Mary's birth and the birth of Jesus (Hennecke and Schneemelcher, *Apocrypha*, 1:370–88).

10. One example is 3 Corinthians, composed around 170 AD.

11. Meade, *Pseudonymity*, 198.

12. Meade, *Pseudonymity*, 198.

13. Meade, *Pseudonymity*, 215–16: "[T]he discovery of pseudonymous origins [. . .] in no way prejudices either the inspiration or canonicity of the work."

14. See chapter 12 below.

15. As a Wagner lover, I have to confess that I find this funnier than Wagner's comic masterpiece *The Mastersingers of Nuremberg*.

But the reason I have chosen Adele's song from Act II is because it highlights an issue of pseudonymous literature: is it meant to deceive or not? Adele, maid to Rosalinde, finds herself in a tricky situation at a party. She is only there because Dr. Falke is playing an extremely elaborate practical joke on Rosalinde's husband, Gabriel von Eisenstein. He has brought him to a party under a false name (Herr Marquis) but has also written a pseud-onymous letter in the name of Adele's sister, Ida, inviting her to the party. Arriving at the party she is told to assume the name "Olga" and pretend to be an "artiste." This song follows her surprise encounter with Eisenstein who asks what his housemaid is doing at the party. Eisenstein is rebuked for assuming "Olga" is his housemaid and she then sings this song.

My dear Marquis, a man like you	Mein Herr Marquis, ein Mann wie Sie
really ought to know better!	sollt' besser das verstehn
I advise you, therefore,	darum rate ich, ja genauer sich
to examine people more attentively!	die Leute anzusehen!
But my hand is so soft and well-kept, ah,	Die Hand ist doch wohl gar zo fein, ach,
my tiny foot so trim and tidy, ah,	dies Füsschen, so zierlich und klein, ach,
my manner of speech,	die Sprache, die ich führe,
my waist, my figure,	die Taille, die Tournüre,
you'll never find the like	dergleichen finden Sie
in a lady's maid	bei eine Zofe nie,
you'll never find the like	dergleichen finden Sie
in a lady's maid!	bei eine Zofe nie!
In fact, you've got to admit	Gestehen müssen Sie fürwahr:
your mistake was really very funny!	sehr komisch dieser Irrtum war!
Yes, the whole thing's, ha ha ha,	Ja sehr komisch, ha ha ha,
extremely funny, ha ha ha	ist die Sache, ha ha ha,
so forgive me, ha ha ha,	drum verzeihn Sie, ha ha ha,
if I laugh, ha ha ha ha ha ha!	wenn ich lache, ha ha ha ha ha ha,
Yes, the whole thing's, ha ha ha,	ja sehr komisch, ha ha ha,
extremely funny, ha ha ha ha ha ha	ist die Sache, ha ha ha ha ha ha
You're very funny, my dear Marquis!	sehr komisch, Herr Marquis, sind Sie!
Nature has endowed me	Mit dem Profil im griech'schen Styl
with a profile of Grecian cut.	beschenkte mich Natur.

If my face is not sufficient,	Wenn nicht dies Gesicht schon genügend spricht
then consider my figure!	so sehn Sie die Figur!
Just take a look at my ball dress, ah	Schau'n durch die Lorgnette Sie dann, ach
through your lorgnette, ah!	sich diese Toilette nur an, ach
I can't help thinking love	Mir scheint wohl, die Liebe
has blurred your eyesight.	macht Ihre Augen trübe,
The image of some pretty lady's maid	der schönen Zofe Bild
has quite filled up your heart!	hat ganz Ihr Herz erfüllt
The image of some pretty lady's maid	der schönen Zofe Bild
has quite filled up your heart!	hat ganz Ihr Herz erfüllt!
Now you see her everywhere!	Nun sehen Sie sie überall,
The whole thing's really funny	sehr komisch ist fürwahr der Fall!
yes very funny, ha ha ha	Ja sehr komisch, ha ha ha
is the whole thing, ha ha ha,	ist die Sache, ha ha ha
so forgive me, ha ha ha	drum verzeihn Sie, ha ha ha
if I laugh, ha ha ha ha ha ha	wenn ich lache, ha ha ha ha ha ha
yes very funny, ha ha ha	ja sehr komisch, ha ha ha,
is the whole thing, ha ha ha ha ha ha	ist die Sache, ha ha ha ha ha ha
Ah! ha ha ha ha ha ha!	Ach! ha ha ha ha ha ha!

So in this case we have Adele being manipulated and deceived. The case with Ephesians, however, is quite different even if there is a certain element of deception for those outside the Ephesian school. This letter does claim to be written by Paul: "Paul an apostle of Christ Jesus by the will of God" (Eph 1:1). The name of Paul reappears in the Epistle. E.g., Eph 3:1: "This is the reason that I Paul am a prisoner for Christ Jesus for the sake of you Gentiles." I think many could cope with a pseudonymous letter if it were simply full of doctrine. But the letter has this personal note which is particularly strong in Eph 6:19–20: "Pray also for me, so that when I speak, a message may be given to me to make known with boldness the mystery of the gospel, for which I am an ambassador in chains. Pray that I may declare it boldly, as I must speak." Is not this a wicked exploitation of the Christians receiving this letter who are now spending nights praying for an apostle who is not actually asking for prayer?

I do not think it is. If Ephesians is pseudonymous we will have the following situation. Someone is writing in the name of the apostle Paul, possibly in the Ephesian school.[16] This pseudonymous letter is not addressed directly to those who may come across the letter. Rather it is addressed to the fictional addressees of Paul.[17] So when people read this letter, knowing it is not directly addressed to them, they will not waste lots of time praying for Paul. They will know that the letter was meant for others. In fact pseudonymous letters were written after the death of the supposed author. So when Christians stumbled across this letter they would know that Paul had died and they would not waste endless hours (or indeed any hours) praying for his needs as expressed in Eph 6:19–20. Nevertheless they would be able to glean much from this letter, just as we can today.

FURTHER READING

Ephesians 6:10–24

---

16. On such an Ephesian School, see Gese, *Vermächtnis*, 14–18, 271–76, who also notes that Eph 6:19–20 is based on 2 Cor 5:20 and Col 4:3–4 (241, 244).

17. Bauckham. "Letters," 475.

2

From Pharisee to Apostle to the Gentiles

PAUL'S BIRTH AND EDUCATION

PAUL WAS BORN IN Tarsus[1] probably between 1 AD and 5 AD. Tarsus, situated in the South East of Asia Minor (modern Turkey), was located on the river Cydnus,[2] just ten miles from the coast, and lying to the north were the Taurus mountains. In 67 BC Cilicia was made a Roman province with Tarsus as capital but it was later divided into the mountainous region of the West and the plainland of the East, of which Tarsus was a part. This Eastern part was united to Syria around 25 BC, and the double province existed until 72 AD. Paul alludes to this double province in Gal 1:21, explaining that after his first visit to Jerusalem after his conversion he went to "the regions of Syria and Cilicia," presumably returning to his town of birth, Tarsus, hence corroborating the witness of Acts that he was born in Tarsus. According to Acts 21:39, he claims to be a citizen of Tarsus and his addition that it was "an important city" is borne out by the fact that it was the home of some illustrious people, such as the Stoic philosopher Athenodorus, who had been a teacher of Emperor Augustus. But from our perspective the greatest and most famous person to have been born there was Paul.

1. See Acts 9:11; 21:39; 22:3 (cf. 9:30; 11:25).

2. For a time in the second century BC it was called Antioch-on-the-Cydnus (after the Seleucid ruler Antiochus IV).

At a young age, we cannot be sure how young, but it could have been before he was old enough to play on the streets,[3] Paul and his family moved to Jerusalem (Acts 22:3). Here Paul moved in two worlds: the world of Hebrew culture and the world of Hellenism. Jerusalem at this time was a "Hellenistic" city, that is, it had been highly influenced by Greek culture. For example, the temple built by Herod the Great was a piece of Hellenistic architecture and it has been estimated that there were at a minimum 10–20 percent of the Jerusalem population who had Greek as a mother tongue.[4]

Paul received one of the best Jewish educations of the time, an education in Jerusalem at the feet of Rabbi Gamaliel. Such an education has been disputed by some, it being suggested that he was educated in Tarsus and therefore the primarily influence on him was "Hellenism" (i.e., Greek culture) and not Judaism (Jewish culture). Indeed, some say that he knew virtually no Hebrew. The reason Paul's Jerusalem education has been questioned is that this fact is not stated by Paul in his letters and is only mentioned by Luke (whom I take to be the author of the Third Gospel and Acts) in Acts 22:3. Here Paul is portrayed as declaring to the crowd in Jerusalem: "I am a Jew, born at Tarsus in Cilicia, but brought up in this city at the feet of Gamaliel, educated according to the strict manner of the law of our fathers, being zealous for God as you all are [to] this day". There are in fact two possible ways of taking "according to the strict manner of the law of our fathers":

1 I am a Jew,

2 born at Tarsus in Cilicia,

3 but brought up in this city,

4 educated at the feet of Gamaliel *according to the strict manner of the law of our fathers,*

5 being zealous for God

6 as you all are to this day

Or

1 I am a Jew,

2 born at Tarsus in Cilicia,

3. Unnik, "Tarsus or Jerusalem," 301.

4. See Hengel, *Hellenization of Judaea,* 10. Working with a population of 80,000 to 100,000 he gives a minimum as between 8,000 and 16,000. These estimations are made on the basis of the inscription on ossuaries (containing the bones of the deceased) in Jerusalem and its environs.

3   but brought up in this city,

4   educated at the feet of Gamaliel,

5   *according to the strict manner of the law of our fathers* being zealous for
    God

6   as you all are to this day

But the key points are that according to Acts 22:3 Paul was born
(*gegennēmenos*) in Tarsus but brought up (*anatethrammenos*) in Jerusalem
and educated (*pepaideumenos*) at the feet of Gamaliel. As indicated already,
Paul in his letters never mentions an education in Jerusalem and this has led
various scholars to argue that Paul received his education not in Jerusalem
but in Tarsus. But there are strong indications that Paul was educated in
Jerusalem. He was educated as a Pharisee, and we know this from his letters. See Phil 3:5: "as to the law, a Pharisee." Before 70 AD (when Jerusalem
was destroyed by the Romans) Pharisaic schools were most likely only to be
found in Palestine. We have no evidence of Pharisaic schools in the diaspora
before 70 AD. One can also add that the largest center of Jewish learning
outside Palestine was Alexandria, in Egypt. Here there were no Pharisaic
schools. Indeed, there is the following polemic against Alexandria in the
Mishnah: "Abtalion said: Ye sages, give heed to your words lest ye incur the
penalty of exile and ye be exiled to a place of evil waters, and the disciples
that come after you drink (of them) and die, and the name of Heaven be
profaned."[5] The "place of evil waters" is most likely Alexandria, situated at
the west end of the Nile delta.

If Paul was educated in Jerusalem, could he have been a pupil of Rabbi
Gamaliel? It is possible that an unnamed pupil of Gamaliel I, who exhibited
"impudence in matters of learning" (mentioned in b. Shabbath 30b of the
Babylonian Talmud), was Paul. However, this is a text coming from around
500 AD so caution is appropriate.

Gamaliel is mentioned in Acts 5:35–39. Some Jewish leaders wished
to kill Peter and his fellow apostles but Gamaliel urged caution, advising his
fellow leaders thus (Acts 5:38–39): "keep away from these men and let them
alone; because if this plan or this undertaking is of human origin it will fail;
[39]but if it is of God, you will not be able to overthrow them—in that case
you may even be found fighting against God!" Despite having the apostles
flogged, the Jewish leaders followed Gamaliel's advice and they were re-
leased. The question then arises: if Gamaliel is so tolerant, is it impossible

5. Aboth 1:11 in Danby, *Mishnah*, 447. Although the editing of the Mishnah took
place around 200 AD it contains earlier tradition and reflects Pharisaic thinking. Indeed, Abtalion was the teacher of Hillel and was active around 50 BC.

that Paul, his pupil, could be so intolerant of the Christians?[6] In reply two points can be made. First, a pupil can be very different from the teacher. Secondly, Gamaliel was faced with Hebrew Christians who kept the law. But Paul, as we shall see, was faced with Hellenistic Jewish Christians who did not keep the law. So the case against Paul's education in Jerusalem (and even his education under Gamaliel) is not compelling.

Paul then received one of the best educations. He says that he received a thorough education in the law, writing in Gal 1:14: "I advanced in Judaism beyond many among my people of the same age, for I was far more zealous for the traditions of my ancestors." Also he could speak fluent Hebrew and Greek. In addition to knowing Greek and Hebrew he may have also known some Latin.

PAUL, THE PERSECUTOR OF THE CHURCH

There may be uncertainty in the scholarly world as to whether Paul was educated in Jerusalem but of one thing there is no dispute: Paul was a persecutor of the church. This is referred to in both his letters (e.g., Phil 3:6) and in Acts (e.g., Acts 8:3). As already stated, Paul persecuted the Hellenistic Jewish Christians, that is those Jewish Christians who spoke Greek and had a liberal attitude to the law. By contrast the Hebrew-speaking Jewish Christians do not seem to have been persecuted by Paul (see Acts 8:1).

Paul persecuted the Hellenistic Jewish Christians for three main reasons, the first being that they did not keep the ritual law and were critical of the temple (see Stephen's speech in Acts 7). Second, they claimed that the crucified Jesus was the messiah. The idea of a crucified messiah was scandalous. According to the 17th Psalm of Solomon (dated first century BC) the Jews were looking for a king messiah who would liberate Israel from the Romans.

> [21]See, Lord, and raise up for them their king,
> the son of David, to rule over your servant Israel
> in the time known to you, O God.
> [22]Undergird him with the strength to destroy the unrighteous rulers,
> to purge Jerusalem from gentiles
> who trample her to destruction.[7]

---

6. Conzelmann, *Apostelgeschichte*, 48, 135, argues the tolerant Gamaliel of Acts 5:34–39 could not be the teacher of the persecutor Paul.

7. Psalms of Solomon 17.21–22, *OTP* 2:667 (translation of R. B. Wright).

Jesus, by stark contrast, died on a cross and was therefore, according to current Jewish thinking, accursed. He was considered accursed because Jews at this time were applying Deut 21:23 to crucifixion. This text explains that after someone has been executed and then hung on a "tree," "his corpse must not remain all night upon the tree; you shall bury him that same day, for anyone hung on a tree is under God's curse." We then find this application to crucifixion in texts from Qumran where, unlike the Deuteronomy text, the "tree" was understood as the *means* of execution.[8] Paul himself was later to make this connection also. He did not deny that Christ was accursed but stresses that he was cursed *for our sake*. And so he writes in Gal 3:13: "Christ redeemed us from the curse of the law by becoming a curse for us—for it is written, 'Cursed is everyone who hangs on a tree.'" Luke also makes this connection when he has Peter saying that the Jewish authorities put Jesus to death "by hanging him on a tree" (Acts 5:30; 10:39).

The third reason Paul persecuted these Christians is that they claimed that salvation was to be found in Jesus alone. So they were saved not by Jesus *and* the law, but by *Jesus alone*. In Jewish culture *only God could save*, as Isa 43:11 makes clear: "I, I am the LORD, and besides me there is no saviour." So these Hellenistic Jewish Christians were then attributing something to Jesus, i.e., that he saves, which can only be attributed to God.

In view of these three serious matters it was not surprising that Paul persecuted the church with ferocious zeal. He was zealous for God rather like Phineas and Elijah. In Phil 3:6 he confesses: "as to zeal [I was] a persecutor of the church." Further in Gal 1:13 he writes: "For you have heard of my former life in Judaism, how I persecuted the church of God violently and tried to destroy it."

Paul himself was later persecuted as a Christian by other zealous Jews. We know of this from Acts and from the letters. For example, in 2 Cor 11:24 he says that on five occasions he received the thirty-nine lashes, a punishment of the synagogue. Paul's theology was like that of the Hellenists but was even more radical. He was then persecuted for the same reasons he had earlier persecuted the Hellenists: because of his attitude to the law, because he claimed that the crucified Jesus was the messiah, and because he claimed Jesus alone was the saviour, i.e., he was divine.

PAUL, THE ROMAN CITIZEN

We only know that Paul was a Roman citizen from Acts and many have argued that because it is absent from the letters, and because they cannot

---

8. 4QpNah 1.7–8; Temple Scroll 64.6–13 (Bell, *Irrevocable Call*, 49–51).

possibly imagine that Paul was a Roman citizen, it must be figment of Luke's imagination. I am convinced that Paul was a Roman citizen but I do not wish to get involved in this here.[9] All I will say is that Roman citizenship could be important for these two issues: his mission and his view of the state. Being a Roman citizen may explain why his missionary activity as a Christian was largely confined to the Roman Empire. So he may have thought that if the Roman Empire were evangelized the whole world would be essentially evangelized. And that is why he was so keen to evangelize Spain, the western extreme of the empire (Rom 15:24, 28). Concerning his view of the state, he was essentially a conservative. As a loyal Roman citizen he told Christians to submit to the governing authorities (Rom 13:1) and although one may well have sympathy with his view that one should pay taxes (Rom 13:6-7), I imagine most of my readers will sharply disagree with Paul's support for the death penalty (Rom 13:4).[10]

CONVERSION OF PAUL

The use of the word "conversion" for the turning point in Paul's life has proved controversial. Stendahl argues: "If [. . .] we use the term 'conversion' for Paul's experience, we would also have to use it of such prophets as Jeremiah and Isaiah. Yet we do not speak of their conversion, but rather of their call. Paul's experience is also that of a call—to a specific vocation—to be God's appointed Apostle to the Gentiles. The mission is the point. It is a call to mission rather than a conversion."[11] Stendahl has overstated his case. It is so that Paul viewed his call in the light of that of Jeremiah and Isaiah (see below). But is it right to remove completely the idea of conversion when considering the turning point in Paul's life? Paul does not use the terms "to convert" or "conversion" for his Damascus experience; but Paul uses such terms very sparingly anyway. So he does use the terms *epistrephō* ("I turn"), *epistrophē* ("turning"), *metanoeō* ("I repent"), and *metanoia* ("repentance"). Of these four terms only *epistrephō* ("I turn") is used by Paul in connection with conversion (2 Cor 3:16), interestingly with reference to Israel's conversion. When I discuss "Paul and Israel" in a chapter 9 I will argue that Paul believed that Israel would come to faith in the same way Paul came to faith: by a direct meeting with the glorified Christ. If Paul then uses *epistrephō* for Israel's conversion perhaps Paul did after all think of the turning point in his life as a conversion. Further, the contrast between the before and after

9. See my *Irrevocable Call*, 366 n. 136.
10. I return to this in chapter 12.
11. Stendahl, *Paul*, 10–11.

in Paul is so marked that perhaps it is right with Gager to speak in terms of Paul's conversion.[12]

The conversion of Paul probably happened within eighteen months of the resurrection of Jesus. That Paul's conversion did not take place that long after the resurrection is implied by 1 Cor 15:3–8 where, after quoting four "creedal statements" (introduced by "that" or "and that"), he lists further resurrection appearances, including the one he experienced:

> [3]For I handed on to you as of first importance what I in turn had received:
> **that Christ died for our sins in accordance with the scriptures,**
> [4]**and that he was buried,**
> **and that he was raised on the third day in accordance with the scriptures,**
> [5]**and that he appeared to Cephas, then to the twelve.**
> [6]**Then he appeared to more than five hundred brothers and sisters at one time,**
> most of whom are still alive, though some have died.
> [7]**Then he appeared to James, then to all the apostles.**
> [8]Last of all, as to one untimely born, he appeared also to me.

The text in bold is material I consider to be pre-Pauline,[13] which Paul may well have learned from Peter and James on his first visit to Jerusalem after his conversion (Gal 1:18–19). His addition of the words "Last of all, as to one untimely born, he appeared also to me" suggests that his conversion did not take place that long after Jesus' resurrection. The precise figure of within eighteen months is based on certain second-century sources where Jesus is said to have appeared after the resurrection for a period of eighteen months.[14]

---

12. Gager, "Conversion."

13. This is suggested by vocabulary and phrases Paul does not typically use. E.g., nowhere else does he use the phrase "according to the scriptures" or refer to "the twelve."

14. Harnack, *Mission und Ausbreitung*, 1:60, points to four texts that give a clue to the time of Paul's conversion, of which I mention three. Irenaeus points out that the Valentinians and the Ophites believed that Jesus appeared to his disciples for a period of eighteen months (*Adversus haereses* 1.3.2 [writing about the Valentinians], *ANF* 1:319; *Adversus haereses* 1.30.14 [writing about the Ophites], *ANF* 1:357). See also *Ascension of Isaiah* 9:16 (*OTP* 2:170: "And when he has plundered the angel of death, he will rise on the third day and will remain in the world for five hundred and forty-five days"). In addition, see the *Apocryphon of James*, which tells of Jesus' "Ascension" as occurring 550 days after his resurrection (Hennecke and Schneemelcher, *New Testament Apocrypha*, 1:336). This scheme of understanding the appearances as taking place and then ceasing does not correspond to Luke's scheme of appearances for a period of forty days (Acts 1:3) and then ascension (Acts 1:9–11) after which the appearance to Paul takes place.

How did the great turning point in Paul's life come about? According to Luke, it was as Paul was on his way to Damascus to persecute the Christians that the risen and glorified Christ appeared to him. The account of Paul's conversion occurs in Acts 9, 22, and 26. Then in Paul's letters the appearance of Christ is mentioned in, for example, Gal 1:15–16, where he writes that God "was pleased to reveal his Son to me." Taking all these accounts together one thing is indisputable: Paul experienced something, and his interpretation was that this "something" was the resurrected Jesus.

This conversion of Paul took place out of the blue. There have been various psychological theories about Paul's conversion. For example, in his persecution of the Christians he secretly envied them. This played on his mind so that one day he simply flipped over, rather as in Thomas Kuhn's understanding of scientific revolutions.[15] Such theories are obviously favoured by those who wish to do away with the story of Christ appearing to Paul.

The conversion of Paul was an act of the pure grace of God. Paul contributed nothing towards his conversion. His conversion was an act of God's grace and it is therefore no surprise to see that Paul later stressed the grace of God more than any other New Testament theologian (with the possible exception of John?).

INFLUENCES UPON PAUL'S THEOLOGY

One of the greatest influences on Paul theology was his conversion.[16] Paul's conversion deeply affected his theology. One key example I have just discussed is that Paul, the persecutor of the church, experienced the grace of God. It is little wonder that one of the central pillars of Paul theology was the justification of the ungodly? Paul contributed nothing to his conversion. He did not even make a decision!

A second great influence on Paul was the Septuagint (LXX), the Greek translation of the Hebrew Old Testament used by early Christians.[17] It appears that Paul, in quoting from the Old Testament in his letters, quotes usually from the Septuagint. The implications of this are not always seen. One implication is that Paul worked with a larger Bible than the Protestant Old Testament. The Septuagint is much bigger than what is usually called the Old Testament and largely corresponds to the Protestant Old Testament with Apocrypha. The Protestant Old Testament consists of books of the

15. Kuhn, *The Structure of Scientific Revolutions*. On relating Kuhn's work to religious conversion see Heirich, "Change of Heart," 675–76.

16. See especially Kim, *Origin*, and *New Perspective*.

17. On the Septuagint as a Christian work, see Hengel, *Septuagint*.

Hebrew canon, the Tanak: the Law, Prophets, and the Writings.[18] The Roman Catholics on the other hand have based their Old Testament on that of the Latin Vulgate. The larger Vulgate canon corresponds approximately to what we know as the Septuagint.[19]

The second implication of Paul's using the Septuagint is that if he worked with ideas of inspiration then he, like the early fathers of the church, considered it to be inspired.[20] This raises interesting theological problems when one realizes that the Septuagint and the Hebrew diverge in many places. Therefore, to understand Paul properly ones needs to know and understand the Septuagint. Paul's letters are filled with quotations from and allusions to the Septuagint. This collection of Jewish works was the most important single literary influence on Paul. But there is something striking. All his quotations, apart from one possible exception, come from the Hebrew canon (albeit usually in the Septuagintal form). Some of the quotations are, as we shall see, fairly free; but they can be reasonably identified.[21] This may suggest that Paul considered the Hebrew canon (later preserved for us in the Masoretic Text) to be the most important. Perhaps because of his call to be apostle to the gentiles he made a conscious decision to switch to the Septuagint text form. But he alludes extensively to the so-called Apocrypha. See especially Rom 1:18ff, which alludes much to Wisdom 13.

So the Septuagint is the most important literary influence on Paul. Greek pagan literature is rarely quoted by Paul. Indeed, in the seven letters there is just one quotation: "Bad company ruins good morals" (1 Cor 15:33). Tertullian and Jerome identified this as from the comedy of Menander,[22] and Clement of Alexandria refers to "a tragic Iambic line."[23] In fact, the line

---

18. The word "**Tanak**" is formed from Law, (*Tôrāh*), Prophets (*Nebi'îm*), and Writings (*Ketûbîm*).

19. The Rabbis defined their canon in opposition to the Christian Septuagint (Gese, "Gestaltwerdung," 25–28); therefore the Jewish Old Testament canon of the "Tanak" was closed *after* most of the New Testament had been written.

20. The idea of the inspiration of the Septuagint goes back to the *Letter of Aristeas*, which claimed that the seventy translators each produced exactly the same translation of the Hebrew. This is then taken up by Irenaeus (*Adv Haer* 3.21.2) and others.

21. The exception is 1 Cor 2:9. Some think Paul has combined Isa 64:3 LXX with Isa 65:17. Others think he quotes from the Testament of Jacob or alludes to Sir 1:10. See the discussion in Thiselton, *1 Corinthians*, 250–52.

22. Menander, *Thais*, Fragment 218. Menander's dates are uncertain. Arnott, "Menander," 956, gives 344/3–292/1 (344/3–392–1 is clearly a printing error); Kraus in *Der Kleine Pauly* 3:1199 gives 342/1–293/2.

23. *Stromata* book 1 chapter 14 (1.5.4). See *ANF* 2:314; Stählin, *Clemens II*, 38.

can be found in Euripides,[24] as Socrates the historian recognized,[25] and it is most likely that the line in Menander is an allusion to Euripides.[26] The quotation in Paul does not mean he had read Menander or Euripides. Indeed, this saying had become a popular maxim[27] and he may well have learned it in the Hellenistic synagogue.[28] In Acts 17:28, part of the speech Paul is purported to have made in Athens, there are two quotations from Greek philosophers. First in Acts 17:28a: "In him we live and move and have our being." This is part of an address to Zeus by his son Minos and comes probably from Epimenides:[29]

> They fashioned a tomb for thee, O holy and high–
> The Cretans, always liars, evil beasts, idle bellies!
> But thou art not dead; thou livest and abidest for ever,
> For in thee we live and move and have our being.

Secondly there is a quotation from the fifth line of Aratus, *Phainomena* in 17:28b, "For we too are his offspring." The first five lines are:[30]

> Let us begin with Zeus. Never, O men, let us leave him
> unmentioned. All the ways are full of Zeus,
> and all the market-places of human beings. The sea is full
> of him; so are the harbors. In every way we have all to do with Zeus,
> for we are truly his offspring.

The arresting factor here is that the God these poets are referring to is *Zeus*, the head of the Greek pantheon of gods. At least in Acts, Paul is presented as recognizing that such pagan poets can disclose the truth, even if a partial truth.[31]

In the deutero-Pauline literature (that is the literature which although ascribed to Paul probably was not written by Paul) there is again probably a quotation from Epimenides in Titus 1:12: "Cretans are always liars, evil

24. Euripides, Fragment 1024 (Collard and Cropp, *Euripides: Fragments*, 578–79).

25. Socrates, *Ecclesiastical History* 3.16 (*PG* 67:424). See Schrage, *Erste Brief an die Korinther*, 4:247.

26. Traill, "Thais," 287 n. 11.

27. Thiselton, *1 Corinthians*, 1254; Koch, *Schrift*, 44.

28. Cf. Hengel, *Pre-Christian Paul*, 2.

29. See Bruce, *Acts*, 339. This quatrain is quoted in Syriac by the ninth-century commentator Isho'dad. The second line is quoted in Titus 1:12 and Clement of Alexandria identifies it as coming from Epimenides (*Stromata* book 1 chapter 14 [1.59.2]; *ANF* 2:313; Stählin, *Clemens II*, 38).

30. See Bruce, *Acts*, 339; Lake, "Poets," 246–47.

31. Stonehouse, *Areopagus*, 29–30.

beasts, lazy gluttons" (this is the second line of what is quoted above). The writer then gives his commentary on this: "This testimony is true". The writer is not affirming that Cretans are liars since he was aware that Epimenides was himself a Cretan, introducing the quotation with "It was one of them, their very own prophet, who said." Hence, we have the so called liar paradox.[32]

So we have in the genuine letters of Paul only one quotation from a Classical Greek source and as I suggested he probably did not learn this by reading Menander but rather heard it as a popular maxim, possibly in the Hellenistic synagogue. Obviously other things in the Hellenistic world influenced him; his vocabulary[33] and the use of the Greek letter form. Also Judaism was heavily Hellenized, as I have already pointed out. But as far as direct influence of Greek philosophy and culture is concerned, we have to say this influenced him little.[34]

PAUL, THE APOSTLE TO THE GENTILES

Earlier I argued for retaining the word conversion for the turning point of Paul's life. But Paul clearly received a call, to take the gospel to the gentiles. The gentile mission is now taken for granted but for the early church it was by no means obvious that its message should be taken to the gentiles. There is a possible problem with Jesus' final words in Matt 28:19–20. Here Jesus commissions the disciples to make disciples of all nations: "Go therefore and make disciples of all nations, baptizing them in the name of the Father and of the Son and of the Holy Spirit, [20]and teaching them to obey everything that I have commanded you. And remember I am with you always to the end of the age." There are signs that these words, challenging and also comforting though they may be, do not go back to the earthly Jesus. Apart from the unmistakable reference to the later liturgy of Christian baptism in the name of the Trinity, there is this simple matter. If Jesus gave this command to evangelize the nations, why did they not so preach? A case can be made that for a period of twelve years the apostles remained in Jerusalem. This is based on a number of pieces of evidence. First, in Acts we see no movement to evangelize the gentiles until Acts 10 and 11. Second, we know of this twelve-year period in Jerusalem from some early Christian texts.[35] Acts of Peter 5 tells that "God was already preparing Peter for what was to come,

32. See Thiselton, "Liar Paradox."

33. A good example is his use of *nous* (mind) which had no clear Hebrew equivalent.

34. Hengel, *Pre-Christian Paul*, 2–3.

35. Harnack, *Chronologie*, 1:243–44.

now that the twelve years in Jerusalem which the Lord Christ had enjoined on him were completed."[36] Clement of Alexandria writes that Peter said that Jesus told the apostles: "If anyone of Israel, then, wishes to repent, and by my name to believe in God, his sins shall be forgiven him. After twelve years go out into the world, that no one may say 'We have not heard.'"[37] Eusebius, writes that according to Apollonius, the opponent of Montanus, "the Saviour ordered his apostles not to leave Jerusalem for twelve years."[38] For those first years it seems that the Jerusalem apostles had the impression that Israel must first be converted. Then the nations will flock to Jerusalem, according to Isa 2:2–4.[39] Only after twelve years did the apostles venture to evangelize non-Jews.[40]

A mission to the gentiles was therefore a new idea. The first to engage in it were the Hellenists, Jewish Christians whose mother tongue was Greek. But the most important apostle to the gentiles was Paul of Tarsus. So how did he understand his mission to the gentiles? One way he understood it was to see his mission in the light of the servant of the Lord of Isa 49:1–6, and he alludes to this text in Gal 1:15–16 (note there is also an allusion to the call of Jeremiah): "But when God, who had set me apart before I was born and had called me through his grace, was pleased to reveal his Son to me, in order that I might proclaim him among the Gentiles, I did not confer with flesh and blood." Compare this to Isa 49:1, 5–6:

> [1]Listen to me, O coastlands, pay attention, you peoples from far away! The LORD called me before I was born, while I was in my mother's womb he named me. [. . .] [5]And now the LORD says, who formed me in the womb to be his servant, to bring Jacob back to him, and that Israel might be gathered to him, for I am honoured in the sight of the LORD, and my God has become my strength – [6]he says "It is too light a thing that you should be my servant to raise up the tribes of Jacob and to restore the

36. Hennecke and Schneemelcher, *New Testament Apocrypha*, 2:284.

37. See the end of Clement of Alexandria, *Stromata* book 5 (6.43.3). ANF 2:490 takes the expression "after twelve years" with Israel's sins being forgiven, which makes little sense. Stählin, *Clemens Alexandrinus II*, 453, places the full stop after "sins" (*hamartiai*) and then renders the final sentence of book 5 *meta <de> dōdeka etē exelthete eis ton kosmon, mē tis eipē ouk ēkousamen.*

38. Eusebius, *Ecclesiastical History*, 5.18.14 (Lake, *History*, 1:492–93).

39. See, e.g., Isa 2:2: "In days to come the mountain the LORD's house shall be established as the highest of the mountains, and shall be raised above the hills; and the nation shall stream to it."

40. Note also that according to Hippolytos of Thebes 3.3; 5.3 (Diekamp, *Hippolytos von Theben*, 4–5, 28) Mary died eleven years after Jesus' death and Prochoros relates that after her death, the apostolic mission began.

survivors of Israel; I will give you as a light to the nations, that
my salvation may reach to the end of the earth."

See also Jer 1:4–5 where Jeremiah says at his call: "Now the word of the
LORD came to me saying, 'Before I formed you in the womb I knew you,
and before you were born I consecrated you; I appointed you a prophet to
the nations.'"

The intriguing aspect of this mission of Paul to the gentiles is that he
came to believe that it was indirect mission to the Jews. Later in his career
Paul came to the belief that in preaching the gospel to the gentiles the Jews
would also be saved. We find evidence for this in Rom 11:11, 13–14: "So I
ask, have they [Israel] stumbled so as to fall? By no means! But through their
stumbling salvation has come to the Gentiles, so as to make Israel jealous.
[. . .] [13]Now I am speaking to you Gentiles. Inasmuch as I am an apostle
to the Gentiles, I glorify my ministry [14]in order to make my own people
jealous, and thus save some of them." Paul believed that by preaching the
gospel to the gentiles, Israel would be provoked to jealousy and so come
to be saved. He has therefore reversed the picture of Isa 2:2–4. The gentiles
do not come to the glory of Israel; rather Israel comes to the glory of the
gentiles. Paul's missionary strategy was therefore the exact opposite to the
missionary strategy of the Jerusalem apostles in those twelve years after the
resurrection.

MAHLER'S *FIRST SYMPHONY*, FOURTH MOVEMENT

I have chosen a piece of music to illustrate something of Paul's psychological
makeup and the mood of his mission to the gentiles. It is the final movement of Mahler's first Symphony.

Paul's mission was an exciting mission but also a dangerous mission:
in 2 Cor 11:24–28 he tells of his beatings, being shipwrecked, adrift at sea,
and many other dangers. But I find it an inspirational mission even though
at some points I may be questioning some of the things Paul taught! This
movement from Mahler is marked "Stürmisch bewegt" ("stormily moved")
and sums up much of Paul's psychological makeup.[41] Just as I do not think
he had much humor, I imagine he would not provide an easy evening of
conversation.

41. On the issue of Paul's health and temperament, see Dodd "Mind of Paul I,"
67–69. etc.

Mahler shared some characteristics with Paul. Just as Paul's mission was a consuming passion, so music was for Mahler. "Music was not merely a profession for Mahler; it was a sacred mission, to which everyone and everything took second place."[42] Like Paul he was also a difficult person to live with. And like Paul, he was Jewish, and converted to Christianity. But there the similarities stop. Paul was a zealous Jew; Mahler had little respect for Jewish religious practice and observance.[43] Paul was converted by an irresistible spiritual experience; Mahler, although having a fondness for Catholic mysticism, seemed to have converted in order to gain the prestigious conducting position at the Vienna State Opera![44]

FURTHER READING

Philippians 3:2–11

42. Kennedy, *Mahler*, 31.

43. One reason for this could be his admiration for Schopenhauer who despised Judaism as "optimistic."

44. He was baptized on 23 February 1897, later saying that "the cloak has been changed" (Carr, *Mahler*, 84).

3

Christ the End of the Law

THE PLACE OF THE LAW FOR PAUL THE PHARISEE

FOR PAUL BEFORE HIS conversion, the law was the center of his religion. The law was the body of Mosaic commandments (later classified as 613 in number),[1] and these laws can be found in the first five books of the Bible, the Pentateuch. As a Pharisee he also had the tradition of the fathers, oral tradition handed down in the Pharisaic schools. This oral tradition is referred to as the "tradition of the elders" in Mark 7:5. In Gal 1:14 Paul refers to the "traditions of my fathers" and this includes the written commandments together with the oral tradition.[2] So Paul writes in Gal 1:14: "I advanced in Judaism beyond many of my people of the same age, for I was far more zealous for the traditions of my ancestors." In writing about his advance in Judaism he is referring to his study and observance of the law. Study was

---

1. The earliest tradition referring to the 613 commandments (365 prohibitions and 248 positive commandments) is probably that going back to R. Simlai, a Palestinian teacher of the second generation of the Amoraim (the Jewish Rabbinic authorities living around 200–500 AD). See b. Makkoth 23b: "Rabbi Simlai when preaching said: Six hundred and thirteen precepts were commanded to Moses, three hundred and sixty-five negative precepts, corresponding to the number of solar days [in the year], and two hundred and forty-eight positive precepts, corresponding to the number of the members of man's body." For further detail see Bell, *No one seeks for God*, 171–72.

2. Fung, *Galatians*, 57.

so important for Jews for it was only through proper study that one can properly observe the law.

Now the torah was not simply a collection of written commandments. In Paul's time it was most likely believed that the torah pre-existed the universe. The reason I say this was "most likely" believed is because the texts that point to the pre-existence of the torah are later than Paul. See Sifre Dt pisqa 37 (pisqa = paragraph): "Torah, the most beloved [of all things], which takes precedence over everything else, was created first of all, for it is said, 'The Lord made me as the beginning of his way, the first of his works of old' (Prov 8.22). And it is further said, 'I was set up from everlasting, from the beginning or ever the earth was' (Prov 8.23)."[3] See also Aboth 3:15, which says that the world was created by the torah. To Israel was given "the precious instrument by which the world was created, as it is written 'For I give you good doctrine; forsake ye not my Law' (Pr. 4.2)."[4]

But although some of these texts may be late, there are indications that the law may well have been seen as pre-existent in Paul's time and instrumental in the creation of the world. For we know that in the later post-exilic period the torah was identified with the figure of Wisdom (Sir 24:23–34) and Wisdom was seen as pre-existent. We see this pre-existence as early as Prov 8:30 and this was then further developed in Sir 24 and Wis 7:22—8.1. And we see a further reflection in Sifre Deut 37 (which cites Prov 8:22–23 in connection with the law and wisdom).

THE PLACE OF THE LAW FOR PAUL THE APOSTLE

At Paul's conversion Christ replaced the law. This can be seen in two respects. First, the Christian Paul came to see that it was not the law that was pre-existent; it was *Christ* who was pre-existent. Secondly, Christ replaced the law regarding salvation. So the Jewish view that the law was a means of salvation was rejected by Paul after his conversion. Paul saw that there was no salvation in the law; salvation was through Christ alone.

The question then arises: what place did the law now have for Paul? The Christian Paul saw that the law had one basic function: to condemn the sinner. This may sound quite shocking; but this is now the central role of the law for Paul.

The clearest exposition of this condemning function is in 2 Cor 3. In this chapter, Paul compares his own ministry to that of Moses. He writes of the two tablets of stone given to Moses on Sinai upon which the Ten

3. Neusner, *Sifre to Deuteronomy*, 1:108.
4. Danby, *Mishnah*, 452.

Commandments were written by God.[5] Paul calls the Ten Commandments the ministry of death. 2 Cor 3:7 affirms that this ministry of death came with splendor; indeed the splendor was so great that the Israelites could not bear to look on Moses' face. He then contrasts this ministry of death with that of the Spirit. See 2 Cor 3:7–8: "Now if the ministry of death, chiselled in letters on stone tablets, came in glory so that the people of Israel could not gaze at Moses' face because of the glory of his face, a glory now set aside, [8]how much more will the ministry of the spirit come in glory?"

The Ten Commandments are then the ministry of death. He makes the same point in 2 Cor 3:6b (and contrasts the law with the Spirit): "The letter [i.e. the written thing, the law] kills, but the Spirit gives life."[6] The law came with splendor but it is a splendor that brings condemnation and death! By contrast the splendor of the gospel is one that brings life. Further the splendor of the law is fading; the splendor of the gospel however becomes stronger and stronger.

The condemning function of the law is seen again in Gal 3:10, 13: "For all who rely on the works of the law are under a curse; for it is written, 'Cursed is everyone who does not observe and obey all the things written in the book of the law.' [. . .] [13]Christ redeemed us from the curse of the law by becoming a curse for us—for it is written, 'Cursed is everyone who hangs on a tree.'" Therefore humanity stands under the curse of the law. And we see here, by the way, the idea that Jesus identified with humanity as he died on the cross in becoming "a curse for us." Further, the law is incapable of making anyone alive, a point Paul makes later in the chapter, Gal 3:21b: "if a law had been given which could make alive, then righteousness would indeed be by the law." Such a claim may appear to go against Phil 3:6 where Paul claims that he was blameless regarding righteousness under the law. But a resolution can be found if Phil 3:6 concerns the external observance of the law and not inner righteousness. In this connection we can think of the words attributed to Jesus in Matt 23:27 against the scribes and the Pharisees: "You are like whitewashed tombs, which on the outside look beautiful, but inside they are full of the bones of the dead and of all kinds of filth."

---

5. The Ten Commandments are given in Exod 20:2–17 and God is described as writing them on the tablets of stone with his finger in Exod 31:18 (see also 34:1).

6. The word *gramma* then means the law. Jude Fawley quotes 2 Cor 3:6 in Thomas Hardy's *Jude the Obscure*, 468 and is cited on the title page of the book. It is, though, a misuse since Paul is not concerned with a "by-the-book adherence to [the] legal contract of 'love.'"

CHRIST SETS THE CHRISTIAN FREE FROM THE LAW

The law brings death and condemnation; but Christ came to set humankind free from the law. I consider three texts where Paul clearly sets this out.

The first is Rom 8:1–2: "There is therefore now no condemnation for those who are in Christ Jesus. [2]For the law of the Spirit of life in Christ Jesus has set you free from the law of sin and of death." The condemnation of the law therefore comes to an end. The Christian is set free from what Paul calls "the law of sin and death," that is, the law that brings sin and death. The Christian now lives in the power of the Spirit.

The second text is Rom 7:6: "But now you are discharged from the law, dead to that which held us captive, so that we are slaves not under the old written code but in the new life of the Spirit." This is truly radical teaching, indeed so radical that even some Christians have found it difficult to cope with this. Many years ago I knew a fine vicar living near my parents' home in East Yorkshire who was a convert from Judaism to Christianity. As a young person, growing up in Jerusalem, he would pass every day a shop with an open New Testament displayed in the window. And one day he stopped to read it. And the next day he noticed the page been turned so he read the next page. So it went on until he had read through a whole gospel and it was through this that he converted to the Christian faith. He was convinced that the truth was to be found in Jesus Christ. But in conversation he was quite honest with me that he felt that Paul had underestimated the importance of the Jewish law and he clearly felt uncomfortable in some Christian circles where he felt the law of Moses was essentially demoted. And one key reason why the law of Moses came to be demoted in the church was because of the teaching of Paul.

The third text I consider is Rom 10:4: "For Christ is the end of the law so that there may be righteousness for everyone who believes." The first issue to address here is what does "end" mean in the phrase "end of the law." The Greek word is "*telos*" and this can mean both "end" and "goal."[7] So some argue that Rom 10:4 is saying Christ is the goal of the law.[8] I take the word to mean "end." One reason is that the word *telos* means end in 2 Cor 3:13. See 2 Cor 3:12–13, which refers to the end of the glory that was associated with the law given to Moses: "Since then we have such a hope, we act with great boldness, [13]not like Moses, who put a veil over his face to keep the people

---

7. And put together "*telos*" goal and "*logos*" word renders the word "*teleology.*" So the teleological argument for the existence of God concerns the design of the universe and so concerns the goal towards which the universe is going.

8. Badenas, *End of the Law.*

of Israel from gazing at the end (*telos*) of the glory that was being set aside." Note also how Paul compares in Rom 10:5–6 the righteousness based on law and that based on faith. Consider Rom 10:4–6 (my translation is slightly different to the New Revised Standard Version):

> ⁴For Christ is the end of the law unto righteousness to everyone who has faith. ⁵For Moses writes concerning the righteousness based on law, "the person who practices them [the command-ments] shall live in them" [Lev 18:5]. ⁶But the righteousness based on faith says, "Do not say in your heart, 'Who shall ascend into heaven' [Deut 30:12]."

In view of this contrast between the way of the law and the way of faith, the contrast between righteousness based on law and righteousness based on faith, *telos* in Rom 10:4 I think must in some sense mean *end*. Note by the way that Paul has the audacity to imply Moses was wrong in Lev 18:5; for not only is it the case that the law *does not* bring life but it simply *cannot* since it was given after the fall.

In what sense then is Christ the end of the law? I suggest the sense is: Christ brings the *condemning* function of the law to an end. He brings it to an end for those who believe in Christ. But the implication is that the law continues to condemn those who do not believe in Christ. The alternative is: Christ brings the *saving* function of the law to an end. But for Paul the apostle the law cannot have such as saving function because of the sinful-ness of the whole of humanity, an issue we will look at in chapter 4. So Christ brings condemning function of the law to an end for Christians.

THE PROBLEM OF ROMANS 2:14–16

I write of the "problem" regarding Rom 2:14–16 because there has been some controversy concerning these verses. When I was a postgraduate the-ology student in Germany I found myself in a place where I should not have been: a seminar on the justification of the godless as a theme of bibli-cal theology. It is not as though I had "gatecrashed" the seminar. Rather someone had made a mistake in issuing the invitation to me, thinking I was a visiting professor and not realizing I was merely a humble postgraduate student. Anyway, never in my life have I been in the same room as so many outstanding theologians. The seminar speaker was talking about the uni-versal sinfulness of humanity and saying that no one has the ability to obey the law. One of the theologians present, a certain Hans Küng, a person very concerned with inter-religious dialogue, drew attention to Rom 2:14–16.

His point was: are there not gentiles who do the good and will be saved on this basis? Romans 2:14–16 runs as follows:

> [14]When Gentiles, who do not possess the law, do instinctively what the law requires, these though not having the law, are a law to themselves. [15]They show that what the law requires is written on their hearts, to which their own conscience also bears witness; And their conflicting thoughts will accuse or perhaps excuse them [16]on the day when, according to my gospel, God, through Jesus Christ, will judge the secrets of all.

So Hans Küng was making the point that there are good people out there who although not possessing the law do instinctively what it requires and if they do so they will be saved at the final judgement. A similar discussion arose in a church I went to in London. On their "missionary Sunday" various missionaries had been invited to speak. In the discussion someone asked about the fate of those who have never heard the gospel. The curate (that is the assistant minister) pointed to these verses in Romans just as Hans Küng had. And the reassuring message was that there may well be gentiles out there who do the good and will be saved. So there is no need to worry too much about those who have never heard the gospel.

But in the seminar I went to in Germany the speaker responded to Küng by making the point that these pious gentiles simply do not exist and again this is something I will discuss further in chapters 4 and 5. But what this text does show is that the law condemns not only Jewish people who have the law but also gentiles for whom the law is written on their heart. So for Jewish people, they have a law. And the central part of this law was chiselled by God on those tablets of stone (2 Cor 3:7; cf. Exod 31:18; 34:1); but for gentiles the law is inscribed on their heart.

These verses in Romans 2 are interpreted in a variety of ways in the commentaries. Some see it as being incompatible with, say, the theology of Martin Luther, who insists that salvation is only possible through the gospel. But I myself would see these verses in the light of Rom 1:18—3:20, which concludes that no one can be saved through works of law. I will return to this in chapters 4 and 5.

THE PROBLEM OF ROMANS 7

Of all the texts where Paul discusses the law, the most difficult is Roman 7. Again, when looking at the commentaries scholars disagree quite radically about what Paul is arguing here.

The easiest part is Rom 7:1–6, where Paul argues that the non-Christian is a slave to the law but the Christian has been set free from the law, something we have seen above in Rom 7:6. But Rom 7:7–25 is difficult. However, I think matters can be clarified if one sees in Rom 7:7–13 references to the fall of Adam and the commandment that brings death to him as the commandment of paradise not to eat of the fruit of the tree of knowledge of good and evil. Then one can understand Rom 7:14–25 as humanity living in the shadow of Adam.

So the commandment in Rom 7:10 that promises him life was not the law of Moses (which cannot give life anyway!) but the law given to Adam in the garden of Eden. See Gen 2:16–17: "And the LORD God commanded the man, 'You may freely eat of every tree of the garden; [17]but of the tree of the knowledge of good and evil you shall not eat, for in the day that you eat of it you shall surely die.'" If Adam refrained from eating of that fruit he could indeed gain life, indeed eternal life, by eating of the tree of life (Gen 2:9). So the commandment in paradise was "do not covet," that is, do not covet the fruit. And this happens also to be the essence of the tenth of Moses' "Ten Commandments": "You shall not covet your neighbor's house; you shall not covet your neighbor's wife, or male or female slave, or ox, or donkey, or anything that belongs to your neighbor" (Exod 20:17). Adam and Eve though broke the commandment "do not covet" for they did covet the fruit and they ate of it (Gen 3:6). The consequence was that they lost the possibility for immortality since they were expelled from the Garden of Eden (Gen 3:24) and no longer had access to the tree of life, whose fruit could have granted them immortality.[9] (Note that they were not *naturally* immortal.) So Paul re-writes Gen 2–3 and, in addition, makes the devastating point that this very commandment "You shall not covet" encouraged him to sin. See Rom 7:7–11:

> [7]What then should we say? That the law is sin? By no means! Yet, if it had not been for the law, I would not have known sin. I would not have known what it is to covet if the law had not said "you shall not covet." [8]But sin, seizing an opportunity in the commandment, produced in me all kinds of covetousness. Apart from the law sin lies dead. [9]I was once alive apart from the law, but when the commandment came, sin revived [10]and I died, and the very commandment that promised life proved to be death to me. [11]For sin, seizing an opportunity in the commandment, deceived me and through it killed me.

9. Wagnerians will recognize a similar pattern in *The Rhinegold* Scene 2: the gods are not naturally immortal but need Freia's golden apples in order to attain it; once they no longer have access to them their strength wanes and they lose their immortality.

Therefore, although in Rom 7:1–6 Paul has been talking about the law of Moses, in Rom 7:7–11 he seems to move over to the commandment as given in paradise, in Gen 2–3. The other complicating matters is that when he says "I" or "me" in vv. 7–11 he may not actually be always talking about himself but rather talking as Adam. In fact, in vv. 9–11 I think he must be talking about Adam and only about Adam.[10] And when he talks about "sin" in vv. 8–11 "seizing an opportunity in the commandment" he is probably talking about the serpent of Genesis 3. So the very commandment encourages him to sin. This is not as strange as it may first appear. This story may not be true but it is quite a good one nevertheless, of a lady who objected to the reading of the Ten Commandments in church in the communion service. Such commandments are read out towards the beginning of the communion service of the *Book of Common Prayer* of the Church of England. The purpose of this is to become aware of one's sins and resolve to keep the commandments in the future.[11] But the lady objected to them being read out because they put so many ideas into her head!

Now Paul emphasizes in Rom 7:12 that despite the commandment provoking one to sin, "the law is holy, and the commandment is holy and just and good." So the law, whether it is that given in the paradise garden or the law that came from Moses, is good and holy. But problems come because of human sin. Paul sets out this problem in v. 13: "Did what is good [i.e., the law], then, bring death to me? By no means! It was sin, working death in me through what is good, in order that sin might be shown to be sin, and through the commandment might become sinful beyond measure." Then in the rest of the chapter he is talking about humanity living in the shadow of Adam. Again we have what may be a confusing use of "I". So in Rom 7:14 Paul says: "We know that the law is spiritual; but I am of the flesh, sold into slavery under sin." And then his argument becomes even psychological in Rom 7:15: "I do not understand my own actions. For I do not do what I want, but I do the very thing I hate."

There is much disagreement as to who this "I" is in vv. 14–25 and I set out three main views. First, he is talking about the non-Christian. The problem here is that the non-Christian Paul thought that as to righteousness under the law he was blameless (Phil 3:6). A second possibility is that he is talking about the Christian.[12] Although this could be supported by the fact

10. Käsemann, *Romans*, 196: "There is nothing in the passage [Rom 7:9–11] which does not fit Adam and everything fits Adam alone."

11. See *Book of Common Prayer*, 237–39.

12. This is supported by Cranfield, *Romans*, 1:345–47. Cranfield points to the long and fine tradition of such an understanding (e.g., Ambrose, Ambrosiaster, Augustine, Aquinas, Luther, and Calvin).

Paul uses the present tense, it seems unlikely that one can say of a Christian that he or she "is sold into slavery under sin" (7:14) given that Rom 6 emphasis throughout that the Christian is now free from sin.[13] A third view, which claims to solve the problem, is that it is the Christian Paul looking at his pre-Christian life through Christian spectacles. So as a Pharisee he would not experience this so-called conflict; but looking back at it as a Christian he can see that he was indeed in some sort of conflict.

None of these solutions work in my view. Of the three the third is probably the best and it is one I used to hold to. All three approaches assume Paul is talking of a conflict.[14] But as I have studied this, I think the essential point is this: Paul is not talking about a conflict or contradiction *within* the human person; rather he is saying that the human person himself or herself *is the contradiction*. Further, he is talking about unredeemed humanity.[15]

The view that the human being is the split was advanced by Kümmel, and developed by Bultmann and Hofius. The essential point is that Paul's statement in Rom 7:14–25 cannot refer to the empirical person. Paul never speaks in positive terms about the will and mind of the empirical human being in relation to the law.[16] On the contrary "the mind that is set on the flesh is hostile to God; it does not submit to God's law" (Rom 8:7). Romans 7:14–24 demonstrates that the human being is a contradiction is this sense: on the one hand, he is a creation of God made to delight in the good and the law; on the other hand, he is living in the shadow of Adam and as such can only displease God and his redemption can only lie in Christ.

THE THREE USES OF THE LAW

According to the Lutheran tradition, there were three uses of the law.[17] First the law to be used by the magistrate; this however has nothing to do with the gospel with which we are concerned. The second use was for bringing the sinner to repentance. I do not think this use is found in Paul, but some

13. E.g., Rom 6:17–18: "But thanks be to God that you, having once been slaves of sin, have become obedient from the heart to the form of teaching to which you were entrusted, and that you having been set free from sin, have become slaves of righteousness."

14. The same conflict model is also assumed by Wasserman, "Death of the Soul," 815, who applies it to the "immoral Gentile."

15. See also Bell, "Reading Romans with Arthur Schopenhauer." Arthur Schopenhauer was a nineteenth-century German philosopher from whom Freud took many of his ideas.

16. Hofius, "Mensch im Schatten Adams," 146–47.

17. See "Formula of Concord" Art VI, in Schaff, *Creeds*, 3:130–31.

see it in Rom 3:20: "through the law comes knowledge of sin." It is argued that through the law comes knowledge of sin in the sense of self-knowledge (Rom 3:20). But one could make a case that for Paul only the gospel shows one to be a sinner and that this verse indicates that the law shows sin to be sin in an objective court of law.

The third use is the law as a guide for Christian conduct. There is some disagreement as to whether Luther himself had this third use of the law corresponding to the first two above. But the Lutheran tradition developed the idea of the third use of the law, the law as a guide for Christian conduct. It is upon this third use of the law (*tertius usus legis*) that I now focus.

There are a number of problems if one is to support a third use of the law in Paul. One problem is Rom 6:14b "you are not under law but under grace." Many may claim that this affirms that Christians are not under the law only in the sense that they do not stand under the *condemnation* of the law. The challenge for this view is that the context of Rom 6:14 is that of Christian living. See Rom 6:12–15:

> [12]Therefore do not let sin exercise dominion in your mortal bodies, to make you obey the passions. [13]No longer present your members to sin as instruments of wickedness, but present yourselves to God as those who have been brought from death to life, and present your members to God as instruments of righteousness. [14]For sin will have no dominion over you, since you are not under law but under grace. [15]What then, should we sin because we are not under law but under grace? By no means!

This final verse is one of the clues. Some could make the inference that since the Christian is not under law in regard to everyday Christian living then one can be licentious. Paul makes it clear that this is a false inference.

Now it is striking how Paul almost never quotes the law in matters of ethical behavior. He often quotes from the law to make a *theological* point; but hardly ever does he quote it to make an *ethical* point. In fact, I think there are only two such texts where Paul quotes the Old Testament law to make an ethical point: Rom 13:8–10 and 1 Cor 9:9. In Rom 13:8–10 various commandments are quoted but they are not the crucial thing; the crucial thing is the law of love. See Rom 13:10: "Love does no wrong to a neighbor; therefore, love is the fulfilling of the law." But Paul does quote the law to establish this: "You shall love your neighbor as yourself" (Lev 19:18). The point though is that it is not that one should follow individual laws but the law of love gives a principle by which one should live.

The second instance where he quotes the law to make an ethical point is in 1 Cor 9:9. Here Deut 25:4 is quoted to prove the point that those who preach the gospel should be paid for it. But Paul's use of the Old Testament law here is somewhat strange. Deuteronomy 25:4 runs as follows: "You shall not muzzle an ox when it is treading the grain." Now what is happening here is that Paul is not really making an ethical point; he is enunciating a principle for Christian service. Note also that although he argues that the preachers have the right to be paid for their service, Paul himself has not made use of this right.

There are two other places in the letters traditionally attributed to Paul where the law is quoted to give guidance in ethical conduct. First 1 Cor 14:34, where Paul says it is not permitted for a woman to speak in church "as even the law says." However, 1 Cor 14:34–35 may be an interpolation, i.e., an insertion from someone other than Paul (see chapter 9 below). Second in Eph 6:2 the author quotes the fifth of the Ten Commandments: "Honour your Father and Mother." But Ephesians is probably not written by Paul (see chapter 1 above).

So Paul rarely quotes the law to make an ethical point. In addition, on many occasions he could have quoted the law but does not. So in 1 Cor 5–6 he addresses issues of sexual morality for which there were Old Testament laws but he does not quote them. In these chapters he is dealing with issues such as adultery, fornication, and homosexual relations but he does not quote the law, although it could be said that he alludes to the law. In fact, some of his arguments where he refrains from quoting the law could be said to become a little bit bizzare. So in 1 Cor 6:15–18a he asks; "Should I therefore take the members of Christ and make them members of a prostitute? Never! [16]Do you not know that whoever is united to a prostitute becomes one body with her? For it is said 'The two shall be one flesh.' [17]But anyone united to the Lord becomes one spirit with him. [18]Shun fornication." His argument is that as the Christian is one body with Christ it is unthinkable that they could also become one body with a prostitute.

Although Paul rarely quotes from the law to make an ethical point he does allude to the law and I will take this up in chapter 4 when I discuss Paul's view of sexual sin. And when he discusses morality he can tend to use a different sort of argument, as in the case of not being one flesh with a prostitute since believers are one flesh with Christ.

Now those who support a third use of the law can refer to three texts, one of which is Rom 13:8–10, which I have already mentioned, and there are two other texts one could consider. In Rom 8:4 Paul writes that "the just requirements of the law might be fulfilled in us, who walk not according to the flesh but according to the Spirit." But this is not saying the Christian is to *fulfil* the law; rather, it says the just requirements of the law might *be fulfilled* in us. So there is a passive rather than an active sense. Also the previous verses make it clear that one is free from the law: "The law of the Spirit of life in Christ Jesus has set me free from the law of sin and death" (Rom 8:2). We have an antithesis: on the one hand, "the law of the Spirit of life in Christ Jesus," the Spirit's vitalizing power; on the other hand, "the law of sin and death," the law of Moses, which brings sin and death. God sent his Son "in order that the just requirement of the law might be fulfilled in us, who walk not according to the flesh but according to the Spirit." The law belongs to the old age, the Spirit belongs to the new. In the old age the written law was followed. In the new age Christians follow the direction of the Holy Spirit. Christians serve no written code, not even the Ten Commandments. Rather, they have God's Spirit in their heart to direct their lives.

There remains only one verse that could support the *tertius usus legis*, namely 1 Cor 7:19: "Circumcision is nothing, and uncircumcision is nothing; but obeying the commandments of God is everything." But Paul is not at all thinking of the law of Moses and the very fact that he writes that circumcision is nothing proves this. Circumcision was one of the commandments of the Old Testament. Paul is most likely referring to the law of Christ as in Gal 6:2: "Bear one another's burdens and so fulfil the law of Christ." The law of Christ includes anything that is consonant with the Spirit of Christ and could include the teaching of Jesus himself, to which Paul occasionally refers.[18]

The Christian is to be a slave to righteousness, as Paul emphasizes in Rom 6. But the law of Moses has no authority in itself. For example, the reason one does not steal is not because of the eighth of the Ten Commandments "You shall not steal" but because of law of Christ (Gal 6:2).

Another problem in taking the law as a guide for Christians is that certain laws we know are not meant to be kept. It is assumed that Christians do not have to keep the food laws. Calvin and others argued that the ceremonial law has been abolished by Christ, but the ethical commandments are to be kept. Calvin writes: "The third and principal use, which pertains more closely to the proper purpose of the law, finds its place among believers in whose hearts the Spirit of God already lives and reigns."[19] There is a possible problem here. For the Jew the law was a whole and generally it was not divided into ceremonial, civil, and moral law.[20] One can say that in Jewish tradition the Ten Commandments have a central role, standing in

18. For a study of Paul's use of Jesus tradition in Rom 12:1—15:13, see Thompson, *Clothed with Christ*.

19. See Calvin, *Institutes* 2.7.12. See also the whole section 2.7.12–15 (McNeill, *Institutes*, 1:360–64).

20. An exception is the Hellenistic Jewish Christians who kept the moral law but not the ceremonial (or at least not all of it).

the center of Jahweh's self-revelation on mount Sinai.[21] But nevertheless the law was not divided into these compartments. In this connection it is worth pointing out that there are so-called ethical commandments that the Christian is not obliged to obey, even in the Ten Commandments. The Christian is certainly not bound to keep the sabbath (fourth commandment). Also the Christian does not have to obey the first part of the second commandment: "You should not make for yourself an idol, whether in the form of anything that is in heaven above, or that is on the earth beneath, or that is in the water under the earth" (Exod 20:4). The law says you shall not make a *pesel*, that is a free-standing object, like a statue. So if this were to be applied churches would need to start taking down statues or any free-standing object. And indeed there have been occasions—for example, at the time of Cromwell in the seventeenth century—where statues in churches were destroyed, reflecting the fact that Calvinists can be legalistic.[22]

CONCLUSIONS

The Old Testament law then has no ultimate authority for the Christian. The law of Christ and the law of Moses may sometimes overlap; but the law of Moses still has no authority. It is rather like travelling from Germany to Britain in the car, a journey I made on the number of occasions. There are laws that are the same in both countries. So when you see a sign with a red circle bisected by a white horizontal line then you are not allowed to enter that street. But some are different. For example, the Germans have the law that you give way to traffic on your right unless indicated by one of those yellow diamond signs. But when you come to Britain this law is no longer valid. Once you leave Germany you are no longer under that code. You are under the law of Britain.

Likewise the Christian is not under the law of Moses, although it may be that the Christian does not steal. But he or she does not steal because of the law of Christ, not the law of Moses. If one were to write a treatise on the ethics of stealing you could *begin* with Moses. But you could also include what Greek moral philosophers said. And ultimately you would conclude with a discussion of the law of Christ. So just as there may be German traffic laws which could teach one something, when in Britain these laws have no authority. Hence the law of Moses has no authority for a Christian.

21. Gese, "Dekalog," 63.

22. Luther deleted what in the UK we know as the "second commandment" in his catechisms and made up for this by splitting our tenth into two. See *BSELK* 507–10 (Smaller Catechism) and 560–638 (Greater Catechism).

According to Paul then the Christian is set free from the law. The law's function is primarily to condemn. Paul's gospel is a liberating gospel. The believer has come of age, as Gal 4:3–5 states: "while we were minors, we were enslaved to the elemental spirits of the world. ⁴But when the fullness of time had come, God sent his Son, born of a woman, born under the law, ⁵in order to redeem those who were under the law, so that we might receive adoption as children." The Christian has received the Spirit of sonship and is no longer to fear. As Paul tells the Christians in Rome: "For you did not receive the spirit of slavery to fall back into fear, but you have received a spirit of adoption" (Rom 8:15).

The Christian is free from the condemnation of the law. The Christian is also free from the law as a guide to our Christian living. But being free from the law does not mean the Christian can be licentious. Many misunderstood Paul in this respect. So he asks in Rom 6:1: "What then are we to say? Should we continue in sin in order that grace may abound?" and he replies "By no means!"

Luther got it right in his treatise "On the freedom of a Christian": "A Christian is a perfectly free lord of all, subject to none. A Christian is a perfectly dutiful servant of all, subject to all." Luther in his treatise goes on to quote 1 Cor 9:19: "For though I am free from all, I have made myself a slave to all."[23] The Christian is subject to none in respect to liberty; but he or she is subject to all in respect to charity.

JOHANN SEBASTIAN BACH, "CUM SANCTO SPIRITU" FROM *THE MASS IN B MINOR*

To get a sense of what freedom in the Spirit may mean I have chosen "With the Holy Spirit, to the glory of God the Father, Amen" from the end of the Gloria of Bach's *Mass in B Minor*. The Latin is: "*cum Sancto Spiritu: in gloria Dei Patris. Amen.*" The conductor Otto Klemperer, whose own great recording can sound at times more like Brahms or Elgar than Bach, considered this piece "the greatest and most unique music ever written."[24] Subjective though this judgement is, I have no doubt that we are in this mass occupying the musical stratosphere.

Of all the composers who will feature in the website, one who in my view preaches the most robust and healthy Christian faith is Johann Sebastian Bach. He has a Christian authenticity and integrity that is welcome at a time when it appears to be in such short supply. Bach will feature again in

23. *LW* 31:344 (modified).
24. Heyworth, *Klemperer, 1933–1973*, 333.

later chapters, and it is there that I will say more as to why he is such a great musician *and* theologian.

FURTHER READING

2 Corinthians 3:1–18.

4

The Need for Reconciliation

JEW AND GENTILE UNDER THE POWER OF SIN

THE PREVIOUS CHAPTER DEALT with the bad news of the sinner being condemned by the law but ended with the good news of freedom from the law of Moses for the Christian. Now I return to the bad news. This is a necessary backdrop for his teaching on justification, which I will look at in chapter 5, on the sacrifice of Christ, which I will look at in chapter 6, and indeed on freedom from law, which I considered in the previous chapter. But as the bad news as Paul sees it is considered, it will be necessary at some points to question whether it can be held on to.

The human problem, according to Paul, is that the whole of humanity, Jews and gentiles alike, is under the power of sin. First of all, it is important to stress that Paul often categorizes humanity in terms of Jews and non-Jews (that is gentiles). And when it comes to sin the important word to stress is *power*, the power of sin. So both Jews and gentiles not only *commit* sins in the sense of stealing, lying, exploiting other people and so on. They are *under the power* of sin, and this is one of Paul's main points in the first three chapters of Romans. See Rom 3:9: "we have already charged that all, both Jews and Greeks [i.e. gentiles], are under the power of sin." In one sense sin is a mythical entity. When we looked at Romans 7 in the previous chapter I said that sin takes on the role of the serpent in Genesis 3 (see Rom 7:8, 11). A related way of understanding sin is that it is like a disease that affects the whole human being. Sin according to Paul affects thinking, sexuality, and relations with other people.

So as well as being understood as a serpent-like figure, sin could be understand as a kind of disease that runs through the whole being. Sin is not just a functional problem (what we *do*); it is an ontological problem (who we *are*). This is one of the most important points to grasp in Paul's theology. Simply as a result of living in this world of space-time, sin is inevitable. This is something we will find reflected in parts of what is called the priestly writing of the Old Testament when we look at the sin offering. It is also found in Luther and in many thinkers who have been influenced by Luther, for example, the German philosopher G. W. F. Hegel.[1]

Therefore, sin affects the human's *very being*. Sin is not just something carried around that can be off-loaded. I once heard a famous evangelist say that we carry a dustbin of sins on our back. When you become a Christian, this bin is turned upside down and emptied. Or taking another illustration, sin is not like a mucky overcoat that you can simply take off. A popular illustration I have heard in evangelical sermons is that sins are like a big heavy book laying on your right hand; such a book can be transferred to the other hand leaving you right hand free. In like manner it is said sins can be simply transferred to Jesus such that we are free of our sins. This image may work for some biblical texts (e.g., Isa 52:13—53:12 or 1 Pet 2:23–25), but it does not work for Paul.

Likewise Paul very rarely talks about sins being covered, rubbed out, expiated. So to expiate sins is essentially to rub them out. But if you take an image of the human being as a pear rotten through to the core, peeling off layers with a knife is not going solve the problem of the rotten pear. All you can do is throw the pear into the ground, allowing it to die, and by some miracle a new pear comes into being.

The reason it is necessary to think like this is because sin is an *ontological* problem; it affects the person's very being. I think it is very clear that Paul has a pessimistic view of the human being and many understandably find that Paul is denigrating human beings in speaking in this way. Many of the great thinkers have shared Paul's view that there is something fundamentally wrong with each of us and it is best to recognize that.[2] But the question arises whether his view of the human person is simply too extreme and whether it can be applied to all. One reason perhaps that Paul has such a pessimistic view of the human person is that during his time as a Pharisee

---

1. See Miller, *Phenomenology*, 281–82 (§468).

2. Augustine and Luther stand out in this respect. Paul's view has also influenced those outside the Christian tradition such as Arthur Schopenhauer (1788–1860).

Paul was the worst kind of religious person, seen especially in his persecuting the Christian church. It may be that he projects this view on to every other human being.

To return to his argument, because of the seriousness of sin Paul claimed that human beings stand under the just judgement of God and they deserve to die (Rom 1:32). When he says "they deserve to die" he is primarily talking about the final judgement, although, as we shall see, he may have the death penalty in mind.

PAUL ON SEXUAL SIN

It is important to say that sexual sin is not the root sin for Paul. The root of sin is turning away from God, worshipping idols, and the darkening of the mind (Rom 1:21–23). But sexual sin is clearly important for Paul and indeed it results from these root sins. I address sexual sin now because it becomes an important part of Paul's argument in Rom 1:18–32 and it was an issue left over from the previous chapter on Paul and the law. There I mentioned Paul's argument that believers should not become one flesh with a prostitute because they are one flesh with Christ and I said that Paul, in prohibiting sexual intercourse with a prostitute, could have appealed to the law but decided not to. But we will now see that although he does not quote the law he does indeed allude to the law when he discusses sexual sin or what he regards as sexual sin.

The text I am concerned with is Rom 1:24–27, which is embedded in his argument in Rom 1:18–32. In Rom 1:24, having argued that human beings have rejected God and turned to idolatry, he says "God gave them up in the lusts of their hearts to impurity, to the degrading of their bodies among themselves." He is speaking here of all types of what he considers sexual sin and the root of this sexual sin lies in idolatry as he makes clear in v. 25: "because they exchanged the truth about God for a lie and worshipped and served the creature rather than the creator." This is a case where he is alluding to chapters 13–15 of Wisdom of Solomon, where idolatry is seen as the root sin.

One reason this passage in Rom 1 is so controversial is because Paul decides to home in on "homosexuality". I use quotation marks because the terms "homosexual" and "heterosexual" are recent terms, coined by Karl-Maria Benkert (Károly Mária Kertbeny) in 1868, who argued that being homosexual is inborn and natural and in fact he campaigned for gay rights.[3]

3. See his letter to Karl Heinrich Ulrichs of 6 May 1868 (Pretsell, *Ulrichs*, 199–205).

So in studying these verses it is important to be aware that Paul did not have the insights we have today into human sexuality.

Paul writes in Rom 1:26–27: "For this reason God gave them up to degrading passions. Their women exchanged natural intercourse for un-natural, [27]and in the same way also the men, giving up natural intercourse with women, were consumed with passion for one another. Men committed shameless acts with men and received in their own persons the due penalty for their error." These verses are, of course, highly controversial and New Testament scholars and theologians have disagreed in interpreting them. My own view is that Paul is condemning all homosexual behavior and in-deed condemning any homosexual thoughts. The fundamental cause of the fall is located in the human mind and much of the emphasis in Rom 1:18–32 is about the darkening of the mind.

Paul's views here on homosexuality are fashioned by the Old Testa-ment, which condemned homosexual activity, although there may have been homoerotic relationships, as between say King David and Jonathan, a relationship that is celebrated in 1 Sam 18:1–4. See also 2 Sam 1:26 where David mourns the death of Jonathan: "I am distressed for you, my brother Jonathan; Greatly beloved were you to me; your love to me was wonderful, passing the love of women." However, there is some dispute whether the relationship with between David and Jonathan was sexual.[4] But going back to Paul, here in Rom 1:26–27 I think he has in mind Lev 18:22 and Lev 20:13. In Lev 20:13 we read: "if a man lies with a male as with a woman, both of them have committed an abomination; they shall be put to death; their blood is upon them." Paul may be alluding to these verses in Rom 1:32 where he speaks of those who practice sins deserve to die.[5]

I will return to the issue of sexuality in the final chapter when I evalu-ate Paul. But I now make two points, both of which are controversial. First, I think Paul is profoundly wrong on the issue of homosexuality. He was clearly steered by the texts in Leviticus, which have had appalling conse-quences. In this connection it is worth saying that a manifestation of the evils of the British Empire is that homosexuality is still illegal in many of the former British colonies because of views held in Britain and propagated by Christian missionaries. Fortunately we understand more now about human nature and sexuality and it has been those outside the Christian tradition

---

4. See the assessment of Anderson, 2 *Samuel*, 19 (on 2 Sam 1:26).

5. Loader, "Homosexuality," 145.

who have been at the forefront of making homosexuality lawful in the UK[6] and fighting for gay rights.[7]

My second controversial point is that despite my criticism of Paul's view of sexuality I also think it is naïve to say simply "sexuality is a good gift of God." Theologically I am happy to say that God has bestowed both heterosexual and homosexual urges in human beings, but in view of our fallen nature I would also say that every sexual act involves sin to some extent. This seems to be the logical conclusion from Paul's view of fallen humanity. The irony is that many evangelical Christians condemn gay people for having sex yet fail to recognize that every time they make love they are also sinning, for no part of our being can be exempt from the effects of the fall. It is also worth emphasizing that in the whole current debate on sexuality in the churches it is often overlooked that in good gay relationships people are simply loving each other and are forming relationships that serve the wider community.

Returning to Rom 1:26–28 we have a difficult text but it is worth highlighting that Paul goes on to list a whole range of sins and not just sexual sins; and I add that the seriousness of sexual sins is actually highlighted in the sins of "deceit" and "faithless[ness]." So in Rom 1:29–31 he writes that human beings "were filled with every kind of wickedness, evil, covetousness, malice. Full of envy, murder, strife, deceit, craftiness, they are gossips, slanderous, God-haters, insolent, haughty, boastful, inventors of evil, rebellious towards parents, foolish, faithless, heartless, ruthless." This then leads to the final verse of the chapter where he says that those who practise such things deserve to die. Now although Paul seems to be alluding to Lev 20:13 he is shifting this in that he is not just thinking of what he considers the sin of homosexuality but also expanding it to other sins. And it is worth emphasizing that the Levitical law commanded the death penalty for a whole range of sins. So the death penalty was not only commanded for murder (Exod 21:14) but also for a female sorcerer (Exod 22:18), apostasy (Exod 22:20), adultery (Lev 20:10), and even for cursing your father or mother (Exod 21:17)! Furthermore, here Paul is not so much thinking of the death penalty but of the day of judgement.

6. Magee, *One in Twenty*, helped make homosexual activity legal in the UK; this book was originally published in 1966, one year before it was legalized. The book is obviously dated and some of the phrases may jar somewhat.

7. I think here especially of Peter Tatchell. This brave campaigner has been much maligned over the years in church circles but now many are coming to see that he was on the right side of history.

THE WRATH OF GOD

Paul speaks of God's wrath being revealed from heaven in Rom 1:18: "For the wrath of God is revealed from heaven against all ungodliness and wickedness of men who by their wickedness suppress the truth." There are two things to note about this verse. First, this is often taken to mean that God's wrath is being expressed in the here and now. This could possibly be the case. But it is more likely that Paul is here talking about the wrath of God that will come at the last judgement.[8] Then God will execute his judgement. In the Greek a present verb is used: "The wrath of God is revealed (*apokalyptetai*) from heaven." But a Greek present can also be used for a future event that is bound to take place.[9] Note also that in Rom 2:5 the wrath is also eschatological wrath: "But by your hard and impenitent heart you are storing up wrath for yourself on the day of wrath when God's righteous judgment will be revealed." See also 1 Cor 3:13 where the same Greek present, *apokalyptetai*, is used for a future event. Here Paul is most certainly speaking of the eschatological wrath. He likens the Christian worker to a builder: "the work of each builder will become visible, for the day will disclose it, because it will be revealed (*apokalyptetai*) with fire, and the fire will test what sort of work each has done." So I understand Rom 1:18 to refer to a future eschatological judgement.

The second point concerning wrath is that for Paul the wrath of God is not like human anger. Wrath is not an emotion of God. Rather it is an objective entity—and the consequence of this wrath is that human beings will be condemned on the day of judgement. Wrath has to do with God's function as a just judge.

This, according to Paul, is the human predicament. If Christ were not to come all would be condemned to death on the day of judgement. Not one person would be acquitted on the last judgement as things stand. In chapter 3 I mentioned that Rom 2:14–16 has been employed to support the view that some are going to be saved because of their holy life; but I argued that such pious Jews and gentiles simply do not exist. So Paul holds the view that everybody is a sinner and, as things stand, everybody is heading for God's just judgement.

---

8. Eckstein, "Gottes Zorn." Such a view is found in a number of patristic writers (Irenaeus, Chrysostom, Theodore of Mopsuestia). Such an eschatological understanding is also found in nineteenth-century commentators (Philippi, *Römer*, 34; Ritschl, *Rechtfertigung II*, 146).

9. For New Testament Greek, see *BDF* §323 and Radermacher, *Grammatik*, 152. For Classical Greek see Schwyzer, *Grammatik*, 2:273.4.

GOD'S LOVE FOR THE SINNER

God's attitude towards sin is the desire to destroy it. God's attitude toward the sinner is the desire to redeem him or her from the tyranny of sin. The Christian saying "God loves the sinner but hates the sin" is thoroughly Pauline. Here it must be stressed that God's attitude towards the sinner does not change as a result of Christ's death. Such a change is assumed in penal substitution. This teaches that God shows wrath towards us; Jesus dies in our place; he pays the price by giving satisfaction to God; God can then and only then accept us. Views of atonement in terms of "satisfaction" can be found among the theories set out in the early Christian centuries[10] but it was Anselm of Canterbury who developed a satisfaction theory systematically.[11] His views were appropriated and developed by Calvin and then by many evangelicals.[12] The implication in this so-called Latin model is that God has to be propitiated. We have an angry God; Jesus is the propitiatory sacrifice; he averts God's wrath.

From Paul's perspective there are two problems with this view. First, the idea of sacrifice is a Greek one that has little to do with the main sacrificial texts of the Old Testament upon which Paul builds. The Greeks worked with propitiatory sacrifices. So in the legend of Troy we read how Paris had carried off the beautiful Helen to Troy. Paris was a son of King Priam of Troy; Helen was the wife of the Menelaus, king of Sparta. A vast Greek force wanted to set off to recover her but they were held up by contrary winds. Calchas prophesied that they would be unable to sail unless Agamemnon sacrificed the most beautiful of his daughters to Artemis. Agamemnon, the Greek general and older brother of Menelaus, had displeased the goddess Artemis, the goddess of hunting; there are various explanations one of which is that when Agamemnon shot a stag he boasted that he was a better

---

10. Kelly, *Doctrines*, 375–99, gives an overview.

11. See his *Cur deus homo?* (*Why Did God Become Human?*)

12. Anselm himself did not hold to a direct change in God's attitude as a result of the satisfaction paid by Christ (Aulén, *Christus Victor*, 85). Rather he thinks in term of the merits Christ gained as passing over to Christians. See *Cur deus homo* II.1: "Upon whom would he more properly bestow the reward accruing from his death, than upon those for whose salvation, as right reason teaches, he became man" (Deane, *Anselm*, 284). And so "[w]hen the transaction is completed, the sinful men are forgiven the debts they owe, for they are given that which by reason of their sins they lacked" (McIntyre, *Anselm*, 180). Anselm's atonement theory was based on the penitential system which Calvin and evangelical clearly do not hold to. In what is called penal substitution the transaction is not between God and human beings (a transfer of merit) but rather Christ paying satisfaction to God.

huntsman than Artemis.[13] Agamemnon had his most beautiful daughter Iphigeneia sent to him at Aulis. Agamemnon sacrificed his daughter to propitiate Artemis. There are versions where at the last minute a hind was substituted. So in Euripides, *Iphigeneia at Aulis*, it is narrated that Iphigeneia vanished just as Agamemnon is about to sacrifice her and is replaced by a hind.[14] But the tradition I am thinking of is where Iphigeneia herself is sacrificed, found in the tragedy of Aeschylus. And so the chorus in Aeschylus *Agamemnon* (224–37) tells us:[15]

> In short, [Agamemnon] brought himself to become
> the sacrificer of his daughter, to further
> a war of revenge over a woman [Helen]
> and as a preliminary rite to the fleet's departure.
> Her pleas, her cries of "father!",
> and her maiden years, were set at naught
> by the war-loving chieftains.
> After a prayer, her father told his attendants
> to lift her right up over the altar
> with all their strength, like a yearling goat,
> face down, so that her robes fell around her,
> and by putting a guard
> on her fair face and lips to restrain
> speech that might lay a curse on his house.

She was sacrificed, Artemis' wrath was satisfied, the west winds then blew and the Greeks were able to reach Troy. Such was the pagan idea of sacrifice.[16]

Penal substitution, understanding Christ death as a propitiatory sacrifice, is a sacrifice rather like that of Iphigeneia. The evangelical leader J. I. Packer was quite happy to understand Christ's death as such a propitiatory sacrifice and even draws parallels to the sacrifice of Iphigeneia. He claims: "The idea of propitiation—that is, of averting God's anger by an offering—runs right through the Bible." Unfortunately he misunderstands the sin

---

13. This is found in the *Cypria*, the earliest evidence of Iphigeneia's sacrifice (Rose/March, "Agamemnon," 35). See also Graves, *Greek Myths*, 2:291.

14. See Way, *Euripides I*, 146–47 (*Iphigeneia at Aulis* ll. 1580–89).

15. Sommerstein, *Aeschylus II*, 26–29.

16. For an overview of this story of Agamemnon's sacrifice of his daughter, I suggest looking first at Graves, *Greek Myths*, 2:291. Agamemnon's sacrificing Iphigenia had ghastly consequences. When he returned from Troy his wife Clytemnestra killed him in revenge. And then Electra, the daughter of Agamemnon, gets her brother Orestes to kill Clytemnestra and her lover Aegisthus, again in revenge. We see the working out of these events in Aeschylus, *Agamemnon*, and *Libation Bearers*.

offering and when he does give an example of God's wrath being averted it is not through an animal sacrifice but through the use of incense (Num 16:41–50).[17]

Now one could hold to penal substitution and emphasize the differences between the sacrifice of Iphigeneia and the sacrifice of Christ. Iphigeneia was sacrificed so the Greeks could sail to Troy. Christ was sacrificed in order to deal with the sins of humanity. And whereas Iphigeneia was simply a human being, Christ is understood as the Son of God. But one should not overlook the fact that such an approach still understands both sacrifices as propitiatory.

Before looking at Christ's sacrifice I turn first to the Old Testament type of sacrifice. There are some instances of propitiatory sacrifices in the early literature (e.g., 1 Sam 26:19 may imply such propitiation) and Isa 52:13—53:12 can be understood as a propitiatory sacrifice in the sense that satisfaction is paid to God for the sins of the people. But in the overwhelming majority of instances where sacrifice is discussed in the Old Testament there is no idea of propitiation. This will be discussed in greater detail in chapter 6 but for now let me say this. In the Old Testament sacrifice of the sin offering, the sinner identifies with the animal and then the animal is slaughtered. There is then a crucial stage that is often overlooked: the blood of the animal is taken into the presence of God. For example, on the Day of Atonement, Yôm Kippur, the blood of bull or goat is sprinkled on the mercy seat in the holy of holies. Paul then applies it to Christ. Christians are identified with Christ, die with him, and are taken into God's presence. There is no idea of propitiation.

The second problem with propitiation is that it assumes that God has to be reconciled to us. But such an idea is not to be found in Paul and possibly nowhere in the New Testament. God does not have to be reconciled to human beings; rather they have to be reconciled to God. God is not their enemy; rather they are God's enemy. To repeat my earlier point, God's wrath is not to be understood as an emotion of God; rather it is concerned with God as just judge and therefore cannot be taken in the sense that God is our enemy. There is in fact no clear single passage in Paul where God is portrayed as our enemy.[18] But human beings are portrayed as God's enemies as in Rom 5:8–10a: "God proves his love for us in that while we were yet

17. Packer, *Knowing God*, 200.

18. The possible exception is Rom 11:28, where Paul writes of Israelites: "As regards the gospel they are enemies of God for your sake; but as regards election they are beloved for the sake of their ancestors." Cranfield, *Romans*, 2:580, argues for a passive understanding of "enemies", corresponding to the passive "beloved". However, an active sense is just as likely (see Bell, *Provoked to Jealousy*, 146).

sinners Christ died for us. [9]Since therefore we are now justified by his blood, much more shall we be saved by him from the wrath of God. [10]For if while we were enemies we were reconciled to God by the death of his Son, much more, now that we are reconciled, shall we be saved by his life."

Therefore, human beings are reconciled to God; God does not need to be reconciled to them. See 2 Cor 5:19: "God was in Christ reconciling the world to himself." God's attitude towards the sinner is then to save him or her. While human beings were yet sinners, Christ died for the ungodly. The sacrifice of Christ is not before God and for God. If this were the case God would be passive in the event of the cross.[19] God himself is active in the event of the cross. There is a unity of action between the Father and the Son.

THE PORTRAYAL OF THE DAY OF JUDGEMENT IN VERDI AND FAURÉ

The day of judgement is just one issue we have looked at in this chapter and it has played a huge rôle in the history of the Christian church. It was to be a day of terror and this terror was to color the lives of many who thereby lived in fear of eternal damnation.

The music I have chosen represents two very different portrayals of the day of judgement. The first is from the requiem of the Italian composer Giuseppe Verdi who had little interest in organized religion[20] (and in fact disliked the established church like many other Italian nationalists) but claimed to be "a very doubtful believer" rather than "an outright atheist."[21] He clearly had an interest in theology and his representation of the day of wrath is terrifying; but at the same time it is great to listen to it! The words are:

Dies irae, dies illa,	Day of anger, Day of terror,
Solvet saeculum in favilla,	All shall crumble into ashes,
Teste David cum Sybilla.	This was David's revelation.
Quantus tremor est futurus,	What a trembling shall possess them
Quando judex est venturus,	When the Judge shall come to judgement,
Cuncta stricte discussurus!	Searching all the souls before Him!

The second representation of the day of wrath is from the requiem by the French composer Gabriel Fauré. His portrayal of the day of wrath is

---

19. Cf. Hofius, "Sühne," 38.

20. Martin, Verdi, 130.

21. Martin, Verdi, 237.

mild; indeed "[h]e presents us with a Mass for the Dead without a real Last Judgement"[22] and some performances offer even a tender interpretation. The words from the movement *libera me*[23] are:

Libera me, Domine, de morte aeterna	Free me, lord, from death eternal
in die illa tremenda	on that day of dread
quando coeli movendi sunt et terra	when the heavens will be shaken and the earth
dum veneris judicare saeculum per ignem	while you come to judge the world with fire.
Tremens factus sum ego et timeo	I am made to shake, and am afraid
dum discussio venerit atque ventura ira.	awaiting the trial and the coming anger.
Dies illa, dies irae, calamitatis et miseriae	That day, day of anger, of calamity and misery,
dies illa, dies magna et amara valde.	that day, the day of great and exceeding bitterness,
Requiem eternam dona eis Domine	Rest eternal give them, Lord,
et lux perpetua luceat eis. . . .	and let light always shine on them. . . .

Fauré explained to Louis Aguettant on July 12, 1902: "It has been said that my *Requiem* does not express fear of death and some have called it a lullaby of death. But it is thus that I see death: as a happy deliverance, an aspiration towards happiness above, rather than as a painful experience."[24]

Is there going to be a day of judgement? Well who knows! If there is going to be a day of judgement, I imagine it is going to be uncomfortable for everyone and for some more than others. But many would deny such a day of judgement, not only atheists but even some Christian theologians.

So do please listen to the music. It gives you a feel for the judgement of God that has been discussed in this chapter. But such judgement is not the last word; for as we shall see in the next chapter, the heart of Paul's theology is not in our condemnation but in our acquittal.

FURTHER READING

Romans 5:6–11.

22. Orledge, *Fauré*, 112.

23. This was first composed in 1877 for baritone and organ and later incorporated into this *Requiem* with chorus and orchestra (Nectoux, *Fauré*, 533, 540–41).

24. Orledge, *Fauré*, 113.

5

The Justification of the Ungodly, *Sola Gratia, Sola Fide*

HOW CENTRAL IS JUSTIFICATION?

ALBERT SCHWEITZER FAMOUSLY DESCRIBED justification as a "subsidiary crater" in Paul's theology[1] and William Wrede argued that justification is not at the center of Paul's theology as the reformers thought.[2] This, I believe, is mistaken. Justification is central to Paul's theology and I hope this will become evident as we look at justification in Paul's letters.

Justification occasionally crops up in other New Testament books. For instance, justification occurs in Luke 18:9–14, the parable of the Pharisee and the tax collector. The Pharisee and the tax collector went to the temple to pray. The Pharisee boasted of his good works; the tax collector simply prayed, "God be merciful to me a sinner." Jesus says the tax collector and not the Pharisee went home justified. This is quite Pauline and there are in fact many similarities between Luke's two-volume work (the Gospel of Luke and Acts of the Apostles) and Paul's theology. This goes back to the fact that Luke, whom I assume was the author of Luke-Acts, was a travelling

---

1. Schweitzer, *Mysticism*, 225: "The doctrine of righteousness by faith is [. . .] a subsidiary crater, which has formed within the rim of the main crater—the mystical doctrine of redemption through the being-in-Christ." As will become clear Schweitzer presents a false dichotomy.

2. Wrede, "Paulus," 67.

companion of Paul. It is striking that in this parable the target is the Pharisee, Paul's pre-Christian identity.

Justification also occurs in Jas 2:14–26, but James present an entirely different view of justification. So whereas Paul says Abraham was justified by faith, James says he was justified by works (Jas 2:21), a point I will return to below and in chapter 7.

So in this chapter I examine Paul's ideas of the "justification of the ungodly"; and it may be worth reflecting on the fact that in my experience this phrase does not occur very often on the lips of many Christians in the English-speaking world.

NO JUSTIFICATION THROUGH WORKS OF THE LAW (ROM 3:20)

Paul in his letters clearly attacked the Jewish view that righteousness could be obtained by works of the law. For Paul there was no justification by works of the law, as he makes clear in Rom 3:20a: "For no human being will be justified in God's sight through works of the law."

There has been some controversy as to the meaning of "works of the law" (*erga nomou*) in New Testament scholarship over the last forty years. I understand the phrase to mean "observance of the torah," the torah being the Jewish law. So observance of the law would involve keeping the Ten Commandments and various other moral laws contained in the Old Testament (for example, the laws concerning sexual behavior in Lev 20). Observing the law also involves the various so-called ceremonial laws, such as the food laws and circumcision. To prove this claim, I point to two texts that are roughly contemporary to the New Testament. First, a text from the fourth cave of Qumran, 4Q Florilegium 1:7: "He has commanded that a Sanctuary of men be built for Himself, that there they may send up, like the smoke of innocence, the works of the Law."[3] Secondly I give a text from 2 Baruch, here speaking of the time of Abraham (which was of course before the law came through Moses): "For at that time the unwritten law was in force among

3. Vermes, *Dead Sea Scrolls*, 493. This is my own literal translation: "And he [God] said that one should build for him [read *lô*, for God] a sanctuary among men [lit. sanctuary of man], to do works of the law in it [read *bô*] for him [read *lô*] a sanctuary among men [lit. sanctuary of man], to do works of the law in it for him in his presence as a smoking sacrifice."

them, and the works of the commandments were accomplished at that time" (2 Bar. 57:2).[4] I therefore take "works of the law" to mean torah observance.[5]

For Paul it was impossible to be saved by keeping the law. Non-Christian Jews had a different view, as can be seen in 2 Bar. 51:7: "Miracles, however, will appear at their own time to those who are saved because of their works and for whom the Law is now a hope."[6] There is some scholarly disagreements as to whether Judaism at this time was a religion of salvation by works.[7] But whatever the case *Paul* understands Judaism as teaching a salvation by works and he wishes to portray it so. Indeed, he portrays Judaism as a legalistic religion. Again this issue of legalism in Judaism has become a controversial issue; but certainly in the Gospels the Pharisees are portrayed as legalistic.

If salvation is not possible through works of the law (Rom 3:20), how can we be saved? For Paul, it is only possible through the mercy of God shown in Jesus Christ. The salvation of God is revealed in the gospel.

RIGHTEOUSNESS OF GOD

To understand this salvation I look first at what Paul means by "righteousness of God" (*dikaiosynē theou*). I start with Rom 1:16–17: "I am not ashamed of the gospel, for it is the power of God unto salvation to all who believe, to the Jew first and also to the Greek. [17]For in it the righteousness of God (*dikaiosynē theou*) is revealed from faith to faith, as it is written 'the one who is righteous through faith shall live.'" There has been a long exegetical battle over these verses and I set out three views and add my own as a variation of the third.

---

4. *OTP* 1:641. This text is in Syriac but has been translated from Greek which in turn is most likely translated from a Hebrew original. It is to be dated around 100 AD (see Klijn in *OTP* 1:616–17).

5. I have stressed this point because some such as Dunn, *Romans*, 158–59, argue that "works of the law" means primarily "participating in the Jewish community." "Works of the law" here take on a sociological dimension. The stress is then on laws like circumcision and food laws, which mark out the Jew from other people. An indication that this is not what Paul has in mind is clear in Rom 4, where an example of not being justified by works is the murderer and adulterer David (Rom 4:6–8). An interesting confirmation of "works of law" being active fulfilment of the law is the way James understands Paul's use of the phrase (Avemarie, "Werke"). On Paul and James see below and chapter 7.

6. *OTP* 1:638.

7. One of the most detailed works concerning Rabbinic literature is Avemarie, *Tora und Leben*. He comes to the conclusion that the view of salvation could be both one of salvation by works and by "grace." My own view is set out in *Irrevocable Call*, 85–156.

First the medieval church understood righteousness of God (*dikaiosynē theou* rendered as *iustitia dei* in the Latin Vulgate) as a distributive justice (*iustitia distributiva*). The verse then means that in the gospel the justice of God (i.e. justice in punishing sinners) is revealed. This verse then haunted the monk Luther as it would haunt any sensitive man or woman. The gospel was then *no* gospel, no good news.

Luther, however, made a discovery. He believed that the righteousness of God is the righteousness that counts before God. So a Lutheran translation will read Rom 1:17 as follows: "For in it [i.e. in the gospel] the righteousness that counts before God is revealed."[8] Such a genitive is a genitive of author (*genitivus auctoris*), God being the author. Righteousness is then a gift that comes from God and is given to the believer and he or she has then a righteousness that counts before God. I do not think Luther was quite right, but it was not a bad start.

A new approach was put forward by the Lutheran Ernst Käsemann. Käsemann argues against a genitive of author (*genitivus auctoris*)—that is, a righteousness that is acceptable in God's eyes and that is bestowed by him upon us. Käsemann understands "the righteousness of God" as a subjective genitive (*genitivus subjectivus*), God's own righteousness.[9]

Such a subjective genitive was proposed before[10] but Käsemann had a particular understanding of it. The righteousness belongs to God and proceeds from him. The gift of righteousness is never separated from the giver; the gift of righteousness is indissolubly connected with righteousness as a power. And so gift and power are linked together.[11] I take first the example of love as power and gift.[12] At the end of Rom 8 Paul says that nothing will be able to separate us from the love of God in Christ Jesus (love as a power).

---

8. "Denn darin (i.e., in the gospel) wird offenbart die Gerechtigkeit, die vor Gott gilt."

9. For anyone new to these terms, a genitive is the case used to link two nouns (usually) to indicate a relationship between them. Consider, for example, the phrase "love of God." Here two nouns, "love" and "God," are related by "of." We have a subjective genitive if the second related word ("God") is the subject of the clause (i.e., God's love). We have an objective genitive if the second word is the object of the clause (i.e., "love for God").

10. E.g., Schlatter, *Gottes Gerechtigkeit*, 36.

11. Such an idea of gift and power is also to be found in Sabatier, *Paul*, 298–99. He understands "righteousness of God" as "the righteousness of which God is the Author" and as existing "already in God as an attribute and active force" (298). The righteousness of God "is more than a simple acquittal of the guilty; it is an actual power [. . .], which enters the world and is organically developed there" (299). So although he understands "righteousness of God" as a genitive of author his thinking is similar to Käsemann's.

12. This is one given by Käsemann himself; see "Righteousness of God," 174.

Then earlier in Rom 5:5 he says that the love of God has been poured into our hearts (love as a gift). The love (*agapē*) of God in Rom 8:39, which is the power from which nothing can separate us, is also the gift poured out into our hearts (Rom 5:5).

So it is in justification: the gift of righteousness is inextricably intertwined with righteousness as power. This power must always seek to realize itself in action. For Käsemann justification and sanctification coincide provided we understand that Christ takes over power over our lives.[13] God does not then impute righteousness to us; righteousness in no simple legal fiction. Righteousness is not saying "let us pretend the sinner is righteous although we know he or she actually is not." Righteousness is a gift to be seen as power and this power is over the whole of creation. When the righteousness of God is revealed the sovereignty of God over the whole creation is also revealed.

Before Käsemann the righteousness of God and the whole doctrine of justification was often seen in individualistic terms. It is interesting to see that there have always been problems as to how Rom 1–8 is to be related to 9–11. Romans 9–11 is about groups, Israel and the gentiles. But 1–8, it was thought, was to do with justification of individuals. According to Käsemann, justification is to do with the righteousness of God over the whole creation. And so this is one way in which Rom 1–8 can be related to 9–11. Romans 1–8 is then not just about individual justification. It is also about God's power of righteousness over the whole of creation.

Therefore, according to Käsemann, the genitive righteousness of God (*dikaiosynē theou*) is a subjective genitive in, say, Rom 1:17. Such righteousness of God is not simply an attribute of God. God's righteousness is his power, his salvation over the whole of creation and this righteousness of God is revealed in God's action in Christ. There are many good things in Käsemann's work on justification. One problem, though, is that justification and sanctification are confused and I will return to this in chapter 7.[14]

If *dikaiosynē* in Rom 1:17 were translated as "salvation" I think you would roughly understand what Paul was getting at. A little later I will explain exactly what I mean by "roughly" but just to say now that "righteousness" is looking at "salvation" in a particular way.

So if we try this out we get this sense of Rom 1:17: For the righteousness of God—that is, the salvation of God—is revealed in it (i.e. in the gospel). Taking "righteousness" to mean "salvation" can be defended by looking first

13. Käsemann, "Righteousness of God," 175.

14. See, for example, the discussion in chapter 7 of 1 Thess 5:9–10, where there is a clear distinction between justification and sanctification.

of all at Rom 10:10 and also looking at the Septuagint. In Rom 10:10 there is a clear parallel between "righteousness" and "salvation." A literal translation is: "For it is believed with the heart unto righteousness (*dikaiosynē*) and it is confessed with the mouth to salvation (*sōtēria*)." This parallelism could suggest that righteousness *dikaiosynē* essentially means salvation or one particular aspect of it.

Now this parallelism is often found in the Septuagint and I will shortly point to what is called "synonymous parallelism." But first I note that in the Old Testament there are a number of texts where the Greek *dikaiosynē* (Hebrew *tsedāqāh*) means God's righteous acts in the sense of his saving acts. The term *dikaiosynē* then takes on the meaning "the saving activity of God" or "God's salvation." This is to be found in the oldest text where *tsedāqāh* occurs, Judg 5:11: "To the sound of musicians at the watering places, there they repeat the triumphs of the LORD, the triumphs of his peasantry in Israel." Here "triumphs" is rendered in the Septuagint (Vaticanus text) as *dikaiosynas*, the plural of *dikaiosynē*. So this text is speaking of the LORD's righteous saving acts.[15]

Very important are a number of passages in Isaiah and the Psalms.[16] There are a number of texts where righteousness takes on the meaning salvation or the saving activity of God. I take Isa 51:6c as an example: "but my salvation (*sōtērion*) will be for ever, and my righteousness (*dikaiosynē*) will never be ended."

So "righteousness of God" in Rom 1:17 can be understood as the "salvation of God." The same goes for Rom 3:21–22a: "But now apart from law, the righteousness of God (i.e., salvation of God) has been disclosed, and is attested by the law and the prophets, [22]the righteousness of God (salvation of God) through faith in Jesus Christ for all who believe." Likewise in Rom 3:25b Paul explains that Christ's atoning sacrifice was "to show his righteousness (i.e. salvation)." But one cannot always simply translate *dikaiosynē* with salvation in Paul. In 2 Cor 5:21, for example, it does not work. Here *dikaiosynē theou* refers possibly to the working out of God's righteousness, the working out of God's salvation. But more likely "righteousness of God" means "the righteous ones of God." "For our sake God made him to be sin

---

15. For a similar understanding of *dikaiosynē* see also 1 Sam 12:7; Mic 6:5; Ps 106:3 (105:3); Dan 9:16. In the Psalms text the reference in brackets is that in the LXX.

16. Isa 45:8, 22–24; 51:6, 8; Pss 71:19 (70:18); 89:17 (88:17); 96:13 (95:13); 98:9 (97:9); 111:3 (110:3). Again in the Psalms texts the references in brackets are those in the LXX. There is a difference of 1 between the Hebrew (Masoretic text, MT) and the LXX because in the LXX Psalms 9 and 10 are run together. So the LXX is always lagging behind after Psalm 10. But the LXX catches up later because the MT Ps 147 is split into two and also we have an extra Psalm, Ps 151.

who knew no sin [referring to Christ] so that in him we might become *the righteous ones of God (dikaiosynē theou).*" "Righteous ones" is not talking about a moral quality; it is rather talking about those who have experienced the salvation of God.

Now it may be asked if there is anything wrong with the understanding of righteousness of God in Rom 1:17 as a genitive of author, that is the righteousness that comes from God and counts before God. This solution of Luther was a good one but I think the view I have given is even better, for it has a much better basis in the Septuagint, and it can be seen as including Luther's view.

TO JUSTIFY

Just as "righteousness" roughly means "salvation", "to justify" roughly means "to save." In Greek the noun "righteousness" and the verb "to justify" are related. The verb "I justify" in the New Testament is *dikaioō* and the noun "righteousness," *dikaiosynē.*[17] When I say the verb "to justify" means *roughly* "to save" I mean that it highlights one particular aspect of salvation. It highlights the aspect of *being declared and made righteous.* In a Jewish law court to justify someone was to acquit them. So in Deut 25:1 we read: "If there is a dispute between men, and they come to court, and the judges decide between them, acquitting the innocent (*dikaiōsōsin ton dikaion*) and condemning the guilty, then if the guilty man deserves to be beaten, the judge shall cause him to lie down and be beaten, etc."[18]

An ironic aspect of Paul's theology is that God does not acquit the righteous but rather the ungodly. What then do we make of Prov 17:15? "One who justifies the wicked and one who condemns the righteous / are both alike an abomination to the LORD." God, according to Paul, justifies the wicked! Proverbs 17:15 is obviously in the context of the human court of law but it would be interesting to know what went through Paul's mind as he read this verse.

Therefore "to justify" stresses *the forensic aspect* of salvation. Christians are justified now and will be justified at the last judgement, i.e., they will be acquitted at the last judgement.

17. Attempts have been made to make English rending of the terms correspond. So in Grobel's translation of Bultmann's *Theology* (e.g., 1:282) "justified" is rendered "rightwised." See also Bryan, *Preface*, 69–70, who renders *dikaiosynē* as "justice" (and *dikaios* as "just"), hence matching them with "to justify."

18. This is a life-threatening punishment Paul underwent on five occasions (2 Cor 11:24).

GOD'S CREATIVE VERDICT

"To justify" in Paul means not only to *declare* someone righteous but also to *make* someone righteous. God makes the sinner righteous by what theologians such as Ernst Fuchs and Eberhard Jüngel have called a "speech event."[19] So God's verdict of "not guilty" is a *creative* verdict and not an *analytical* verdict. We see this clearly in the case of Abraham whom Paul regards as a justified sinner. In Rom 4:3 Paul quotes Gen 15:6: "Abraham believed [in] God and it was reckoned to him as righteousness." Abraham was therefore justified by faith alone (*sola fide*).

Being reckoned righteous is *the declaration of God that creates salvation*. Justification is then no legal fiction. We do not have the situation where we pretend Abraham was righteous but actually he was not. God's word of "not guilty" actually means that the sinner is made righteous. It is a creative word of judgement.

We have to be clear that Abraham's faith, according to Paul, was a *gift* of God. In contrast, the Jewish way of understanding Gen 15:6 is that the faith of Abraham was a *work* of Abraham. He worked and produced faith. So he believed God's promise in Gen 15:5 that his descendants would be as numerous as the stars in heaven. God reacted and reckoned this faith as righteousness. So Abraham's faith was like a work. God's verdict of declaring Abraham righteous was then an analytical judgement. This is precisely the view we find in Jas 2:21–24 and to his credit this seems to be the sense in the original Genesis text. See Gen 15:5–6 which tells that Abraham believed the LORD (i.e. that his descendants shall be as the stars in heaven) and the LORD reckoned it to him as righteousness.

For Paul the situation is quite different. The verdict is not analytic but creative and declaratory. So God's verdict does not declare what is but *it creates what was not there*. God calls into being what was not already there. Put another way, in Judaism two thing happened concerning God's verdict on Abraham. First, Abraham did something: he believed God. Second, God reacted and reckoned this to him as righteousness. For Paul there is only one element: God's creative verdict of righteousness for Abraham. There is a simultaneous reckoning of righteousness with a gift of faith.[20]

19. Fuchs, "Sprachereignis in der Verkündigung Jesu"; "Was ist ein Sprachereignis?" ("What Is a 'Language-Event'"); Jüngel, *Mystery*, 12.

20. See Hofius, "Rechtfertigung des Gottlosen," 129. Note also that Hofius (129 n. 42) understands Paul to read Gen 15:6 as Abraham believed in God, not simply that he "believed God."

ATTACKS ON THE LUTHERAN UNDERSTANDING OF JUSTIFICATION

What I have presented so far is roughly a Lutheran understanding of Paul and I have taken this approach because I think Luther got the essential things right in his reading of Paul even though some matters such as "righteousness of God" need some modification. However, Luther's approach in terms of a grace/works dichotomy and the centrality of justification have been questioned, including in the Protestant tradition.

Justification has become an especially controversial subject in Pauline scholarship since Krister Stendahl's essay of 1963 "The Apostle Paul and the Introspective Conscience of the West."[21] Luther's understanding is that justification is not by doing works of the law, by which he meant essentially good works, but by grace through faith. You had basically a works/faith dichotomy. Stendahl said that Luther had misunderstood Paul. Luther suffered from what he called the introspective conscience of the West. This introspective conscience began roughly with Augustine in his *Confessions* and reached its peak in Luther. On the secular side, it reached its peak in Freud. In contrast, Paul was a man with a robust conscience. He was a successful Jew. He had no pangs of conscience like the monk Luther. Stendahl then argues that justification in Paul has nothing to do with the question "how can I find a gracious God?" Rather the question is that of Jew and gentile in God's plan of salvation. Stendahl has essentially changed (and one can even say reduced) justification from a doctrine of salvation to a doctrine of the church.[22]

I think Stendahl has grossly misunderstood Paul.[23] First, it may be that Paul did not have the extreme sensitive conscience that the monk Luther had, but there was a very important tradition in Judaism about the wretchedness of the human being. Did Paul not know texts like the penitential Psalm 51? Second, the Christian Paul knew that the question facing humankind was: "how can I find a gracious God?" It may be that he did not have this question as a Pharisee but *as a Christian* he saw that the fundamental human problem was, how can one find a gracious God?

21. This was published in the *Harvard Theological Review* and later reproduced in Stendahl, *Paul*, 78–96 (1977). The article arose from a paper given in 1961 to the American Psychological Association which in turn was a revision of an article in Swedish, "Paulus och Samvetet" ("Paul and the Conscience").

22. Cf. Käsemann, "Salvation History."

23. Note that although Stendahl's understanding of justification goes completely against that of Luther, after his controversial writings on Paul he became the (Lutheran) bishop of Stockholm (1984–88).

Another attack on a "Lutheran" approach to Paul is that of E. P. Sanders. Sanders has exerted an enormous influence on English scholarship; e.g., he has had a decisive influence on two influential British New Testament scholars, James D. G. Dunn and N. T. Wright. Luther understood the Judaism of Paul's time as a religion of works righteousness. Salvation was by doing good works. By contrast Sanders argues for a view of salvation by grace in Judaism. Sanders argues that one of Luther's problems was equating Judaism of Paul's day with the Roman Catholic Church of the sixteenth century.[24] So the Roman Catholic Church was Judaism; Luther was Paul. Such tendencies to read the Bible as though it is directly addressing our own issues certainly exist. But actually the Judaism of Paul's time does bear resemblances with the Roman Catholic Church of the sixteenth century. So both ancient Judaism and sixteenth-century Roman Catholicism can speak of "grace" but when this is unpacked it often turns out to be quite unlike how Paul would understand "grace."

There has been an enormous amount of literature on Paul and what has been called the "new perspective" on Paul and I have addressed it elsewhere.[25] The relevant Jewish literature is diverse, some of it having a stronger emphasis on works. I maintain that in comparing Jewish literature to Paul we find that Paul has a much stronger emphasis on grace, this being because he had a much more pessimistic view of the human person. Judaism was generally more optimistic about the human person and so could accommodate works within the concept of salvation. The additional point to bear in mind is that even if Judaism has more room for "grace" than the Lutheran approach allows, Paul himself expressed the view that Judaism placed the emphasis on works and appeared to find little room for grace. See, e.g., Rom 10:2–3, where he writes of the Jewish people: "I can testify that they have a zeal for God, but it is not enlightened. For, being ignorant of the righteousness of God and seeking to establish their own, they have not submitted to God's righteousness."[26]

When I worked in a church in Edgware in North West London I got to know the local Orthodox Rabbi and when I told him about the work of the new perspective he thought it was frankly ridiculous. He said: "we as Jews believe in salvation by works." One of the odd things about the new perspective is that the proponents are trying to make Jews look like liberal

24. Sanders, *Paul and Palestinian Judaism*, 57. Artinian, "Luther's View," 87, refutes Sanders' view that Luther was equating Paul's first-century Jewish opponents with sixteenth-century Roman Catholics.

25. See, e.g., my *No one seeks for God* and *Irrevocable Call of God*.

26. My own translation.

Protestants;[27] it is assumed that "grace" has to be superior to "works." This reminds me of some graffiti in New York I was told about. Christians had written "Jesus saves." Then on an opposite wall Jews had written "Moses invests." So I think the best thing to say is that Christians and Jews have quite different views of salvation. And a Jewish person could legitimately argue that salvation by works is a better theology. I happen to be a Christian and for a number of reasons I consider the truth to be in salvation by grace and through faith in Christ.[28]

CLARIFICATION OF "WORKS RIGHTEOUSNESS"

As we have seen, Luther considered Judaism to be a religion of "works righteousness." There is, however, an important distinction to be made when we talk of works righteousness from a Christian perspective. Luther's own view is that the Jews tried to fulfil the law and they did not succeed. We find this in Paul of course: there is no justification by works of the law because all men and women are in Adam; they have all fallen short of the glory of God. This can be called a *quantitative* criticism of works righteousness. It is simply impossible to fulfill the law.

Bultmann took this a stage further. He wrote that according to Paul men and women are incapable of fulfilling the law but he goes on to write this: "But Paul goes much further still; he says not only that man *can* not achieve salvation by works of the Law, but also that he is not even *intended* to do so."[29] This can be called a *qualitative* criticism of works righteousness. So if the Jew fulfills the law from A to Z, that is one of the biggest sin he or she could commit. The pious Jew then boasts is this performance. Pious Jews feel they have a claim upon God. This idea of the self-righteous Jew is found not only in Bultmann but also in his pupils, Käsemann and Bornkamm, where the Jew is seen as the religious person par excellence. Bornkamm writes: "For Paul, the Jew represents man in general, and indeed man exactly in his highest potential: the pious man who knows God's demands in the law but who has yet failed to meet God's claim and is lost in

27. Cf. Alexander, "Review of *Jesus and Judaism*," 105, and Neusner, "Response to Sanders," 92, both referred to by Matlock, "Almost Cultural Studies," 445.

28. An added point to note is that the new perspective presents Paul as "sounding surprisingly liberal, Western pluralist" (Matlock, "Almost Cultural Studies," 442). This is indeed strange in view of the supposed distance between Paul and ourselves that Stendhal, "Biblical Theology," 420, emphasizes. Hence "Luther's Paul comes to grief more for his failure to fit the twentieth century than the first" (Matlock, "Almost Cultural Studies," 443).

29. Bultmann, *Theology of the New Testament*, 1:263.

sin and death." In Romans therefore Paul addresses the Jew "hidden within each Christian."[30]

Two points should be made in response. First, there is some substance to the idea that for Paul the Jewish person represents the religious and pious person striving to fulfil the law. But this is only half the truth since for Paul the Jewish person represents the person who receives the promises of God, a theme I will investigate in chapter 9. There is grace for the Jewish people but this is not through the "religion of Judaism" but rather through the "religion" Paul presents in his letters, a religion of salvation by grace through faith in Christ.[31] Secondly, is Paul guilty of gross generalization in claiming the Jew represents the pious person? Yes he is, but it is worth bearing in mind that he was a former Pharisee and Luke 18:9–14, the parable of the of the Pharisee and the tax collector, certainly presents a Pharisee who boasts in his performance of doing the law. Perhaps Paul is guilty of projecting his own former life of a Pharisee onto all Jews and claiming that they boast in doing the works of the law (see Rom 3:27–4:2). Also in virtually all religions there is the tendency to self-righteousness including in the Christian religion.

JUSTIFICATION BY GRACE ALONE (*SOLA GRATIA*), BY FAITH ALONE (*SOLA FIDE*)

Two of the great slogans of the Reformation were "by grace alone" (*sola gratia*) and "by faith alone" (*sola fide*). We come here to fundamental questions of soteriology, the part God plays and the part the human being plays in his or her salvation. Such Reformation views were very much based on Paul, who teaches justification *sola gratia, sola fide*. So Paul can say Christians are justified by faith (Rom 5:1); he can also say they are justified by grace (Rom 3:24). Paul clearly contrasts justification by faith with justification by works of the law. Paul argues that through works of the law (i.e., torah observance) there is no justification (Rom 3:20).

Justification by faith is therefore to be contrasted with justification by works of the law. The question could then be put: is not faith itself a work? Luther in his *Freedom of a Christian* (1520) addresses this question, arguing that faith is a "work" but it is a work of *God!*[32] This is precisely Paul's own

30. Bornkamm, "Testament," 26.

31. What Paul presents is sufficiently distinct from his former Judaism that it can legitimately be considered a different religion with a different understanding of God.

32. See *LW* 31:347: "[W]hen the Jews asked Christ, as related in John 6[:28], what they must do 'to be doing the work of God,' he brushed aside the multitude of works

view: faith is the gift and work of God. Another way of putting this is that faith is not the condition of salvation; it is rather the mode of salvation,[33] an issue I will take up again in chapter 7.

For Paul works have no place in the salvation of humankind. This was a scandal for many Christians in Paul's day and it is still a scandal today. In addition to the fact that it seems "unfair" that grossly immoral people can find salvation through faith in Christ, human beings also have a natural tendency to work with ideas of merit. They feel they must pay for everything and must earn everything. It is striking that even in some theories of the atonement merit has come to play a key role. So in the satisfaction theory of the atonement developed by Anselm of Canterbury Jesus had to offer a human work of satisfaction to God.[34] Likewise "merit" is central to Calvin's view of the atonement. Although Calvin argues that Christ's merit does not exclude God's grace,[35] the role he gives for merit does not in my view fit with Paul's view of the atonement. Calvin writes: "Apart from God's good pleasure Christ could not merit anything; but did so because he had been appointed to appease God's wrath with his sacrifice, and to plot out our transgressions with his obedience."[36] Among the many problems with this sentence[37] is precisely the idea of "merit"![38]

To highlight two aspects of salvation by grace I turn to two terms used by E. P. Sanders: "getting in" and "staying in." Sanders makes a distinction

---

which is saw they did in great profusion and suggested one work, saying, 'This is the work of God, that you believe in him whom he has sent' [John 6:29]; 'for on him has God the Father set his seal' [John 6:27]."

33. Hofius, "Wort Gottes," 172.

34. Aulén, *Christus Victor*, 88. See also my comments on Anselm in chapter 4 above. As well as having his supporters Anselm's satisfaction theory with its associated idea of merit have been criticized from various angles. See, e.g., Moberly, *Atonement*, 370, who argues that Anselm's theory "makes sin in its essence quantitative, and, as quantitative, external to the self of the sinner, and measurable, as if it had a self, in itself." This all relates to the problem of merit in his theory.

35. Calvin, *Institutes*, 2.17.1–5 (McNeill, *Institutes*, 1:528–34). See the discussion in Wendel, *Calvin*, 227–28.

36. Calvin, *Institutes*, 2.17.1 (McNeill, *Institutes*, 1:529). See the discussion in Wendel, *Calvin*, 227–28.

37. See chapter 4 above on appeasement and God's wrath.

38. Note also the tendency among some to see Christ's merit not only in his sacrifice but also in his fulfilling of the law during his life. See the idiosyncratic understanding of Rom 10:5 in Cranfield, *Romans*, 2:521. He suggested Paul applies Lev 18:5 to "the achievement of the one Man who has done the righteousness which is of the law in His life and, above all, in His death, in the sense of fulfilling the law's requirements perfectly and so earning as His right a righteous a status before God." See also Lietzmann's view that Jesus engages in a substitutionary fulfilling of the law (*Römer*, 64).

between getting in the covenant and staying in the covenant. It so happens to be a distinction I do not think is helpful[39] but it is often found in the secondary literature. According to Sanders "getting in" is by grace in both Judaism and Pauline Christianity; "staying in" is by works in both Judaism and Pauline Christianity.

I first examine "getting in." According to the vast majority of rabbinic texts, you do not get in by "grace" in the sense that Paul speaks of grace. The Rabbis had three main theories as to why God chose Israel. God chose Israel because of the merit of the patriarchs, Abraham, Isaac, and Jacob. Or God chose Israel because the law was offered to all nations and only Israel accepted it. Or God foresaw that in the future Israel would obey the law. This is not grace; it is synergism. God does a bit, and human beings do a bit. There was another theory and this is the only theory that points to a doctrine of grace: God chose Israel simply because he loves Israel. This view is, of course, found in Old Testament passages like Deut 7:6–8. I therefore grant that there are texts where there is a doctrine of grace regarding "getting in" and it can debated as to how frequent such a view is to be found.[40]

Concerning "staying in," Sanders is right that Jews stay in by works. But if you stay in by works then that is no salvation by grace even if getting in is by grace. If you are on the road between election and final salvation and if failing to produce the goods means being cast out then salvation is ultimately by works.

By contrast Paul could be said to hold to a view of salvation *sola gratia*. This can be considered again from two points of view, "staying in" and "getting in," again the terms used by Sanders. Getting in had to be by grace for Paul because of his view of the human situation. Human beings were so twisted that the only way to save them was through God's grace. Judaism had no such doctrine of the total corruption of humankind and therefore could envisage a religion where getting in was partly on the basis of works.

One could argue that Paul had a doctrine of the total corruption of humankind. Romans 3:23 tells that all have fallen short of the glory of God, and since "glory" and "image" are related in Paul (1 Cor 11:7), this suggests that Paul considered the human being to have lost the image of God after

---

39. Cf. Gundry, "Grace," 12: "Sanders' bisection of getting in and staying in cuts a line through Paul's religion where the pattern shows a whole piece cloth."

40. Avemarie, *Tora und Leben*, and "Erwählung und Vergeltung" argues that in ancient Rabbinic Judaism the ideas that everlasting life can be seen as a reward for torah observance and as a gift of election stand side by side. Further, both ideas are richly attested in Talmud and Midrash. He therefore rejects an approach which places either "works" or "grace" in any kind of hierarchy.

the fall.[41] According to Paul, only Christ bears the image of God (2 Cor 4:4), an image that is being built up again in Christians in that they are being conformed to the image of Christ (Rom 8:29). For Paul then, human beings are incapable of coming to faith by their own strength because of their absolute corruption.

But what about staying in? Here Paul is inconsistent. In some texts he affirms what has been called the "perseverance of the saints." God will see that the Christian comes through the final salvation, a view strong in the Calvinist tradition. Such a view is supported by texts such as Phil 1:6 and Rom 8:31–39.[42] However, there are texts that could imply that if you are disobedient you will fall from grace (e.g., Gal 5:4). These are quite involved issues and I will return to them in chapter 7.

"IT IS GOD WHO JUSTIFIES" (ROM 8:33): GOETHE'S *FAUST*; MAHLER'S *EIGHTH SYMPHONY*

Finding a suitable drama or piece of music to illustrate justification by faith was not easy and this may be saying something! The drama that I think encapsulates such justification is the end of Goethe's *Faust* part one. This closes with Margareta in prison. Earlier in the drama this simple girl has been seduced by Faust. He is an elderly scholar, who has studied philosophy, law, medicine, and even theology. There is even a scene where he tries to translate John 1:1.[43] Weary of all this study he recovers his youth with the help of the demonic figure Mephistopheles. Faust falls in love with Margareta (Gretchen) but this leads to a series of tragic events. So that they may consummate their relationship Faust provides Gretchen with a sleeping drug to be given to her mother, which accidentally kills her. Then Faust kills Gretchen's brother in a duel. He has to flee and Mephistopheles distracts Faust such that he forgets about Margareta. She gives birth to his child but in desperation she murders the child by drowning.[44]

On realizing that Gretchen faces execution Faust insists that she be rescued from prison. This final scene of *Faust* Part I is remarkable because Faust together with the demonic figure of Mephistopheles, having managed

---

41. Käsemann, *Romans*, 95.

42. Such texts are emphasized by Gundry Volf, *Paul and Perseverance*.

43. Luke, *Faust I*, 39 (ll. 1224–37).

44. Goethe's idea for this drama was partly based on the execution for infanticide in 1772 of Susanna Margaretha Brandt. She was imprisoned just 200 yards from Goethe's home in Frankfurt (Luke, *Faust I*, xix).

to get into the prison, offer to Margareta the option to escape. But she refuses to leave and some of the final words of the drama are thus:[45]

Margareta (in prison):

Oh Father, save me, do not reject me,	Dein bin ich Vater! Rette mich!
I am yours! Oh holy angels, receive	Ihr Engel! Ihr heiligen Scharen,
Me under your wings, surround me, protect me! . . .	Lagert euch umher, mich zu bewahren!

Mephistopheles:

She is condemned!	Sie ist gerichtet!
A voice (from above):	Stimme, von oben:
She is redeemed!	Ist gerettet!

Mephistopheles embodies the biblical devil as the great accuser, a view we find for example in Zech 3:1 of the Old Testament. Paul alludes to this tradition when he asks in Rom 8.33: "Who will bring any charge against God's elect?" The answer: "It is God who justifies." So this close of *Faust* Part I illustrates powerfully justification by faith. Margarita has murdered her child but she is saved because of her faith.

I tried to find a suitable setting of this scene but I did not particularly like what was on offer. So I decided to turn to the end of *Faust* Part II. The very final scene presents us with famous sinners from the Bible and they together with Margareta and even Faust himself come to be saved. I have to say that some of the words do not present fully the grace of God but it is nevertheless a beautiful conclusion. Gustav Mahler set this to music and so here you have the very close of his eighth Symphony often called a "Symphony of a Thousand" because it requires a vast orchestra and choir. The meaning of the very final words are ambiguous and makes it especially interesting: "Eternal Womanhood, Draws us on high." "Eternal womanhood" could refer to Margarita, or the Virgin Mary. I take it to mean "love personified." So the words the choir sing are:[46]

Chorus mysticus:

All that must disappear	Alles Vergängliche
Is but a parable;	Ist nur ein Gleichnis;
What lay beyond us, here	Das Unzulängliche

45. Luke, *Faust I*, 148 (ll. 4607–12).
46. Luke, *Faust II*, 239 (ll. 12104–11).

All is made visible;	Hier wird's Ereignis;
Here deeds have understood	Das Unbeschreibliche
Words they were darkened by;	Hier ist es getan;
Eternal Womanhood	Das Ewig-Weibliche
Draws us on high.	Zieht uns hinan.

FURTHER READING

Romans 3:21–31.

6

The Sacrifice of Christ

INTRODUCTION

IF WE ARE TO understand Paul's view of Jesus' sacrificial death it is best not to have in mind the sacrifices of the pagan Greek religions. In chapter 4 I noted that some wish to understand Christ's death rather like the sacrifice of Iphigeneia. Agamemnon had displeased the goddess Artemis and he sacrificed Iphigeneia to appease Artemis. Another way of wording it is that he sacrificed her to propitiate the goddess. It is worth clarifying that one propitiates (or appeases) a *person*, not the *sins*.[1] Also if the terms "expiation" or "expiates" are used, these relate to *sins*: so one expiate sins, that is rubs them out or covers them. In chapter 4 I argued that "propitiation" is an alien idea to Paul's theology and "expiation" is an inadequate concept, and as we look more closely at Paul's view of sacrifice this should become clear.

To understand the sacrifice of Christ in Paul's theology I turn to the sacrifices of the Old Testament, especially those in the "priestly writing" of the Old Testament. This material was composed around the sixth century BC and is found, for example, in passages of Exodus, Leviticus, and Numbers.

---

1. Hence, the Authorised Version of 1 John 2:2 "he [Jesus Christ] is the propitiation for your sins" (quoted in the *Book of Common Prayer* communion service) can be a little confusing.

65

TWO EXAMPLES OF OLD TESTAMENT SACRIFICES

I consider two texts from Leviticus on sacrifices, and the sacrifice that is particularly important for our purposes is the sin offering.

Leviticus 4:27–31

Lev 4:27–31 runs as follows:

> [27]If anyone of the ordinary people among you sins unintentionally in doing any one of the things that by the LORD's commandments ought not to be done and incurs guilt, [28]when the sins that you have committed is made known to you, you should bring a female goat without blemish as your offering, for the sin that you have committed. [29]You shall lay your hand on the head of the sin offering; and the sin offering shall be slaughtered at the place of the burnt offering. [30]The priest shall take some of its blood with his finger and put it on the horns of the altar of burnt offering, and he shall pour the rest of its blood at the base of the altar. [31]He shall remove all its fat, as the fat is removed from the offering of well-being, and the priest shall turn it into smoke on the altar as a pleasing odor to the LORD. Thus the priest shall make atonement on your behalf, and you shall be forgiven.

This tells of the key stages the sacrifice of the sin offering, and the essential ones for our purposes are as follows: the hand is placed on the head of the sacrificial animal, here "a female goat without blemish" (vv. 28–29); the animal as sin offering is slaughtered (v. 29); some of the blood is placed on the horns of the altar of burnt offering (v. 30); thus the priest makes atonement for the Israelite and is forgiven (v. 31). Atonement literally means "at-one-ment"; God and the Israelite are reconciled. But it is worth emphasizing here that such a sacrifice is for *unintentional* sins (v. 27), a point to which I shall return.

A clue to what is going on here is that the laying on of the hand (singular)[2] in Lev 4:29 is not a transference of sins but rather *an act of identification*. We see the same thing in 2 Chr 29:23–24:

> [23]Then the male goats for the sin offering were brought before the king [Hezekiah] and the assembly; they laid their hands on them, [24]and the priests slaughtered them and made a sin offering with their blood at the altar, to make atonement for all Israel.

---

2. The issue of whether one hand or two hands are placed is not always clear. A helpful table is set out in Janowski, *Sühne*, 200.

> For the king commanded that the burnt offering and the sin of-
> fering should be made for all Israel.

So the laying on of a hand was not a transfer of sins but an act of identification. Hartmut Gese, who has done so much to clarify the matter
of sacrifice in the priestly writing, writes of a "transference of subject"
("Subjektübertragung").[3] I will keep to this language of a "subject" although
this is really a term belonging to modern philosophy, starting with Des-
cartes. An alternative is to speak of "soul" (or life). See Lev 17:11: "For the
soul/life of the flesh is in the blood; and I have given it to you for making
atonement for your souls/lives on the altar; for through the soul/life the
blood makes atonement." But using the language of "transference of subject"
through laying on of hands on the *head*, one can compare Moses appointing
Joshua as his successor (Num 27:18–20, 23; Deut 34:9).

For the purposes of understanding Christ's sacrifice, the crucial point
in the Levitical sin offering is that the laying on of a hand represents not
an *"exclusive* place-taking" ("ausschließende Stellvertretung") but an *"inclusive"* one ("einschließliche Stellvertretung").[4] An "exclusive place-taking" is
essentially a *substitution* whereas an "inclusive place-taking" is an *identification*. With the "inclusive place-taking" the death of the animal is a death
in which the Israelite participates and in bringing the blood of the animal
in contact with the holy (here the horns of the altar) the result is that the
Israelite has fellowship with God. The end result of the sacrifice is therefore something entirely positive. The result is not simply that "sins are dealt
with"; the end result is *fellowship with God*.

Leviticus 16

As a second example I take the Day of Atonement (*Yôm Kippur*)[5] ritual in
Lev 16. The chapter is clearly the result of a process of editing and sometimes it is rather repetitive. For our purposes the most important things to
bear in mind are the following.

First in vv. 1–14 Aaron the high priest makes atonement for himself
and for his family by offering the bull as a sin offering *ḥaṭṭat*.[6] After the bull

---

3. Gese, "Sühne," 97. Gese's essay "Die Sühne" has been translated as "The Atonement" in a collection *Essays on Biblical Theology*. The translation is not entirely satisfac-
tory. I have offered by own translation of some of the key passages from his essay in my
article on "Sacrifice and Christology."

4. Gese, "Sühne," 97.

5. *Yôm* is the Hebrew word of "day" and the Hebrew root for atonement is *kpr*.

6. There is also a ram as a burnt offering but this is not so important for us. Also

as sin offering has been slaughtered Aaron takes some of the blood of the bull and sprinkles it on the mercy seat. This was a top-piece, made of solid gold, for the ark of the covenant, which was kept in the holy of holies. In the tabernacle or temple there was the holy place and then behind a veil the holy of holies. Once a year, according to the Levitical code, the high priest, and the high priest only, went into this holy of holies. So the high priest makes atonement for himself and his family.

In the next stage (vv. 15–22) Aaron takes two goats. One goat is killed and the blood is sprinkled on the mercy seat in the holy of holies. This acts as atonement for the people of Israel (vv. 15–19). Aaron then lays his hands on the head of the other goat and confesses the sins of his people. This goat, the one bearing the sins of the people, is then driven into the wilderness (v. 22).

Many assume that Lev 16:21 points to the laying on of hands as a transference of sins: "and Aaron shall lay both his hands upon the head of the live goat, and confess over it all the iniquities of the people of Israel, and all their transgressions, all their sins, putting them on the head of the goat." It is then assumed that in all other cases of laying hands on an animal's head, the sins are transferred to the animal. In fact, Lev 16:21 is the *only* instance of the simultaneous laying on of hands and confession of sins. It may be that in Lev 16:21 laying on of hands does represent a transference of sins or it may be that the two acts of laying on of hands and confession of sins are entirely independent.[7] And it is not clear whether sins are transferred through the hands and fingers or from the mouth of Aaron and then onto the head of the live goat. But whatever the case, it must be stressed that *this goat is not the one sacrificed;* rather it is driven into the wilderness to Azazel. We have therefore in Lev 16 an elimination rite of the "scapegoat" together with the sin offering of the goat and an earlier sin offering of the bull. The laying on of a hand is not mentioned but I think it can be assumed.

HOW DID THE SIN OFFERING "WORK"?

The first key to understanding the sin offering is that the laying on a hand (Lev 4:29; see also e.g., 4:15) or hands (2 Chr 29:23) is an act of identification. The second is that in the sacrificial cult of Israel the animal is not simply killed. There is another very important stage in the sacrifice, namely the blood of the animal is brought into the presence of God. So on *Yôm Kippur*

---

vv. 7–10 mentions the two goats, one for the LORD and the other for Azazel, to which I shall return.

7. Gese, "Sühne," 96.

the high priest sprinkles the blood of the bull and of the goat on the mercy seat in the holy of holies (Lev 16:14). Hence, the sacrifice of the sin offering works in this way: the people are identified with the animal, this often being done through the laying on of hands; the animal is killed and the blood is taken into the presence of God (e.g., in the Day of Atonement ritual this is done by sprinkling the blood on the mercy seat); the Israelite, having being identified with the animal, is therefore also taken into God's presence. I trust that it is now clear that the sin offering has nothing to do with the pagan idea of propitiatory sacrifice.

I offer one final word about Old Testament sacrifices before we move onto the New Testament. In the Old Testament the Israelite brought the animal to be sacrificed and the priest carries out the sacrifice. How is this human activity related to the atonement with God? Bernd Janowski puts it like this: the principle is not *do ut des* (I [the human being] give so that you [God] give) but *do quia dedisti* (I [the human being] give because you [God] have already given).[8] So in the Old Testament sacrifices the Israelite was not twisting God's arm so to speak. The Israelites offered sacrifices because God had already reached out to Israel. It may be worthwhile emphasizing here that there is indeed grace in the Old Testament. But in Paul's time there were certainly many strands of Judaism that had minimized this and had instead emphasized the role of works. Hence we have Paul's attack on justification by works, something we saw in chapter 5.

SACRIFICE OF CHRIST IN PAUL'S LETTERS

Paul's understanding of Jesus death roughly corresponds to this understanding of the sin offering as found in the priestly writings of the Pentateuch. Therefore Paul does not understand Jesus' death as Jesus carrying our sins and taking God's judgement upon himself as we have in the case of the suffering servant of Isa 53. See Isa 53:4–6:

> [4]Surely he [that is, the servant of the LORD] has borne our infirmities
> and carried our diseases;
> yet we counted him stricken,
> struck down by God, and afflicted.
> [5]But he was wounded for our transgressions,
> crushed for our iniquities;
> upon him was the punishment that made us whole,
> and by his bruises we are healed.

8. Janowski, *Sühne*, 361.

> [6]All we like sheep have gone astray;
>   we have all turned to our own way,
> and the LORD has laid on him
>   the iniquities of us all.

This is one of the most powerful passages of the Old Testament and has been used much by Christians. But this text cannot be simply applied in the case of Paul. For Paul sins cannot be simply transferred, a point I noted in chapter 4 where I emphasized that for Paul sin was an ontological problem. Therefore, sins simply cannot be removed as we can take off a dirty coat. One cannot separate a human being from his or her sins; to separate human beings from their sins is to separate them from themselves![9] How Paul applies Isa 53 we shall presently see when I discuss below 2 Cor 5:21.

Therefore, according to Paul, Jesus did not then die as a substitute as many have suggested. Rather the sinner is identified with Christ as the Israelite was identified with the animal and taken into God's presence. Therefore, Jesus' death is not about substitution; it is about *identification*. The human being is identified with Jesus in his death such that when he died all died. Paul expresses this so in 2 Cor 5:14: "For the love of Christ urges us on, because we are convinced that one has died for all; therefore all have died." Further, his death is our death and his resurrection our resurrection. Therefore, for Paul, Jesus' death was not to avert the wrath of God; that is, it was not a propitiatory sacrifice. Neither is the death of Jesus just a taking away of sins; that is, it is not just an expiatory sacrifice. The purpose of Christ's death is that the human being may become a new creation. The old person dies and a new person comes into being. See 2 Cor 5:17: "So if anyone is in Christ, there is a new creation; the old has passed away, behold, the new has come."

Paul has then taken over this Old Testament scheme of sacrifice. Indeed, in Rom 8:3 Paul most likely is referring to God sending his Son as a sin offering (*peri hamartias*), and I will discuss this verse below.

HOW PAUL DIFFERS FROM THE OLD TESTAMENT

The clue to Paul's understanding of Jesus' death is the Levitical sin offering. But Paul has introduced important mutations, and I mention six.

First, in the Old Testament the human being brings the animal to be sacrificed. For Paul, *God alone* is involved in the work of sacrifice: "All this comes from God, who through Christ reconciled us to himself" (2 Cor

---

9. Cf. Hofius, "Sühne," 46.

5:18). The Old Testament was characterized by *do quia dedisti*, "I give because you have already given." In the New Testament it is *tu solus omnia dedisti*, "you alone have given everything."[10]

Secondly, in the Old Testament the sacrifices had to be repeated. Christ's sacrifice however was done *once* for all sins (Rom 6:10). It is God's eschatological saving act, which requires no repetition or completion.[11]

Thirdly, in the Old Testament the sin offering was only valid for sins done unwittingly and not for sins done with a high hand, i.e., deliberate sins. I pointed to this earlier in Lev 4:27, but I turn to another text that makes this point starkly, Num 15:27, 30–31: "[27]An individual who sins unintentionally shall present a female goat a year old for a sin offering. [. . .] [30]But whoever acts highhandedly whether native or an alien affronts the LORD and shall be cut off from among the people. [31]Because of having despised the word of the LORD and broken his commandments, such a person shall be utterly cut off and bear the guilt." By contrast Christ died for *all* sins. He died for the godless, for those who sin deliberately.[12]

Fourthly, the sacrifices of the Old Testament were only valid for Israel. For Paul, Jesus' death is valid for *the whole world*, Jew and gentile.[13]

Fifthly, in the Old Testament sacrifices the Israelite was identified with the animal through the laying on of hands before the animal was sacrificed. For Paul such identification is done *after* the sacrifice of Christ, faith being the equivalent to the laying on of hands.

Sixthly, on the Day of Atonement the blood of the animal was sprinkled on the mercy seat (Lev 16:14–15). The mercy seat, which would include not only the golden top-piece of the ark of the covenant but also the space above it, represented the presence of God and place of atonement. Jesus, in being described as the mercy seat (*hilastērion*) in Rom 3:25,[14] therefore represents the presence of God and the place of atonement. In Leviticus the mercy seat was hidden away in the holy of holies to which the high priest alone had access, and then just once a year. For Paul, the mercy set was "publicly set

---

10. Hofius, "Sühne," 48.

11. Hofius, "Sühne," 49.

12. Hofius, "Sühne," 49.

13. Hofius, "Sühne," 49.

14. Such a translation and understanding of *hilastērion* is found in Origen (Scherer, *Commentarie*, 156–63) and Luther (who in *Die gantze Heilige Schrifft Deudsch* translates *hilastērion* as "Gnadenstuhl" in Rom 3:25). Note also Tyndale's translation "seate of mercy." Such an understanding is found in modern times by a range of exegetes (e.g., Stuhlmacher, "Röm 3,24–26"; Wilckens, *Römer*, 1:193; Bailey, "Mercy Seat"). Among those who object to such an understanding, see, e.g., Wolter, *Römer*, 1:259, who argues that *hilastērion* refers to something abstract, not concrete.

forth" on Golgotha, open to public view: "God set forth Christ publicly as a mercy seat" (Rom 3:25).

This now leads us to the crucial text Rom 3:23–26a.

ROMANS 3:23–26A

The key verse Rom 3:25 is set within Rom 3:23–26a and my translation is as follows:

> [23]for all have sinned and fall short of the glory of God [24]being justified freely by his grace through the redemption that is in Christ Jesus [25]whom God publicly set forth as a mercy seat perceived through faith, by means of his blood, for the establishing of his righteousness on account of the passing over of former sins [26]in the forbearance of God.

This text can be understood as a chiasmus. The name chiasmus comes from the Greek letter Chi, which looks like an X, and the chiasmus has a mirror structure such as AB BA, ABC CBA. In Rom 3:23–26a we have something rather complex: ABCDE EDCBA.

A for all have sinned and fall short of the glory of God

   B being justified freely

      C by his grace

         D through the redemption

            E which is in Christ Jesus

            E[1]whom God publicly set forth

         D[1]as a mercy seat perceived through faith,

      C[1]by means of his blood,

   B[1]for the establishing of his righteousness

A[1]on account of the passing over of former sins in the forbearance of God.

One key to understanding these verses is that the Greek word *hilastērion* in v. 25 is best translated as "mercy seat." In the Septuagint *hilastērion* nearly always translates *kapporet*,[15] which means the mercy seat. Conversely the Hebrew *kapporet* is nearly always rendered by *hilastērion*. The only other New Testament occurrence of *hilastērion* is in Heb 9:5 where it clearly means mercy seat. See Heb 9:1–5:

---

15. Note the root *kpr* as in *Yôm Kippur*.

[1]Now even the first covenant had regulations for worship and an earthly sanctuary. [2]For a tent was constructed, the first one, in which with the lampstand, the table, and the bread of the presence; this is called the Holy Place. [3]Behind the second curtain was a tent called the Holy of Holies. [4]In it stood the golden altar of incense and the ark of the covenant overlaid on all sides with gold, in which there were a golden urn holding the manna, and Aaron's rod that budded, and the tablets of the covenant; [5]above it were the cherubim of glory overshadowing *the mercy seat* (*hilastērion*). Of these things we cannot speak now in detail.

So if *hilastērion* means mercy seat why are so many reluctant to translate *hilastērion* as mercy seat in Romans 3:25? Well, it is claimed that had Paul wished to refer to the mercy seat he would have used the definite article "the" (*to* in Greek). But in this construction we have what is called a *predicativum* and here in Greek the definite article has to drop out.[16] An example of a *predicativum* in English is "I understand Johann Sebastian Bach *as* a great composer." In Rom 3:25 it is "God publicly setting forth Christ *as* a mercy seat." Another objection to translating *hilastērion* as mercy seat is: how can Jesus be identified with an inanimate piece of temple furniture? Is it not a bit like saying my grandmother is a wardrobe? Now the mercy seat is the top-piece for the ark of the covenant.[17] The mercy seat may be dismissed as an inanimate piece of temple furniture but it represents the presence of God and the place of the atonement. Considering Christ as a mercy seat is actually entirely fitting for it points to the intersection of the human with the divine.

Some nevertheless translate *hilastērion* by "propitiation," but there are serious problems here of a linguistic nature.[18] Put briefly, if the translation "propitiation" is employed you have to understand *hilastērion* not as a noun but as an adjective and supply a noun "sacrifice" "*thyma*." Hence, you have a "propitiatory sacrifice." I find this translation in the Authorised Version of 1611 unsatisfactory: "[25]Whom [that is Christ] God has set forth to be a propitiation [i.e., propitiatory sacrifice] through faith in his blood,

16. This point is not recognized by what is otherwise one of the best commentaries on Romans produced in the Anglo-sphere. See Cranfield, *Romans*, 1:214–15. He has been endlessly copied (e.g., Stott, *Romans*, 114). That the article has to drop out has been amply demonstrated by Bailey, "Mercy Seat" (see also his important appendix "*Hilastērion*," in Stuhlmacher, *Biblical Theology*, 824–68). Note also the earlier article of Stuhlmacher, "Röm 3,24–26," 124–25, that has inspired so much fresh work on the *hilastērion* in Rom 3:25.

17. It is not a "lid" since for a lid (e.g., of a jar) one can take the lid off and then look inside; the mercy seat cannot be so removed.

18. Bell, "Sacrifice and Christology," 19–20.

to declare his righteousness for the remission of sins that are past, through the forbearance of God; [26]To declare, *I say*, at this time, his righteousness: that he might be just, and the justifier of him which believeth in Jesus." In my translation you will see that I relate the *hilastērion* to "through faith" and I take the passage to mean the mercy seat is accessible through faith or perceptible through faith. Further, Paul talks about the passing over of former sins and I think we have an allusion here to the Day of Atonement ritual when the sins of the past year were passed over.

If I am correct in this understanding of the passage there are three key points to be made about the person of Christ and what he achieves through his death. First, there is a unity of action of God and Jesus Christ. This passage is not concerned with God's *justice*, understanding "righteousness" (*dikaiosynē*) as retributive justice or showing God to be "just" in punishing sin. Such a view sets God over against Jesus. Rather, the passage is about the salvation event. So when Paul speaks of the establishing of God's righteousness he is referring to God's *salvation*, not his *justice*. And when Paul describes God as "righteous" (*dikaios*) he is stressing that God is the one who saves. The second christological point is that we see here the intersection of the divine and the this-worldly through Christ, the mercy seat. The third point is that this setting forth of Christ as a *hilastērion* can be perceived only through faith and only through faith can it be a salvation event. The role of faith is a dual one for it is through faith that one is identified with Christ but at the same time it is through faith that the atoning death of Christ is perceived and understood.

ROMANS 8:3; 2 CORINTHIANS 5:21

Earlier I mentioned that Paul presents Jesus as a sin offering in Rom 8:3. This however is not clear in some translations. For example, the NRSV of Rom 8:3 runs as follows: "For God has done what the law, weakened by the flesh, could not do: by sending his Son in the likeness of sinful flesh, and to deal with sin (*peri hamartias*), he condemned sin in flesh." The phrase "and to deal with sin" is best translated "and as a sin offering." The two translations come about because of the Greek *peri hamartias*, which can be translated "concerning sin" or "sin offering," *peri hamartias* being the term used for the "sin offering" in the Septuagint. Paul may simply be saying that Christ's mission "had to do" with sin. But the frequent use of *peri hamartias* in the Septuagint for the sin offering suggests that this is also what is in Paul's mind here.[19]

19. Moo, *Romans*, 480.

Therefore I translate Rom 8:3 as follows: "For God has done what the law, weakened by the flesh, could not do: by sending his Son in the likeness (*homoiōma*) of sinful flesh [or in the form (*homoiōma*) of sinful flesh], and as a sin offering, he condemned sin in flesh." As well as raising the issue of Jesus as a "sin offering" this text also raised questions about Christ's sinlessness. One question is how to understand *homoiōma*. Is it to be understood as "likeness" or "form"? Here I think it is best understood as form rather than likeness. So Paul is talking about the perceptible expression of a reality. This I think is the sense in Phil 2:7 when Paul says that Christ became in the form of a human being. But if we adopt the translation "in the *likeness* of sinful flesh" it could suggest that Christ was not truly the same as we are and was indeed sinless.

Now it might be that Paul did hold to the sinlessness of Christ but I do not think he is concerned with that here. Romans 8:3 is saying that Christ was sent into the area of human existence and part of the very structure of this existence is sin. He is not saying Jesus committed sins but he is saying that Jesus fully participated in the sphere of humanity where a sinful existence is inevitable. What is so interesting is that this is precisely the view of sin in the priestly writing. So the sin offering is concerned with ontological views of sin, not functional views. The sin offering was concerned with Israel's sinful *being*, not so much with his sinful *doing*. But whereas the animal victim of the sin offering did not participate in the sinful existence of the Israelites, Paul seems to be saying that Christ as sin offering did so participate. Christ fully shared in our human existence and can be considered a "sinner" in this sense.

However, he became a "sinner" *for our sake*, a point Paul sets out in 2 Cor 5:21: "For our sake he made him to be sin who knew no sin, so that in him we might become the righteousness of God." Christ was made to be "sin" for our sake; that is, he was made to be a "sinner" but a sinner in what one can call a "cosmic" rather than an "ethical" sense. Here Paul takes Isa 53:6 and introduces an ontological view of sin. So rather than Jesus carrying sin or bearing sin, he is rather made to *be* a "sinner".

The reference to his "not knowing sin" could either be to this preincarnate existence or to his earthly life. But his being made to be sin could be a reference to the incarnation or it could be a reference to the cross. Whichever is the case, the key point is that his being made to be a sinner was *for our sake*. And so we have this remarkable exchange: Christ is made to be a "sinner" and Christians are made to be the righteousness of God, that is "the righteous ones of God."[20]

---

20. See the discussion of 2 Cor 5:21 in chapter 5 above.

THE MYSTERY OF PLACE-TAKING

The word "place-taking" corresponds to a German word "Stellvertretung"[21] and is not found in the New Testament, but does serve to render the idea of Christ stepping into our place. So this is found in texts such as Gal 3:13; 2 Cor 5:14; 5:20, all of which were discussed above.

Writing in 1793 Immanuel Kant questioned whether place-taking can make any sense at all. His argument was as follows:

> Moreover, so far as we can judge by our reason's standards of right, this original debt, or at any rate the debt that precedes whatever good a human being may ever do (this, and no more, is what we understood by *radical* evil; cf. the first Section), cannot be erased by somebody else. For it is not a *transmissible* liability which can be made over to somebody else, in the manner of a financial debt (where it is all the same to the creditor whether the debtor himself pays up, or somebody else for him), but the *most personal* of all liabilities, namely a debt of sins which only the culprit, not the innocent, can bear, however magnanimous the innocent might be in wanting to take the debt upon himself for the other.[22]

Such a view is reflected also in Exod 32:30–34 where after Moses offers his own life for the sins of the people, Yahweh responds: "Whoever has sinned against me I will blot out of my book" (Exod 32:33). A similar view is expressed in Ezek 18:20: "The person who sins shall die. A child shall not suffer for the iniquity of a parent, nor a parent suffer for the iniquity of a child; the righteousness of the righteous shall be his own, and the wickedness of the wicked shall be his own."[23] However, not all would agree with this line of argument. Janowski writes that "[a] drama of delayed recognition in Isaiah 53 provides an alternative to Immanuel Kant's narrow understanding of representation of 'taking another's place' (German *Stellvertretung*), which insists that no person can represent or take the place of another in matters of personal guilt."[24] Janowski criticizes Kant' subject theory of guilt "which makes the sinner merciless toward himself and blind to the 'other.'"[25] How-

21. Jüngel, "Stellvertretung," 250–51, notes how this word has come into the German language rather late; it is not found in Luther and probably came into being with the opposition to the orthodox Lutheran satisfaction theory.

22. Kant, *Religion within the Boundaries of Mere Reason*, 104 (*AA* 6:72).

23. Hofius, "Fourth Servant Song," 169; "Gottesknechtslied," 111–12.

24. Janowski, "He Bore Our Sins," 48.

25. Janowski, "He Bore Our Sins," 51. In 51 n. 8 he points to the work of Lehmann, "Er wurde für uns gekreuzigt," 315–16, and Breuning, "Sühne," 79–80, who appeals to

ever valid these points may be, I can see no evidence that they represent the thinking of Paul in terms of "place-taking."

If for Paul a human being cannot stand in our place who can? Paul's answer is the God-man Jesus Christ. He is the one human being who is able to take our place.[26] Further, one can make the point that inclusive place-taking is not human but *divine* place-taking.[27] This brings us to the argument of Hegel that "God cannot be satisfied by something else, only by himself."[28]

Many find the idea of sacrifice difficult. But many of the problems can be avoided if it is stressed that we are not dealing here with appeasing an angry God but rather that Jesus takes our place as the divine Son of God and includes us in his sacrificial death in what I have termed "inclusive place taking." Further, the sacrifice of Christ is not a metaphor but a myth. Metaphors merely depict reality. Myth brings us in contact with reality itself. The sacrifice of Christ is therefore part of Paul's rich mythology and the power and truth of this myth is that it enables an existential displacement for the one who encounters the Christ of this mythology.

JOHANN SEBASTIAN BACH, *ST JOHN PASSION*

As a convinced Lutheran,[29] Bach was naturally drawn to what is called the "passion" of Christ, the events leading to his redemptive death on the cross. Bach's *St John Passion* was first performed on Good Friday 1724 in St. Nicholas Church, Leipzig. Bach made three subsequent revisions together with an uncompleted revision.[30] In this work Bach gives a musical setting of the passion narrative of John's Gospel (John 18:1—19:42). But in addition to

---

Levinas' category of the "other." Levinas, "La trace de l'autre," 273 ("The Trace of the Other," 353), refers to Isa 53.

26. Iwand, *Gesetz und Evangelium*, 101, writes that Christ can take our place "where no other can take or place." Quoted in Hofius, "Fourth Servant Song," 173.

27. Hofius, "Fourth Servant Song," 173; "Gottesknechtslied," 115.

28. Hegel, *Philosophy of Religion*, 3:219. Hegel continues: "The satisfaction consists in the fact that the first moment, that of immediacy, is negated; only then does God come to be at peace with himself, only then is spirituality posited. God is the true God, spirit, because he is not merely Father, and hence closed up within himself, but because he is Son, because he becomes the other and sublates this other. [. . .] Through death God has reconciled the world and reconciles himself eternally with himself. This coming back again is his return to himself, and through it he is *spirit*. So this third moment is that Christ has risen. Negation is thereby overcome, and the negation of negation is thus a moment of the divine nature." Hegel, *Philosophy of Religion*, 3:219, quoted in Hodgson, *Hegel and Christian Theology*, 172.

29. See Leaver, "Music and Lutheranism" and *Bach's Theological Library*.

30. Wolff, *Bach*, 294–95.

the text of John, he adds "chorales" and choruses and arias which comment on those events leading up to the crucifixion of Christ.

I have chosen the opening chorus which captures the seriousness of the Christian enterprise. "Lord, our Ruler, whose fame is glorious through all the world, show us through your Passion that you, the true Son of God, have been glorified for all time, even when you were humbled and brought very low." Bach's setting of these words[31] presents the grandeur and dignity of the person of Jesus Christ but also the pain he endured.[32]

FURTHER READING

2 Corinthians 5:14–21.

31. The author of the words of this opening chorus is unknown. For the libretto division of the first version of 1724 see Wolff, *Bach*, 293.

32. The opening chorus is discussed by Mellers, *Bach*, 92–95 within an extended chapter devoted to the whole work (77–156).

7

Word of God, Faith, and Grace

WORD OF GOD

THIS CHAPTER CONCERNS ISSUES that are intimately related: word of God, faith, and grace. Faith and grace may be immediately seen as related but the connection of these to word of God may not be so immediately clear and it is to this that I now turn.

In God's saving work in Jesus Christ there are, according to Paul, two elements. First there is the saving act, the reconciliation achieved in the death and resurrection of Jesus, something considered in the previous chapter. Second, there is the word of God that brings God's salvation to human beings. Both these elements, the *act* of salvation and the *word* of salvation belong together. The central text here is 2 Cor 5:18–21 and I quote now just 2 Cor 5:19: "God was in Christ, reconciling the world to himself [the reconciling act] [. . .] and entrusting to us the word of reconciliation [the reconciling word]." Here Paul speaks on the one hand of the act of reconciliation through Christ; and on the other hand of the word of reconciliation, the gospel. In 2 Cor 5:18–21 God appears as the subject of the reconciling act and the subject of the reconciling word. He has entrusted to Paul and others the "word of reconciliation" (*logos tēs katallagēs*, 5:19c). He has given them the "ministry of reconciliation" (*diakonia tēs katallagēs*, 5:18c). God appeals through the preachers with the message of reconciliation (5:20). So according to 2 Cor 5, as Eichholz puts it, "the Christ event and the witness to this event must be understood as an integrated but dual activity of God."[1]

We see the same dual pattern of act of reconciliation and word of reconciliation in other letters of Paul. In the first two chapters of 1 Corinthians we find talk of the "cross of Christ" (in 1 Cor 1:17), the reconciling act, and the gospel as the "word of the cross" (1 Cor 1:18). In Romans we see the same pattern. I argued in chapter 5 that the expression "righteousness of God" (*dikaiosynē theou*) refers to the salvation of God. Paul speaks of two aspects of this righteousness: the proving or establishing of his righteousness (*endeixis tēs dikaiosynēs*) through the sacrificial death of Christ (Rom 3:25–26). This is the reconciling act. The other aspect is the revelation of this righteousness, the reconciling word. This we find in Rom 1:16–17: in the gospel the righteousness of God is revealed (*apokalyptetai*). Here the passive "is revealed" (*apokalyptetai*) is a divine passive (*passivum divinum*). So rather than saying in the active voice form "God himself reveals his own righteousness" it is implied that the righteousness of God is revealed *by God*.

The gospel is in the strictest sense God's own word. It is therefore not to be identified with the apostolic preaching.[2] But I think one can say the apostolic preaching has the capacity to witness to the gospel. The gospel is signified by the synonyms *to euangelion* (the gospel) and *ho logos* (the word) and sometimes a genitive of author (*genitivus auctoris*) is used as in *to euangelion tou theou*, the gospel from God (Rom 1:1; 15:16) and *ho logos tou theou*, the word from God (1 Thess 2:13).

FAITH

The content of faith is the same as the content of the gospel, namely Jesus Christ. So we find two corresponding and correlate expressions in Paul: *euangelion tou Christou*, the gospel from Christ, and the *pistis Christou*, the faith in Christ. This expression *pistis Christou*, literally "faith of Christ," can be understood either as a subjective genitive, Christ's own faith, or, as

---

1. Eichholz, *Theologie*, 200: "das Christusgeschehen und das Zeugnis von diesem Geschehen [müssen] als einheitliches, aber zweifältiges Handeln Gottes begriffen werden."

2. Bultmann claimed that the gospel is to be equated with the apostolic preaching (*Theology* 1:87; *Theologie*, 89). Note also that the gospel or its synonyms can appear as the object of proclamation (*euangelizesthai* [proclaim, 1 Cor 15:1]; *kērussein* [proclaim, Gal 2:2]) as well as the object of the negative verbs (*metastrephein* [pervert, Gal 1:7]; *kapēleuein* [peddle, 2 Cor 2:17]). It could be argued that it makes no sense to equate the gospel with the preaching if Paul speaks not only of the preaching of the gospel but also of the perversion of the gospel. See Hofius, "Wort Gottes," 151–52.

I think is correct, as an objective genitive, faith in Christ. See, for example, Rom 3:22 where the NRSV gives two alternative translations "faith in Jesus Christ" and "faith of Jesus Christ". The same question of translation arises also in Rom 3:26; Gal 2:16, 20; 3:22; Phil 3:9.[3]

So what is this faith? First, it is *a rational activity*. Paul says Christians believe "that Jesus died and rose again" (1 Thess 4:14), "that God raised him from the dead" (Rom 10:9). In faith the Christian confesses that "Jesus is Lord" (Rom 10:9). Faith in Christ is therefore the receiving of the gospel of Christ and the knowledge and recognition of the content of God's act of salvation. Faith holds as true what the preaching has told of the gospel.[4] Faith is therefore believing certain things to be true and is hence a rational activity. Because of this a number question Luther's theology of infant baptism. Luther argued that at baptism the parents and Godparents do not believe for the child (as in the Calvinist tradition); rather the infant itself believes.[5] So this may be a problem if one stresses this rational activity of faith that to believe is to know and I will return to this below.

Secondly, faith is *confessing*. In this connection Paul can speak of obeying the gospel or the "obedience of faith" (*hypakoē pisteōs*, Rom 1:5). Obeying here has nothing to do with ethics. The obedience of faith is simply the obedience that consists in faith.

Thirdly, faith can involve *trust*.[6] The clearest example of this in Paul is Rom 4:4–5: "Now to one who works, wages are not reckoned as a gift but as something due. [5]But to one who does not work but trusts him who justifies the ungodly, such faith is reckoned as righteousness."

Fourthly, faith is related to *union with Christ*.[7] It corresponds to the laying on of hands in the sin offering. This sense of faith is either non-rational or supra-rational, and is an antidote if one were needed to the rational stress I gave earlier. There are clearly cases where people simply do not have the mental equipment to engage in rational faith. Paul does not address this directly but he must have known of cases. So infants cannot engage in this rational activity; neither can those who are severely mentally disabled. And indeed one hears of cases where Christians suffering from degenerative mental diseases in later life come to blaspheme. But despite this one is in union with Christ and Paul says on a number of occasions that nothing can

---

3. The whole issue is discussed in Bird and Sprinkle, eds., *The Faith of Jesus Christ*.

4. Hofius, "Wort Gottes," 155.

5. Jewett, *Infant Baptism*, 167–68.

6. Faith as trust was central to Luther (e.g., see "The Freedom of a Christian," *LW* 31:350). On faith as trust, see Morgan, *Faith*, 214–24; Morgan, *Being 'in Christ'*, 203–42.

7. See again Luther, "The Freedom of a Christian," *LW* 31:351.

destroy this. The most striking instance is in Rom 8:38–39; "For I am convinced that neither death, nor life, nor angels, nor rulers, nor things present, nor things to come, nor powers, [39]nor height, nor depth, nor anything else in all creation, will be able to separate us from the love of God in Christ Jesus our Lord."

HOW DOES FAITH COME ABOUT?

According to Paul, it is the preached word of God that creates faith. Faith is a creation of the word (*creatura verbi*). According to Rom 1:16, the gospel is the power of God unto salvation to all those who believe. The gospel has this power simply because it is *God's* word. Romans 10:8 suggests that the gospel does produce faith in the hearers. The *rēma tēs pisteōs*, the word of faith, the gospel, (10:8) must is this context mean the word *that produces* faith.[8]

The word therefore has creative power. It brings faith into being out of nothing. We therefore have a creation out of nothing (*creatio ex nihilo*). Another way of looking at it is that it is like the resurrection of a corpse. These two images are used in Rom 4:17: first the resurrection image, second the creation out of nothing. Paul writing of Abraham's faith says that God "gives life to the dead and calls into existence the things that do not exist" (Rom 4:17). The creation out of nothing is clearly to be seen in 2 Cor 4:4–6. See 2 Cor 4:6: "For it is the God who has said 'Let light shine out of darkness,' who has shone in our hearts to give the light of the knowledge of the glory of God in the face of Jesus Christ." There is here in v. 6 a clear allusion to the first day of creation when God created electromagnetic radiation: "Let there be light" (Gen 1:3). God has likewise shone in the heart of Paul giving him the light of the knowledge of God in the face of Christ.

Therefore the word of God, the gospel, has creative power. This idea of course goes back to the Old Testament where the word has creative power. In Gen 1 there is the repeated refrain "And God said . . . ." So in Gen 1:3: "Then God said, 'Let there be light'; and there was light." And in Ps 33:6 we read: "By the word of the Lord the heavens were made, and all their host by the breath of his mouth."

The word of God then creates faith. The other parallel creative activity is that of the Holy Spirit. In the Old Testament the Spirit has also creative activity, as in Job 33:4: "The Spirit of God has made me, and the breath of the Almighty gives me life." There is a remarkable passage in the text known as Joseph and Aseneth that points to the creative and renewing power of the Spirit. Joseph and Aseneth is a tale written sometime between the first

---

8. Hofius, "Wort Gottes," 159–60. The genitive here means that it produces faith.

century BC and the second century AD. It tells of how the Egyptian Aseneth is converted to the faith of Joseph and marries him. The prayer of Joseph is for Aseneth's conversion (Jos. Asen. 8:9):

> Lord God of my father Israel,
> the Most high, the Powerful One of Jacob,
> who gave life to all (things)
> and called (them) from the darkness to the light,
> and from error to the truth,
> and from the death to the life;
> you, Lord, bless this virgin,
> and renew her by your spirit,
> and form her anew by your hidden hand,
> and make her alive again by your life.[9]

This, by the way, does present grace, but it may not be simply a "Jewish" text since there are signs of Christian interpolations.[10] One of my students many years ago was facing Joseph's dilemma: he was in love with a woman who did not share his faith (he was a Christian). He was so taken by this prayer that he posted it on the wall in his student room and recited it almost daily. He told me his prayer was answered!

Just as in this beautiful Jewish (and probably Christian) prayer so too in Paul the Spirit has this creative power to bring faith into being. See, e.g., 1 Cor 2:4–5: "and my speech and my message were not in plausible words of wisdom, but in demonstration of the Spirit and of power, that your faith might not rest on human wisdom but on the power of God."

FAITH, BAPTISM, AND RECEIVING THE SPIRIT

We come now to a controversial question: is the Spirit given by baptism or on hearing the gospel? This is a central question since receiving the Spirit is the very thing that makes one a Christian.

Bultmann claims that Paul "shares the general Christian view, that the spirit is conferred by baptism."[11] Although Bultmann was Protestant in his theology many in the Catholic and other traditions would agree with him; and such a view is to some extent suggested by the many images we know of Jesus being baptized and the Spirit in the form of a dove descending upon

9. Translation of Burchard in *OTP* 2:213.

10. Holtz, "Christliche Interpolationen," points to the problem of passages reminiscent of the Eucharist. However, West, "Joseph and Asenath," 78, considers that "the basic narrative is indisputably Jewish."

11. Bultmann, *Theology*, 1:333; *Theologie*, 335.

him. However, according to Paul, the Spirit is not given through baptism; it is given on hearing the gospel. See Gal 3:2b, 5: "Did you receive the Spirit by doing the works of the law or by believing what you heard? [...] ⁵Well then, does God supply you with the Spirit and work miracles among you by your doing the works of the law, or by your believing what you heard?"

Why then does Bultmann think that according to Paul the Spirit is given in baptism.[12] He offers three texts. The first is 1 Cor 6:11: "And this is what some of you used to be [that is idolaters, adulterers, etc]. But you were washed, you were sanctified, you were justified in the name of the Lord Jesus Christ and in the Spirit of our God." But this says nothing about the Spirit being given upon baptism. Conzelmann rightly comments on this verse: "The Spirit is not given in baptism, but the efficacy of the sacrament is the efficacy of the Spirit."[13] The second text is 1 Cor 12:13: "for in the one Spirit we were all being baptized into one body—Jews or Greek, slaves are free—and we were all made to drink of one Spirit." Again this text says nothing about the Spirit being given in baptism; it simply says the Spirit is active in baptism. The third text may have nothing to do with baptism, 2 Cor 1:21–22: "But it is God who establishes us with you in Christ, and has anointed us, ²²by putting his seal on us and given us his Spirit in our hearts as a first installment." It is not clear that this concerns baptism and even if it does it does not say that the Spirit was given first at baptism.

The conclusion is then that baptism is in the power of the Holy Spirit but the Holy Spirit is not given first at baptism.[14] The Holy Spirit then creates faith and the Spirit is given on hearing the gospel. Another way of looking at it (see above) is that the gospel that is preached produces faith in those who hear.

FAITH AS THE CONDITION OR MODE OF SALVATION

Some think, on the basis of Rom 1:16, that faith is to be seen as the *condition* of salvation: "For I am not ashamed of the gospel; it is the power of God for salvation to everyone who has faith, to the Jew first and also to the Greek." So the gospel is the power of God for salvation, but it is argued that the phrase "to all who believe" (*panti tō pisteuonti*) places a condition on this power. Bernhard Weiß wrote: "Faith is a condition on the side of men

12. Bultmann, *Theology*, 1:333; *Theologie*, 335.

13. Conzelmann, *1 Corinthians*, 107 n. 46 (*1 Korinther*, 137, n. 46), quoted in Hofius, "Wort Gottes," 169.

14. Hofius, "Wort Gottes," 170.

and women, without which the gospel has no power to save."[15] But if this is
the case it would paralyze God's power. An alternative approach is that of
Schlatter. The person who hears the gospel "is made a believer through the
gospel" ("durch die Botschaft zu einem Glaubenden gemacht") and therefore, having become a believer, is saved.[16]

I suspect that Schlatter has correctly understood Paul's intention. Faith
for Paul is not a *condition* of salvation but rather the *mode* of salvation. For
Paul, salvation is not *propter fidem* but *per fidem*, it is not *because of* faith,
rather it is *through* faith.[17] One reason for taking this approach is that, like it
or not, Paul's theology is highly predestinarian. And so if faith is the mode
of being saved, unbelief is the mode of being excluded from salvation. We
come here specifically to what is called double predestination, a teaching
associated with Calvin but having its root in Paul, especially Rom 9–11.
Whereas Augustine had a single predestination to salvation, those being
saved being take out of the "mass of perdition" (*massa perditionis*), Calvin
held that salvation and damnation were equal but opposite forces. We see
this, although not so explicitly, in 1 Cor 1:18: "For the word of the cross
is folly to those who are perishing, but to us who are being saved it is the
power of God." Conzelmann in his commentary rightly emphasizes that
"the word itself creates the division between the two groups."[18] This view is
found explicitly in 2 Cor 2:15–16: "For we are the aroma of Christ to God
among those who are being saved and among those who are perishing, [16]to
one a fragrance from death to death, to the other a fragrance from life to
life."

We come then to the essential point that for Paul faith is a *gift* of God
and, as noted earlier, it is the work of the Holy Spirit. That such is the nature
of faith and it not being a human work is beautifully expressed in the Schwabacher Article 6: "Such faith is not a human work nor is possible through
our own efforts, but rather is the work and gift of God, which given by the
Holy Spirit through Christ works in us."[19]

15. "Der Glaube ist auf Seiten des Menschen die Bedingung, ohne welche ihm das
Evangelium jene Kraft (sc. zur Rettung) nicht sein kann." (Weiß, *Römer*, 70).

16. Schlatter, *Gottes Gerechtigkeit*, 33. See Hofius, "Wort Gottes," 158–59, concerning the positions of Weiß and Schlatter.

17. Hofius, "Wort Gottes," 172.

18. Conzelmann, *1 Corinthians*, 42 (*1 Korinther*, 60).

19. Schwabacher Article 6, *BSELK* 59,16–17: "Daß solcher Glaube sei nicht ein
menschlich Werk noch aus unsern Kräften muglich, sondern es ist ein Gotteswerk und
Gabe, die der heilige Geist durch Christum gegeben in uns wirket [. . .]." The seventeen
Schwabacher articles were the first of the Lutheran confessions, formulated in 1529 and
forming the basis for the first part of the Augsburg confession (1530).

SALVATION BY GRACE

Salvation by grace is a corollary of salvation by faith, provided faith is seen as this gift of God. I have argued above that faith is indeed the work and gift of God, according to Paul. To highlight this point it is worthwhile comparing Paul to the epistle of James. I take the author to be the brother of Jesus writing around 60 AD.[20] He opposed Paul by arguing that Abraham was justified by works. Paul argued that Abraham was justified by faith, a view that goes against the whole of Jewish tradition. In the Jewish tradition, including James, Abraham was seen as justified by works. By contrast, for Paul Abraham was a godless man, a point not always immediately appreciated. But this is clearly implied in Rom 4:4–5. This was quoted above, but the key thing to note here is that the verses are in the context of Abraham's justification: "Now to one who works, wages are not reckoned as a gift but as something due. [5]But to one who does not work but trusts him who justifies the ungodly, such faith is reckoned as righteousness." Abraham was therefore a godless man but he was justified by faith. Paul uses Gen 15:6 to prove this. Rom 4:2–3: "For if Abraham was justified by works, he has something to boast about, but not before God. [3]For what does the scripture say? 'Abraham believed God and it was reckoned to him as righteousness.'"

When we come to James we read that Abraham was justified by his works. It seems clear that James is opposing Paul, especially as he quotes from precisely the same verse that Paul quotes, Gen 15:6. Jas 2:21–23: "Was not our ancestor Abraham justified by works when he offered his son Isaac on the altar? [22]You see that faith was active along with his works, and faith was brought to completion by the works. [23]Thus the scripture was fulfilled that says, 'Abraham believed God, and it was reckoned to him as righteousness,' and he was called the friend of God." Abraham was then justified by works because he offered his son Isaac. Even Abraham's faith, according to James, was a work. This is clearly seen in that he quotes Gen 15:6 to prove that Abraham was justified by works.

Another telltale sign that James is attacking Paul is that Rom 3:28 is mirrored in Jas 2:24:

> Rom 3:28: For we reckon that a human being is justified by faith (alone) apart from works of the law.

> Jas 2:24: You see that a human being is justified by works and not by faith alone.

---

20. Hengel, "Jakobusbrief," 252–53.

Note that the word "alone" occurs in James and not in Romans! There is some dispute as to whether that word "alone" should be understood in Rom 3:28. Luther translated it as "faith alone" and I think this is the correct interpretation. And it is interesting that the Catholic scholar Schlier (who actually converted from Protestantism) so understood it in his commentary, and this commentary received the imprimatur, that is, the licence issued by the Catholic Church to be printed.[21] But in the sixteenth century there was certainly much bitter debate between Protestants and Catholics on this idea of justification by faith alone.

My own judgement is that Luther was right to question James. Some of a theologically conservative approach argue that Luther, the great hero of the Reformation, changed his mind about James.[22] This, I think, is simply not true. Luther died in 1546 and in 1542 he said "I almost feel like throwing Jimmy into the stove, as the priest in Kalenberg did."[23] The context of this is that there was a story of the priest of Kalenberg who, on being visited by the duchess, heated his room by burning wooden statues of the apostles. The statue of James was the last to go in and he said "Jimmy you must go into the stove; no matter if you were the Pope or all the bishops, the room must become warm."[24] This was a pre-Reformation story told by Philipp Frankfurter (c. 1450–1511) of the priest Gundacker von Thernberg.

COROLLARIES OF SALVATION BY GRACE ALONE (*SOLA GRATIA*) AND BY FAITH ALONE (*SOLA FIDE*)

Paul has a *sola gratia* theology as far as "getting in" is concerned. He also had a *sola gratia* theology as far as "staying in" is concerned. The Christian life is a life of grace from beginning to end. This has various implications and corollaries, some of which I have already mentioned. I conclude by mentioning four of them.

The first is the *absolute corruption of humankind*. Paul even went to the point of implying that human beings had lost the image of God. So in

21. Schlier, *Römer*, 117 (1st ed. 1977; 3rd ed. 1987).

22. The basis for this claim is probably that in the Preface for the 1545 Bible the negative references to James we find in the 1522 preface do not appear. But the omission of such material can be accounted for by the fact that the 1545 Preface is much shorter (see *Die gantze Heilige Schrifft*, 2:1962–65).

23. *LW* 34:317 (The Licentiate Examination of Heinrich Schmedenstede, 7 July 1542).

24. *LW* 34:317 n. 21 (see also *WA* 39.2, 199, n. 2).

Rom 3:23 he says that all have sinned and fall short of the glory of God, implying, as we saw in chapter 4, that the image of God has been lost. If this is true then there are serious implications for Christian ethics where a foundation stone is that human beings bear the image of God. One way of universalizing this image is to say we do not know in whom this image is being recreated by being conformed to Christ's image and hence all should be treated with the same respect. The other is to say that if all are going to be saved through Christ, as some maintain, then one can anticipate this conforming to Christ's image in the here and now.

A second corollary is that since salvation is by grace alone we must *lack free will.* Luther writes: "I herewith reject and condemn as sheer error all doctrines which glorify free will as diametrically contrary to the help and grace of our Savior Jesus Christ. Outside of Christ death and sin are our masters and the devil is our god and lord, and there is no power or ability, no cleverness or reason, with which we can prepare ourselves for righteousness and life or seek after it."[25] Note, however, that Luther is not writing here of general free will; rather, using the language of his *On the Bondage of the Will,* one can say human beings lack free will as regards "things above" but not regarding "things below."[26] One reason Paul's view of salvation is so different to the Jewish ones is that Jewish views do not have the idea of original sin and retain the idea of freedom of the will.[27]

The third corollary is *predestination* and this obviously accompanies the lack of free will. We find this in Rom 8:29a: "For those whom God foreknew he also predestined to be conformed to the image of his Son." Here we have a predestination to salvation, which is found later in Augustine. But Paul had also a doctrine of double predestination, a predestination to salvation and a predestination to damnation. E.g., Rom 9:18: "So then God has mercy upon whomever he wills, and he hardens the heart of whomever he wills." We have to take care, for Paul's primary concern in this passage is the unbelief of Israel; but I think it fair to say that a doctrine of double predestination can be discerned here. The predestination to damnation is a difficult doctrine and I will come back to this problem later when we discuss Paul and Israel. But for now I will say that in Rom 9:19–23 Paul speaks of two groups of people, vessels of wrath and vessels of mercy. So God has predestined one group to damnation and the other to salvation. But there is also a different sort of double predestination in Rom 5:18–19 whereby *everybody,*

25. Confession concerning Christ's Supper, 1528 (*LW* 37:362–63).

26. See Luther, *The Bondage of the Will*: "free choice is allowed to man only with respect to what is beneath him and not what is above him" (*LW* 33:70).

27. On Jewish views and Paul's view of the fall see Bell, *No one seeks for God*, 118–25, 125–31.

one could argue, is a vessel of wrath and a vessel of mercy! "Therefore just as one man's [Adam's] trespass led to condemnation for all, so one man's act of righteousness [Christ's] leads to justification and life for all. ¹⁹For just as by the one man's disobedience the many [i.e., all!] were made sinners, so by the one man's obedience the many will be made righteous."²⁸

The fourth corollary is the *perseverance of the saints*. This is a term often used in the period of the sixteenth-century Reformation. Calvin spoke of the perseverance of the believers through the power and faithfulness of God.²⁹ The perseverance of the saints means this: if God has chosen someone then that person will come to final salvation on the last day. See for example Phil 1:6: "I am sure that he who began a good work in you will bring it to completion at the day of Jesus Christ." Or at the end of Rom 8 Paul says that nothing can separate us from the love of God in Christ Jesus.³⁰

Some have objected to this idea of the perseverance of the saints, saying that in Galatians, for example, there exists the possibility of falling from grace (Gal 5:4). He says those who wish to be circumcised and take on the burden of fulfilling the whole law will fall from grace. But it seems that no one had yet taken this step and Paul is sure it will not happen (Gal 5:10).³¹ There are also other verses in Paul that have been held to go against a perseverance of the saints and have been widely discussed in the secondary literature and in Christian circles.³² Nevertheless, the emphasis in Paul, I maintain, is on perseverance.³³

But two additional points should be made about Paul's theology of the perseverance of the saints. First, it only comes into full bloom in Romans. There is in fact a correlation in Paul between his doctrine of perseverance and his doctrine of Israel. The early letters such as 1 Thessalonians and Galatians see no hope for those Jews who do not believe in Christ now. However, in Romans Paul believes that *all Israel* will be saved (Rom 11:26) for God's gift and call are irrevocable (Rom 11:29). If God has called Israel then he will see that Israel comes to salvation.

---

28. Note that "many" is a Semitic way of saying "all" (Isa 53:11–12).

29. Calvin, *Institutes* 3.2.15–28; 3.24.6–8 (McNeill, *Institutes*. 1:561–74; 2:971–75).

30. See also 1 Cor 1:8–9; 1 Thess 5:23–24; 2 Cor 1:22; 2 Cor 5:5.

31. Gundry Volf, *Perseverance*, 214.

32. Consider 1 Cor 5:1–13; 6:9; 10:1–12; 2 Cor 13:5; Gal 5:19–21. All of these texts are open to different interpretations. E.g., 1 Cor 10:12 suggests the sin of idolatry calls into question the authenticity of professed faith in Christ; in 2 Cor 13:5 *adokimos* most likely refers to rejection of a non-convert. See Gundry Volf, *Perseverance*, 120–30, 217–25.

33. Such a view is also found among "Arminians" such as John Wesley.

The second additional point is that perseverance is not automatic since one is dependent on divine grace. Romans 11:17–24 tells of an olive tree whereby some branches were broken off (v. 17a, referring to Jews) and others grafted in (gentile Christians, v. 17b). Paul says God has the power break off natural branches (Jews) and also to break off the gentile Christians also (vv. 20–21). There is therefore nothing natural about the relation of *the grafted-in gentile branches* in their relation to the "rich root" (Abraham) (although the Jewish branches do have a natural relation). Continued salvation is not automatic but depends on the continual intervention of God and it must be stressed that God can graft in again any broken-off branches (v. 23). Perseverance is rather like continuous creation. Some believe that God created the world and everything then runs automatically, God being like an absentee landlord. But in continuous creation God constantly upholds the universe, an idea found in Heb 1:3 where Christ "sustains all things by his word of power." The same occurs in salvation through Christ. God is totally free in working out his saving purpose for the elect. There is nothing automatic in the saving process and God continually intervenes to bring humanity to salvation.[34]

The fifth corollary is *limited atonement*. The idea that Christ died only for the elect is not explicit in Paul but as the Calvinists realized it belongs to the logic of a *sola gratia* theology. As I understand Paul, it is impossible that Jesus should die for someone and that this person should not have the benefits of his death. The doctrine of a limited atonement is then implicit in Paul. Christ died only for the elect. Many, understandably, find this an odious idea. The only solution seems to be to say the elect equals the whole of humankind. There are some texts in Paul that could point to such a universalism and I have quoted one above, Rom 5:18–19.

Those familiar with the Calvinist tradition may well recognize traces of the "five points of Calvinism" in what I have written. These five points are expressed in English with the acronym TULIP: Total depravity, Unconditional election, Limited atonement, Irresistible grace, Perseverance of the saints. These points emerged at the Synod of Dort (1618), which was convened to examine the five points of Arminianism. In 1610 five articles of faith were drawn up by followers of James Arminius, who had died the previous year. The Arminian articles are sometimes seen as the polar opposite to the Calvinist five points, but this is too simplistic. The Arminian articles can be summarized as follows. 1. God elects or reproves on the basis of foreseen faith or unbelief (opposed to unconditional election). 2. Christ died

34. On Rom 11:17–24 and the relation to perseverance, see Gundry Volf, *Perseverance*, 196–201.

for all, although only believers are saved (opposed by limited atonement). 3. Humans are depraved such that God's grace is needed for faith or any good work (a toned-down version of total depravity). 4. This grace may be resisted (opposed by irresistible grace). 5. Whether believers will persevere in faith needs further investigation (compare perseverance of the saints).[35]

In my experience most Christians would tend to follow the Arminian view rather than the Calvinist. However, if my arguments in this chapter are sound the Calvinists in general seem to have Paul on their side. However, I am by no means aligning Paul with Calvin and Calvinism in every respect, as I hope is clear from my views on Paul and the law (chapter 3), on universal salvation (the present chapter and chapter 11), and on Christology (discussed in the next chapter).

EPILOGUE: SALVATION OF ALL CREATION

Paul, like the Synoptic Gospels (Matthew, Mark, and Luke), has a view of the salvation of the whole human being. For Paul salvation includes the salvation of our body and soul. The effects of this salvation are seen now. Although Paul himself was not healed (2 Cor 12:7–9)[36] he was himself a miracle worker.[37] He claimed that salvation had already come but he, like the Synoptics, also works with the scheme of the already and the not yet.

Final salvation occurs at the second coming, the parousia, when the dead will then be raised. This is the ultimate and final salvation of human beings. Paul understood the final glory to be concrete in that he talks about a resurrection body (1 Cor 15:35–58). Hence, redemption is seen in "physical" terms.

The final salvation will also include the redemption of the non-human creation. Many years ago when I was visiting my parents in East Yorkshire in the Easter break, I watched a TV programme where the then Archbishop of York, Stuart Blanch, was answering questions about the Christian faith, which viewers had sent in. I thought this fine Christian and biblical scholar answered the questions well—apart from one. A lady, who was mourning the death of her dog, wanted to know if she will be reunited with him in heaven. No, said the Archbishop, because animals have no souls. Despite

35. The way I have set this out is indebted to Nicole, "Arminianism," 64, cited in Steele and Thomas, *Romans*, 141. For an overview of Arminius himself see Brian, *Arminius*, who among other things makes clear the differences between Arminius and Pelagius (73–85).

36. On 2 Cor 12:1–10, see Heckel, *Kraft in Schwachheit*.

37. See Twelftree, *Paul and the Miraculous*.

the gentle tone of his answer the lady must have been devastated. We can discuss at length whether and in what way animals have "souls" but Rom 8:18–21 affirms the redemption of the non-human creation:

> [18]For I consider that the sufferings of this present time are not worth comparing with the glory about to be revealed to us. [19]For the creation waits with eager longing for the revealing of the children of God; [20]for the creation was subjected to futility, not of its own will but by the will of the one who subjected it, in hope [21]that the creation itself will be set free from its bondage to decay and will obtain the freedom of the glory of the children of God.

Here the whole non-human as well as the human creation has a purpose in God's future creation. Animals will be redeemed. Perhaps today more than ever before, in view of the ecological crisis, and the cruel methods of farming found in many countries (including advanced countries such as the United States of America and Australia), we know what it means to speak of a redeemed animal. Not only the animals but also non-living material has a place in heaven. As Arthur Moore put it when he was preaching on this passage in Wycliffe Hall chapel (around 1981), the very tiles of the chapel floor have some glorious plan in God's future kingdom.

Some years ago when health and safety was not so strict, I brought in my rabbit Tufty to a lecture concerned with the salvation of the whole creation. Although Tufty brought joy to the class, one student did put a problem to me: why is there a universal salvation for rabbits but not necessarily for human beings? This again raises the question of a universal salvation to which I return in chapter 12.

WAGNER'S *PARSIFAL:* GOOD FRIDAY MUSIC

Although Richard Wagner did not possess a rabbit he enjoyed the company of various dogs and parrots and was known as an animal lover and an opponent of the cruel methods of vivisection. The redemption of the whole created order is wonderfully portrayed in his final stage work *Parsifal*. Kundry, a tormented woman, comes to faith and is baptized, and her death with Christ is expressed by the remarkable sound of muted cellos and basses. This is followed by the Good Friday music that expresses the consequent redemption of creation.

Paul thinks that this redemption of the whole of creation is integrally related to the redemption of human beings but he does not make an organic connection between the redemption of human beings. Wagner does offer one though. The Good Friday music follows directly from Kundry's baptism and faith in Christ. The renewal of creation may be explained by Wagner's appropriation of Arthur Schopenhauer's idea that there is always a correlation between the subject (who observes) and the object (which is observed). If Kundry is renewed, her representation of the world is also renewed; see the very first sentence of Schopenhauer's World as Will and Representation: "The world is my representation (Vorstellung)."[38] In the "magic of Good Friday" it is as though we are all perceiving the renewed world through Kundry's eyes.[39]

Parsifal:

My first office I thus perform:

(*He bends over Kundry, still kneeling before him, and sprinkles her head*)

Receive this baptism,

and believe in the Redeemer!

(*Kundry bows her head to the ground and appears to weep bitterly. Parsifal turns and gazes in gentle rapture on wood and meadow, which are now glowing in the morning light.*)

How fair seems the meadows today!

Once I came upon magic flowers,

which twined their tainted tendrils about my head;

but never did I see so fresh and charming

the grass, the blossoms and flowers,

nor did they smell so sweet of youth

or speak of such tender love to me.

Gurnemanz:

This is . . . the magic of Good Friday, my lord!

Mein erstes Amt verricht' ich so:

Die Taufe nimm

und glaub' an den Erlöser!

Wie dünkt mich doch die Aue heut' so schön!

Wohl traf ich Wunderblumen an,

die bis zum Haupte süchtig mich umrankten;

doch sah ich nie so mild und zart

die Halme, Blüten und Blumen,

noch duftet' all' so kindisch hold

und sprach so lieblich traut mir.

Das ist . . . Karfreitagszauber, Herr!

---

38. Schopenhauer, *World as Will and Representation*, 1:1; *Welt als Wille und Vorstellung*, 1:31.

39. For Wagner's "theology of Good Friday" and his understanding of redemption through love, see Bell, *Parsifal*, 152–61. The translation of the following text is by Lionel Salter.

Parsifal:

Alas for the day of utmost pain!	O wehe des höchsten Schmerzentag's!
Now, I feel, should all that blooms,	Da sollte, wähn' ich, was da blüht,
that breathes, lives and lives anew	was atmet, lebt und wieder lebt,
should only mourn and weep!	nur trauern, ach! und weinen!

Gurnemanz:

You see that it is not so.	Du siehst, das ist nicht so.
It is the tears of repentant sinners	Des Sünders Reuetränen sind es,
that today with holy dew	die heut' mit heil'gem Tau
besprinkle field and meadow:	beträufet Flur und Au:
thus they make them flourish.	der ließ sie so gedeihen.
Now all creation rejoices	Nun freut sich alle Kreatur
at the Saviour's sign of love	auf des Erlösers holder Spur,
and dedicates to Him its prayer.	will ihr Gebet ihm weihen.
No more can it see Him Himself on the Cross;	Ihn selbst am Kreuze kann sie nicht erschauen;
it looks up to man redeemed,	da blickt sie zum erlösten Menschen auf;
who feels freed from the burden of sin and terror,	der fühlt sich frei von Sündenlast und Grauen,
made clean and whole through God's loving sacrifice.	durch Gottes Liebesopfer rein und heil.
Now grasses and flowers in the meadow know	Das merkt nun Halm und Blume auf den Auen,
that today the foot of man will not tread them down,	daß heut' des Menschen fuß sie nicht zertritt,
but that, as God with divine patience	doch wohl, wie Gott mit himmlischer Geduld
pitied him and suffered for him,	sich sein' erbarmt' und für ihn litt,
so man today in devout grace	der Mensch auch heut' in frommer Huld
will spare them with soft tread.	sie schont mit sanftem Schritt.
Thus all creation gives thanks,	Das dankt dann alle Kreatur,
all that here blooms and soon fades,	was all' da blüht und bald erstirbt
now that nature, absolved from sin,	da die entsündigte Natur
today gains its day of innocence.	heut' ihren Unschuldstag erwirbt.

FURTHER READING

Romans 10:5–15.

8

The Person of Christ

INTRODUCTION TO JESUS' DIVINITY

SO FAR WE HAVE looked at what theologians call the "work of Christ," especially in chapter 6 on the sacrifice of Christ. Now I focus on the question as to how Paul understood the person of Jesus. In fact, already we have considered various issues concerning his person in the discussion in chapter 6 of Rom 8:3 and 2 Cor 5:21 regarding Jesus "sinlessness."

The fundamental Christological question is that of Jesus' divinity. It is generally accepted that Paul understood Jesus to be divine in some sense. But one of the key issues to discuss is whether Paul understood Jesus to be *fully* divine, e.g., whether Paul believed in Jesus' pre-existence. So one can only speak of the incarnation if one thinks that in some sense Christ was pre-existent. A further complication is that it is unclear what "divinity" actually means and as we shall see the meaning of the term "God" as assumed in the ancient Jewish tradition actually changed as a result of the Christ event.

Before looking at specific texts regarding Christ's divinity three general points can be made. First, Paul understood Jesus as a saviour. Paul only once uses the terms "Jesus" and "saviour" together (Phil 3:20) but the idea is implicit throughout much of the seven letters and the use of "saviour" in the deutero-Pauline letters is an authentic development of Paul's Christology.[1] Further, Paul uses the verb "save" or the noun "salvation" in relation to Jesus'

1. See 2 Tim 1:10; Titus 1:4; 2:13 3:6.

96

saving work. Now for Paul there was salvation in Jesus and only in Jesus. We do not know exactly when he came to this view but it was certainly something he derived from his conversion experience. For a Jew there was only one person who could save and that was God. See Isa 43:11: "I, I am the LORD and besides me there is no saviour." Therefore Jesus, if he was a saviour, must have been divine in some sense. However, some caution is needed here since Jesus could have been a *means* of salvation just as the law and keeping it could be a *means* of salvation.

This brings us to an interesting pattern of salvation in the early church that I think elucidates Paul's Christology. Those who believed that salvation was in Jesus *and* in the law soft-pedalled Jesus' divinity or perhaps even believed Jesus was simply an inspired prophet. So in the New Testament you can find a rough correlation. Those who have a radical view of the law and stress the law has absolutely no place in salvation have a high Christology. Here we have Paul, the author of the Fourth Gospel, and Hebrews. On the other hand, those who have a conservative view of the law, those who stress that the law has some role in salvation, tend to have a lower Christology. Here we have James and the later Ebionites. The enemies of Paul in the Galatians controversy may also have been in this category. These enemies of Paul were teaching that salvation is through Christ and the law. Paul however believed that salvation was through faith in Christ and through faith in Christ alone. For Paul, works are not a condition of salvation. Paul naturally desires that Christians love God and love their neighbor but even if the Christian makes no progress in sanctification he or she will be saved on the day of judgement. Paul then believed Christ was fully divine because salvation was through Christ alone.

My second general point concerning Jesus' divinity is that if Paul worshipped Jesus from the beginning of his Christian life (and there are grounds for believing this to be so), then if Jesus was not God Paul would be an idolater.[2] So Paul was not just venerating Jesus as say someone may venerate the Virgin Mary. He was *worshipping* him as one would worship God.

The third general point is that Paul spoke of Christ in the way one would usually speak of God. Paul prayed to Jesus (Rom 10:13–14; 2 Cor 12:8–9). Further he could speak of sin against Christ (1 Cor 8:12), tempting Christ (1 Cor 10:9), the day of Christ (1 Cor 1:8), the church of God (1 Cor 10:32) and of Christ (Rom 16:10), the Spirit of God (1 Cor 2:11) and of Christ (Rom 8:9).

---

2. On the issue of devotion to Jesus, see Hurtado, *How on Earth Did Jesus Become a God?*

PHILIPPIANS 2:6–11 (PART I)

I now turn to one of the most important texts in Paul concerning Jesus being divine, Phil 2:6–11. This is often called the Philippian hymn because it is widely believed that Paul has taken up a traditional hymn of the church. My own translation is as follows:

> [6]He, who was in **the form of God**,
> did not count the equality with God *as something to be used for*
> *his own advantage* or *as robbery* (usually translated "as something to be grasped"), (*harpagmos*)
> [7]but rather[3] *made himself poor* (usually translated "emptied himself"),
> taking **the form of a servant.**
> Becoming in the likeness of human beings
> and being found in the form of a human being,
> [8]he humbled himself
> and became obedient unto death,
> even death on a cross.
> [9]Therefore, God has highly exalted him,
> and given him the name above all names,
> [10]so that at the name of Jesus
> every knee shall bow in heaven and on earth and under the earth
> [11]and every tongue confess
> "Jesus Christ is Lord"
> to the glory of God the Father.

The hymn has been often described as a great parabola describing Jesus' descent to earth and his exaltation into heaven. The hymn begins by speaking of Christ's pre-existent glory, then goes on to his becoming a human being and his death on a cross. Then we have a sweep upwards to Christ's exaltation. This I believe to be a correct understanding of the hymn, although such an understanding has been questioned.[4]

I now want to start at the beginning and put three questions, and they all relate to vv. 6 and 7. First, what does Paul mean by "being in the form of God" (*en morphē theou hyparchōn*)? Does it mean:

(i) Christ as being equal with God;

(ii) Christ being in the "image of God" (cf. Adam)?[5]

---

3. On translating *alla* as "but rather" cf. Hofius, *Christushymnus*, 137.

4. See, for example, Dunn, *Christology*, 114.

5. This second view is that of Dunn, *Christology*, 115–16.

In view of the parallelism between "the form of God" in v. 6 and "the form of a servant" in v. 7 (marked in bold above), (i) is almost certainly correct.

The second question is what does *harpagamos* mean? It could mean one of four things:[6]

(i) "a thing to be grasped." The Revised Standard Version adopts this: "did not count equality with God *a thing to be grasped*." The secondary literature discussion of *harpagamos* employs Latin expressions. So "a thing to be grasped" is rendered *res rapienda*. *Res* is Latin for "thing" and *rapienda* is from *rapio*, "I grasp." *rapienda* is then the gerundivum.

(ii) *harpagamos* could mean "a thing having-been-grasped" ("a grasped thing"). This is the *res rapta* and is adopted by the Authorised Version: "thought it not *robbery* to be equal to God." Christ's equality with God had not been obtained by snatching. We find this understanding in the Latin fathers.

(iii) *harpagamos* "as something to be held on to." This is the *res retinenda* (gerundivum), *retineo* meaning "I hold." Philippians 2:6b then means "did not count the equality with God *as something to be held on to*." Such an understanding can be found in the Greek fathers.[7]

(iv) *harpagamos* can be understood such that Phil 2:6b means "did not regard equality with God as *something to be used for his own advantage*."[8] We find something similar in NRSV: "did not regard equality with God as something to be exploited."

Of these I think that (ii) and possibly (iv) are correct and the decision has to be made by considering the context.

The third question is what happened when Jesus became a human being? Two solutions are as follows:

(i) He emptied himself and gave up his divinity (so his divinity is exchanged for humanity). This idea is often called "kenosis." The term "kenosis" is taken from that Greek verb *kenoō*, used in v. 7, and possibly to be translated as "I empty." Ideas of kenosis were developed by Gottfried Thomasius (1802–75), who made a distinction between God's "immanent attributes" (absolute power, truth, holiness, love) and the "relative attributes" (omnipotence, omniscience, omnipresence). So the immanent attributes were retained but the relative attributes were

6. Especially helpful on this is Wright, "Philippians 2.5–11," 62–90.

7. On the Latin and Greek fathers' understanding of *harpagmos*, see Lightfoot, *Philippians*, 134–37.

8. This is the solution of Hoover, "Harpagmos Enigma."

not only not *used* but were not *possessed* by Christ.[9] Such a division was severely criticized as a "completely mechanical and impossible division of the divine attributes" ("eine recht mechanische und unmögliche Teilung der göttlichen Eigenschaften")[10] and as a "thoughtless division of the divinity" ("Ungedanke einer Teilung der Gottheit").[11] Further, the "relative attributes," so-called because they relate God to the world, may not be so easily put to one side. Ritschl asks, "is not this very relation the limit within which alone any knowledge of God is possible, outside of which God is wholly inconceivable?"[12] Baillie too is critical of setting aside the "relative attributes," calling them Christ's "*distinctively* divine attributes."[13]

(ii) The alternative solution to kenosis, that is, "he emptied himself," is to understand the verb as "He made himself poor."[14] This is what Paul says in 2 Cor 8:9: "For you know the generous act of our Lord Jesus Christ, that though he was rich, yet for your sakes *he became poor*, so that by his poverty you might become rich". So Christ retained his divinity but did not take advantage of it. If this solution is chosen, I think it is necessary to redefine what one means by "God." It makes little sense to say he *voluntarily chose* not to make use of his omnipotence, omniscience, omnipresence. A way forward may be to ask searching questions about finitude and infinity and introduce a distinction, as did Hegel, between a bad and good infinity, to which I will return.

So here are the three questions and one can take various combinations of the solutions I have given. One such combination is to say that Jesus was in the image of God, as Adam was. But unlike Adam he did not consider the equality with God as a thing to be grasped. Such is the approach of James D. G. Dunn. But if there was a reference to Adam (Gen 1:27) one would

---

9. Thomasius, *Christi Person und Werk*, 2:239.

10. Frank, *Geschichte*, 262. See Beutel, "Thomasius," *TRE* 33:490.

11. Althaus, *Wahrheit*, 454. See Beutel, "Thomasius," *TRE* 33:490.

12. Ritschl, *Justification and Reconciliation*, 410.

13. Baillie, *God Was in Christ*, 94–95 (my emphasis). One of Baillie's objections to a kenotic Christology is that with a scheme of a divine pre-existence—human earthly life—divine resurrected life there is no place for Christ's permanent humanity (*God Was in Christ*, 97).

14. Although Charles Gore is often described as having a "kenotic Christology" he understood the "self-emptying" as "a continuous act of Self-sacrifice" and related Phil 2:7 to 2 Cor 8:9 (Gore, "Holy Spirit and Inspiration," 360 n. 2).

expect *kat' eikona theou*, not *en morphē theou*. Further, Wanamaker makes this important point:[15]

> [Dunn] maintains that Christ as the Second Adam, "faced the same archetypal choice that confronted Adam". But unlike Adam, Christ "chose to empty himself of Adam's glory and to embrace Adam's lot", namely man's slavery "to corruption and the powers." This view lacks coherence, however, because Dunn gives no account of what glory Christ could have had which was not available to other men and how he surrendered it up. In effect Dunn mythologises the humanity of Christ by making him qualitatively different from the rest of humanity without any explanation of the origin of the supposed difference. Dunn does not seem to realise that it was precisely this problem which the idea of Christ's pre-existence explained for Paul.

The Philippian Hymn has little to do with Adam Christology. Just to add that Dunn argues that it was only with the Logos Christology of John[16] and the Wisdom Christology of Colossians[17] that the idea of an incarnation shines through. This essentially means that there is nothing clear in the genuine letters of Paul on incarnation. As opposed to Dunn I shall argue that Paul believed in Jesus' pre-existence and believed that he was divine and fully divine.

This brings me to a second way of understanding the hymn. Paul's argument is that Jesus was pre-existent, but he did not consider his equality with God to be robbery or something to be used for his own advantage. Rather, he made himself poor (v. 7). The best commentary on this is, as I have already suggested, 2 Cor 8:9, which is worth repeating: "For you know the generous act of our Lord Jesus Christ, that though he was rich, yet for your sake he became poor, so that by his poverty you might become rich." Jesus in becoming human remained God. But he made himself poor. This refers not only to the incarnation but to the whole of Jesus' earthly life. He took the form of a servant and humbled himself even to death on a cross.

---

15. Wanamaker, "Philippians 2.6–11," 182–83, citing Dunn, *Christology*, 117. Wanamaker is quoted by Hofius, *Christushymnus*, 114.

16. See John 1:1: "In the beginning was the Word (*logos*), and the Word was with God, and he Word was God."

17. See Col 1:15–17, where Christ's role reflects that of pre-existent Wisdom: "[Christ] is the image of the invisible God, the first born of all creation; [16]for in him all things in heaven and on earth were created, things visible and invisible, whether thrones or dominions or rules or powers—all things have been created through him and for him. [17]He himself is before all things, and in him all things hold together."

As indicated above I think a way forward in considering how God can become incarnate is to ask searching questions about finitude and infinitude. Hegel addresses this in his *Science of Logic* but a more accessible entry to the issue is in his *Philosophy of History* where he understands Jesus Christ "as a *particular person*, in abstract subjectivity, but in such a way that conversely, finiteness is only the *form* of his appearance, while infinity and absolute independent existence constitute the essence and substantial being which it embodies."[18] Whereas many may think that the contradictions in theology (such as God becoming a human being) are an embarrassment, Hegel thought the truth of matters actually lie in such contradictions and he developed his famous speculative Christology, which means not undisciplined thinking but dialectical thinking.[19] In his *Phenomenology of Spirit* he presents the unfolding of Spirit in self-consciousness, in historical events, in morality and religion. It reaches its climax as he speaks of the death of God in Christ and the emptying of the absolute spirit in finitude and knowing itself in finite spirits.[20] So although he speaks of the "death of God" (cf. Phil 2:8) he goes on to speak of the giving of the Spirit into human hearts as a result of this death. This is Hegel's re-writing of the resurrection, and it is to Paul's account that I now turn in the second part of the Philippian hymn.

PHILIPPIANS 2:6–11 (PART II)

I now focus on the closing verses of the hymn. We have seen that Phil 2:6–8 refer to Christ's pre-existent glory, his incarnation, and his crucifixion. In vv. 9–11 we then have the sweep upwards: "Therefore God has highly exalted him and bestowed on him the name which is above every name, [10]that at the name of Jesus every knee should bow, in heaven and on earth and under the earth [11]and every tongue confess that Jesus Christ is Lord, to the glory of God the Father." Three things at the end of this hymn point to the fact that Jesus is God.

(i) The "name that is above every name" could be simply the name "Jesus" but more likely it is the name Yahweh, the tetragrammaton, the divine name consisting of four consonants YHWH.

(ii) The second pointer to Jesus divinity is the allusion to Isa 45:23:

By myself I have sworn,
from my mouth has gone forth in righteousness

18. Hegel, *Philosophy of History*, 318.
19. Macquarrie, *Jesus Christ*, 212.
20. Macquarrie, *Jesus Christ*, 218.

a word that shall not return:
"To me every knee shall bow,
every tongue confess."

Paul has applied words that originally referred to Yahweh to Jesus!

(iii) Paul says every tongue shall confess that Jesus Christ *is Lord*. The Greek word for "Lord" is *kyrios*. In the Septuagint this word translates the Hebrew *ādôn*, which means lord; this could be used by a servant for his master or by a wife for her husband. But *kyrios* could also be used for the divine name, the tetragrammaton, rendered in English Bibles as "LORD." Here in Phil 2:11 *kyrios* refers to the divine name.

It seems fairly clear to me from this text that for Paul Jesus was God. He had not yet thought through all the implications. He had developed no clear doctrine of the Trinity (although, as I shall argue in the next chapter, there is a proto-trinitarian theology in Paul's letters). But I think he clearly believes that Jesus was fully divine.

JESUS AS *KYRIOS*

We have seen the use of *kyrios* in Phil 2:11 and I have argued that it refers to the divine name. But there are many other texts where the title *kyrios* is used of Jesus but the precise meaning of *kyrios* is disputed. Does it refer to Jesus as divine, or simply as master? I consider three texts.

(i) The first text is 1 Cor 8:5–6: "Indeed, even though there are so-called gods in heaven or on earth—as in fact there are many gods and many lords (*kyrioi*)—yet for us there is one God, the Father, from whom are all things and for whom we exist, and one Lord (*kyrios*), Jesus Christ, through whom are all things and through whom we exist." Paul speaks of God the Father, and the Lord Jesus Christ. As I said earlier Paul had not thought through any clear doctrine of the Trinity, although I think he presents all the essential elements for the doctrine. In 1 Cor 8:5–6 Jesus seems to take the role of Wisdom as in the later texts of the Jewish tradition. Paul is here speaking in the context of paganism: there are many gods and lords in paganism. But for Paul there is only one God and one Lord. Paul is alluding here to the "Shema" of Deut 6:4: "Hear (*šemaʿ*) O Israel: The LORD is our God, the LORD alone."

(ii) Some have said that it was only possible to name Jesus as Lord in a Hellenistic (i.e., Greek) environment. The problem with this view is that in 1 Cor 16:22 the term "Maranatha" is used, an Aramaic expression transliterated into Greek, meaning either "Our Lord, come" or "Our Lord has come."

This ambiguity arises because the early Greek manuscripts (written with capital letters) had no separation of words. So the text can be read: Marana tha ("Our Lord, come"); or Maran atha ("Our Lord has come").[21] From the context the imperative is most likely. The Lord in this Aramaic expression is clearly Jesus and being Aramaic means that the expression goes back to the Palestinian Jewish church.

Some have argued that this is simply an invocation and not an acclamation. So it is a call upon Jesus to come as Lord, not that he is already Lord, as in 1 Cor 8:6. It is then argued that there is a development between the early Palestinian community and the Hellenistic community. Perhaps that is right, but we must tread carefully for both passages occur in one letter of Paul and there is no idea in the letter that there is a development from 8:6 to 16:22.

(iii) A third text to consider is Rom 10:13, which quotes Joel 3:5: "everyone who calls upon the name of the Lord will be saved."[22] In the Hebrew we have Yahweh (LORD), in the Septuagint we have *kyrios*, and Paul applies this verse Jesus.[23] These texts therefore point to Jesus being fully divine.

THE QUESTION OF SUBORDINATION

Although I have argued that Paul understood Jesus to be fully divine, some texts appear to speak of Jesus' subordination to the Father. One key text here is 1 Cor 15:24–28:

> [24]Then comes the end, when he (Jesus) delivers the kingdom to God the Father after destroying every rule and every authority and power. [25]For he must reign until he has put all his enemies under his feet. [26]The last enemy to be destroyed is death. For "God has put all things in subjection under his feet." [27]But when it says. "All things are put in subjection (*hypetaxen*)," it is plain that this does not include the one who put all things in subjection under him. [28]When all things are subjected (*hypotagē*) to him, then the Son himself will also be subjected (*hypotagēsetai*) to the one who put all things in subjection (*tō hypotaxanti*) to him, so that God may be all in all.

Paul is here quoting from and alluding to two texts from the Psalms. First Ps 110:1 (109:1 LXX): "The LORD said to my lord, 'Sit at my right

---

21. See Rüger, "Aramäisch II," 607.

22. Joel 3:5 is the reference in the MT and LXX. In the English Bible it is 2:32.

23. Capes, *Yahweh Texts*, 116–23.

hand, till I make your enemies a footstool for your feet."[24] In the Hebrew the first LORD (*YHWH*) is Yahweh and the second lord (*ādôn*) is the king. Paul applies the first LORD to God and the second to Jesus. Psalm 110:1 is alluded to in 1 Cor 15:25: "For he must reign until he has put all his enemies under his feet."

The other psalm is Ps 8. This begins by speaking about the majesty of the heavens and asks in v. 4 "what are human beings that you are mindful of them, mortals that you care for them?" The answer is "yet you have made them a little lower than God, and crowned them with glory and honor" (v. 5). Then it is the next verse, v. 6, which Paul quotes in 1 Cor 15:27: "You have given them dominion over the works of your hands; you have put all things (*hypetaxas*) under their feet."

So what are we to say about Christ being subject to God? Ziesler comments: "Things traditionally said about God may now be properly said about Christ, but not that he *is* God, for the element of subordination remains."[25] I think this is mistaken. There is subordination in this passage of 1 Corinthians but it is not subordination in the sense that Jesus is not fully God; it is subordination in the sense that Jesus submits himself to God. The verb used here for submit is *hypotassō*. Jesus is subject to his heavenly Father in the same way as the author of Ephesians understands a woman to be subject to her husband: "Just as the church is subject to Christ, so also wives ought to be, in everything, to their husbands" (Eph 5:24). Although the Ephesians text may not be from Paul it shows how the verb *hypotassō* can be used. A case can be made that just because the wife is subject to her husband— granted, an approach to marriage that we today may well take issue with— she is not any less a human being. Likewise, just because Jesus is subject to his Father it can still be maintained that he is no less divine. Further, the final phrase of 1 Cor 15:28 "so that God may be all in all" does not minimise Christ's divinity[26] and should be understood a referring to the scheme of salvation and not as some sort of metaphysical statement.[27]

Another text pointing to the subordination of Jesus to his Father is 1 Cor 11:3. "I want you to understand that Christ is the head (*kephalē*) of every man, and the husband is the head (*kephalē*) of his wife, and God is the head (*kephalē*) of Christ." The word *kephalē* usually means "head" but it can

24. This verse was applied to Jesus not only by Paul but also in a number of independent text such as Mark 12:36; Acts 2:34; Heb 1:13.

25. Ziesler, *Pauline Christianity*, 39–40.

26. Fee, *1 Corinthians*, 759, points out that "all in all" are a "Pauline idiosyncrasy" and should be understood in the light of 1 Cor 15:54–57 or Rom 11:36.

27. This is a point made by several commentators, including Barrett, *1 Corinthians*, 316, and Fee, *1 Corinthians*, 759.

sometimes mean "source." So God is the *head* of Christ or God is the *source* of Christ. Whichever way it is taken, there is some element of subordination. But again it does not mean Christ is any less God than the Father. Subordination is functional, not ontological.

Therefore, Jesus is God. It is not that he is to be equated with the Father. But he is, as the Nicene Creed (325 AD) puts it, "of the same substance (*homoousios*) as the Father."[28] This is the one phrase in the Creed that is not found in the New Testament. Paul does not work with words concerning "substance" (*ousia*)[29] but were Paul living three hundred years later I think he would not object to the *homoousios*.

THE QUESTION OF ADOPTIONISM

Adoptionism is the view that Jesus was born a normal man but was appointed God's divine son at his baptism or at the exaltation. Such a view obviously soft-pedals Jesus' divinity. The key text concerning adoptionism is Rom 1:3–4, which, by the way, is often viewed as a pre-Pauline composition. Paul writes of "the gospel concerning his Son, who was descended from David according to the flesh [4]and designated Son of God in power according to the Spirit of holiness by his resurrection from the dead, Jesus Christ our Lord." Does it not appear that it was only at the resurrection that Jesus was appointed Son of God? However, a crucial question to pose is this: does "in power" (*en dynamei*) qualify "Son of God" or "designated"? If it qualifies "designated" we have: "designated in power Son of God." This implies adoptionism. Only at the resurrection was he designated Son of God, and designated in power. But if "in power" qualifies Son of God we have: "designated Son-of-God-in-power."[30] This means that we have no adoptionism. At the resurrection he was designated Son of God in power as opposed to his being Son of God in weakness in his earthly existence.[31]

Against adoptionism one should also note the simple fact that already in v. 3 (speaking of his descent from David according to the flesh) he writes "concerning his Son" (*peri tou hiou autou*). A further argument against an adoptionism is that for Paul *"adoption* as sons" (*huiothesia*) applies only to

---

28. For the Greek see Denzinger, *Enchiridion*, §125. On the adoption of the *homoousios* see Studer, *Trinity*, 105–10.

29. In the whole New Testament the word *ousia* only occurs in Luke 15:12–13 and here simply means "property" (so the younger son asks "Father, give me the share of the property that will belong to me" Luke 15:12).

30. Cranfield, *Romans*, 1:62.

31. Bruce, *Apostle*, 117.

Christians (Rom 8:15; Gal 4:5) and to Israel (Rom 9:4) and not to Christ; Christ *is* God's own Son (*tou idiou huiou*, Rom 8:32), and is not adopted as God's son.

JESUS AS SON OF GOD

The title "Son of God" in Paul is important even though "Son of God" or simply "Son" is used much less frequently than the title "Lord" (*kyrios*). One striking aspect about this title is that it is used in connection with Jesus' pre-existence and his sending into the world and in connection with his being given up to death. Therefore, Son of God occurs in central parts of the Pauline letters.

So first I turn to the use of Son of God in relation to Jesus' pre-existence and sending into the world. See:

- Gal 4:4–5: "But when the time had fully come, God sent forth his Son, born of woman, born under the law, ⁵in order to redeem those who were under the law, so that we might receive adoption as children (*huiothesia*)."

- Rom 8:3: "For God has done what the law, weakened by the flesh, could not do: sending his own Son in the likeness of sinful flesh . . . ."

In chapter 6 I noted that Rom 8:3 raises the question as to whether Jesus took on fallen human nature. The Greek for "in the likeness of sinful flesh" (NRSV) is *en homoiōmati sarkos hamartias*. If *homoiōma* is translated as "likeness" it could imply that Jesus took unfallen human flesh. But when *homoiōma* is used in Phil 2:7 it is certainly not implied that Jesus simply appeared as a man, that he was the imitation of a human. It means he really did become human: "being found in the form (*en homoiōmati*) of a human being." Going back to Rom 8:3, it is best to understand *homoiōma* as "form" and I understand Paul to be saying that Jesus took on fallen human nature. He was born under the power of sin as all are born under the power of sin. But unlike mere human beings he was able to conquer sin. Unlike other human beings he did not fall short of God's glory (cf. Rom 3:23). He was the only one to bear the image of God! There is, of course, the important theological point that if Jesus was not made like us he would not be able to help us. There was the famous theological controversy with Apollinarius who claimed Jesus had no human soul but the divine Logos replaced the soul. Gregory of Nazianzus made a good point in response: "that which He has not assumed He has not healed."[32] The same point can be made in relation to Jesus taking our sinful human flesh. Had he not taken upon himself sinful human flesh he could not have redeemed it.

In addition to the Son of God title being used in connection with Jesus' pre-existence and sending into the world, it was used in connection with Jesus' being given up to death. See Rom 8:32a: "He did not withhold his own Son but gave him up for all of us," echoing the sacrifice (or attempted sacrifice) of Isaac by his father Abraham in Gen 22. Another key text is Gal 2:20: "It is no longer I who live, but it is Christ who lives in me. And the life I now live in the flesh I live by faith in the Son of God, who loved me and gave himself for me."

The New Testament use of "Son of God" shares with the Old Testament and ancient Jewish texts the messianic dimension. The messiah (literally "the anointed one") was related to the king, priest, and prophet in the Old Testament, all anointed figures. Especially important was the kingly messiah and we see this in Ps 2:7: "I will tell of the decree of the LORD: He said to me, 'You are my son; today I have begotten you." Also important is 2 Sam 7:13–14 where the prophet Nathan tells David that his son (Solomon) "shall build a house [i.e. the temple] for my name, and I will establish the throne of his kingdom forever. [14]I will be a father to him, and he shall be a son to me." The use of 2 Sam 7:14 as a messianic text in Qumran[33] confirms that the title "Son of God" had this messianic dimension.

Applying "Son of God" to Jesus therefore tells us that Jesus is the messiah and he was put to death as a messianic pretender. But for Paul "Son of God" means not just that he was the messiah but also points to what he shares with the "Father," namely divinity.

Related to Jesus' sonship is the "sonship" of the Christian. In the two key texts on sonship, Gal 4 and Rom 8, the adoption of the believer as a son of God features. The key word is *huiothesia*, which can be translated literally as "adoption as sons."[34] We have seen this already in Gal 4:5 and it is also used in Rom 8:15. "For you did not receive a spirit of slavery to fall back into fear, but you have received a spirit of adoption (*huiothesia*)."

---

32. Gregory Nazianzen, Epistle 101 (*NPNF2* 7:440).

33. 4Q Florilegium (4Q174) 1:10–12: "*The Lords declares to you that He will build you a House* (2 Sam. vii,11c). *I will raise up your seed after you* (2 Sam. vii,12). *I will establish the throne of his Kingdom* [*for ever*] 2 Sam vii,13). [*I will be*] *his father and he shall be my son* (2 Sam. vii,14). He is the Branch of David who should arise with the Interpreter of the Law [to rule] in Zion [at the end] of time. As it is written, *I will raise up the tent of David that is fallen* (Amos ix,11). That is to say, the fallen *tent of David* is he shall who shall arise to save Israel" (Vermes, *Dead Sea Scrolls*, 494).

34. Scott, *Adoption*.

JESUS AS SECOND ADAM AND AS "GOD"

I now look at two descriptions of Jesus that may appear to be at the opposite ends of the spectrum: first Jesus as second Adam and secondly Jesus as God.

Christ is seen as undoing the effects of Adam in 1 Cor 15:20–23, 45–49 and Rom 5:12–21. See, e.g., 1 Cor 15:22: "For as all die in Adam, so all will be made alive in Christ." Adam and Christ are then representative figures. Then one of the striking aspects of Rom 5:12–21 is that it refers to Christ as *the* human being, *ho anthrōpos*. For Paul, Christ's divinity is expressed in the sense that he is a human being who reversed the effects of Adam. This clearly differentiates the Christian faith from other so-called monotheistic faiths and again suggests that for Paul the meaning of the word "God" changed after his conversion.

As far as Jesus being directly called "God" is concerned we have in the seven letters of Paul only one single text where he could be so described, Rom 9:5. There are various translations of this verse, the NRSV giving three possibilities:

"to them [Israelites] belong the patriarchs, and from them, according to the flesh, comes the

> (i) Messiah, who is over all, God blessed forever. Amen."

> (ii) Messiah, who is God over all, blessed forever. Amen."

> (iii) Messiah. May he who is God over all be blessed forever. Amen."

There are grounds for holding to (ii), where the term "God" (*theos*) is applied to Christ: "Messiah, who is God over all, blessed forever. Amen." First of all, if Christ is referred to as "according to the flesh" one would naturally expect a continuation concerning his divinity.[35] Secondly, we are not dealing with an independent doxology. As Cullmann points out, independent doxologies begin with the word "blessed."[36] E.g., 2 Cor 1:3: "Blessed be the God and Father of our Lord Jesus Christ."[37] Thirdly, with a doxological apposition, the subject stands first, as in Rom 1:25, 2 Cor 11:31. So this doxology refers naturally to the subject, to Christ.[38]

It is often objected that Paul cannot have thought such a thing of Jesus in view of his Jewish monotheism. But two things should be borne in mind. First, in Judaism there were elements like Wisdom, which obviously proved

---

35. Cullmann, *Christology*, 313 n. 1, refers to Cremer/Kögel, *Wörterbuch*, 448, who compares the Old Testament contrast of flesh/God (*bāśār/elohîm*).

36. Cullmann, *Christology*, 312–13.

37. Compare Eph 1:3a: "Blessed be the God and Father of our Lord Jesus Christ."

38. For a detailed discussion, see Harris, *Jesus as God*, 143–72.

a useful background for Paul's Christology. Personified "Wisdom" was pre-existent and instrumental in the creation of the world (Prov 8:22–31) and was seen as "a breath of the power of God, and a pure emanation of the glory of the Almighty" (Wis 7:25). Second, Paul obviously broke through his former Jewish views. Paul remained monotheist but saw that monotheism does not have to mean that there can be no divine Son such as Jesus. There was a radical discontinuity at Paul's conversion. Simply put, the meaning of the word "God" had changed as a result of his conversion.

How Jesus can be both God and human has exercised theologians over the centuries. One solution was the two-nature Christology: a divine and a human nature are brought together in the person of Jesus Christ.[39] Such a view of Christ was even developed by assigning certain sayings of Christ to his human nature and others to his divine nature.[40] Or taking another example, it was said that on Good Friday his humanity died but not his divinity.[41] Hegel rightly objects to such a "monstrous compound." Rather, "what has thereby been brought into human consciousness and made a certainty for it is the unity of divine and human nature, implying that the otherness, or, as we also say, the finitude, weakness, and frailty of human nature, does not damage this unity, just as otherness does not impair the unity that God is in the eternal idea. It is the appearance of a human being in sensible presence; God in sensible presence can take no other shape than that of human being."[42] So as Hodgson puts it: "God and humanity are connected in such a way that God works within humanity without cancelling but strengthening

39. The Symbol of Chalcedon (451 AD) speaks of the Lord Jesus Christ "to be acknowledged in two natures (*ek duo physeōn*), inconfusedly (*asygchytōs*), unchangeably (*atreptōs*), indivisibly (*adiairetōs*), inseparably (*achōristōs*); the distinction of nature being by no means taken away by the union but rather the property of each nature being preserved, and concurring in one person and one Subsistence (*eis hen prosōpon kai mian hypostasin*), not parted or divided into two persons, but one and the same Son, the only begotten, God the Word, the Lord Jesus Christ" (Schaff, *Creeds*, 2:62).

40. E.g., Tertullian ascribed Christ's cry of dereliction (Matt 27:46) to his humanity; it was "the voice of flesh and soul, that is to say, of man—not of the Word and Spirit, that is to say, not of God" (*Against Praxeas* 30, ANF 3:627).

41. Again, taking the example of Tertullian, he declared that "we do not maintain that he died after the divine nature, but only after the human" (*Against Praxeas*, 29, ANF 3:626). However, Tertullian may appear to be inconsistent. Fighting against Marcion he wrote: "God was found little, that man might become very great. You who disdain such a God, I hardly know whether you *ex fide* believe that God was crucified" (*Against Marcion*, 2.27; ANF 3:319). A little earlier he wrote "it is part of the creed of Christians even to believe that God did die, and yet that he is alive for ever more" (*Against Marcion*, 2.16; ANF 3:309). One can account for this inconsistency in that Praxeas held that it was the Father who entered the Virgin's womb, suffered, died, and rose again (Kelly, *Doctrines*, 121). See also Jüngel, *Mystery*, 64–65.

42. Hegel, *Philosophy of Religion*, 3:315–16.

human subjectivity and personality. The awkward apparatus of orthodox Christology—'two natures', 'one person', 'hypostatic union'—is replaced by a new philosophical intuition."[43]

BORN OF THE VIRGIN MARY?

If I am right that Paul believed Jesus to be fully divine both before his birth, during his life, and in and after his exaltation, one may be left with a puzzle. Where is the so-called virgin birth or what I would rather refer to as virginal conception?[44] We know of this from the birth narratives of Matthew's Gospel and Luke's Gospel. Paul appears to be silent on the issue.

Some have argued that there could be a hint of the virginal conception in that Paul, when he refers to the birth of Jesus, uses a particular Greek verb *ginesthai*.[45] This is found in Rom 1:3, Phil 2:7, and Gal 4:4. It is true that in the Septuagint this verb *ginesthai* can be used for any normal birth together with a different verb *gennasthai*. But the striking thing in Galatians is that Paul uses *ginesthai* in v. 4 for Jesus' birth but when he later in the chapter refers to the birth of Ishmael (v. 29) he switches to a different verb *gennasthai*.

I think it unlikely that Paul knew of the virginal conception, although one would have to account for why Luke, if he was both the travelling companion of Paul and the author of the third gospel, felt able to include the birth narratives in his gospel (Luke 1:4–2:52) which tell of this virginal conception. It is worth adding this striking observation: the three New Testament theologians who have the highest Christology do not mention the virginal conception, namely Paul, the author of the Gospel of John, and the author of the letter to the Hebrews. I suggest that even if Jesus were born of a natural father and mother he could nevertheless be the divine Son of God.[46] Some argue for the necessity of the virginal conception on the basis that Jesus was born without original sin. This, however, works on the assumption that sin is somehow passed on down the generations almost like a genetic

43. Hodgson, *Hegel and Christian Theology*, 168.

44. The problem with "virgin birth" is that it could imply a miraculous *birth* as found in later tradition; "virginal conception" simply means conception without a human father.

45. Cf. Cranfield, *Romans*, 1:59.

46. This view has also been held by those who are not considered theological liberals. See, e.g., Ratzinger, *Introduction*, 208: "According to the faith of the church the Sonship of Jesus does not rest on the fact that Jesus had no human father: the doctrine of Jesus' divinity would not be affected if Jesus had been the product of a normal marriage. For the Sonship of which faith speaks is not a biological but an ontological fact, an event not in time but in God's eternity."

transmission. However, sin for Paul is to do with participating in the sin of Adam and is best understood as a mythological entity.

Apart from the historical problems involved with the virginal conception, it not being mentioned in the earliest New Testament texts (Mark and the letters of Paul), there is a dogmatic problem that Macquarrie sets out as follows: "[I]f we suppose Christ to have been conceived and born in an altogether unique way, then it seems that we have separated him from the rest of the human race and thereby made him irrelevant to the human quest for salvation or for the true life. We would be saying not that he is the revelation of God shedding light in our darkness, but that he is an altogether unintelligible anomaly, thrust into the middle of history."[47]

MOZART, *ET INCARNATUS EST* (AND BECAME INCARNATE), *MASS IN C MINOR*

Mozart is one of the most remarkable composers of all time, and he died at the age of thirty-five. He was a serious Catholic as can be seen in his letter to his father of July 3, 1778 on the death of his mother: "I am solaced, come what may—because I know that God, who arranges all things (however arbitrary it still appears to us) for the best, has so willed; for I believe (and this I will not be dissuaded from) that no doctor, no man, no misfortune, no accident, gives life to a man, nor takes it away, but God alone."[48]

The *Mass in C Minor* was composed as a thank offering for his marriage to Constanza, who sang the solo soprano part in the first performance in Salzburg (October 26, 1783). The words are very simple but point to the profound truth that God became a human being: *Et incarnatus est de Spiritu Sancto ex Maria Virgine, et homo factus est* ("And was incarnate of the Holy Spirit of the Virgin Mary, and was made a human being"). The phrases of this confession are repeated in "a sinuous dialogue with wind instruments."[49]

FURTHER READING

Philippians 2:6–11.

---

47. Macquarrie, *Jesus Christ*, 393.

48. Stone, "Beliefs," 147; Bauer/Deutsch, *Mozart: Briefe*, 2:387.

49. Humphreys, "Sacred Music," 312. The music can be found in Holl/Köhler, *Mozart: Geistliche Gesangswerke I.5*, 122–31.

9

The Church and Israel

TEMPLE, SYNAGOGUE, AND CHURCH

FOR PAUL A FUNDAMENTAL distinction in humanity is between Jews and gentiles. We have seen this, for example, in Rom 1:16: "For I am not ashamed of the gospel; it is the power of God for salvation to everyone who has faith, to the Jew first and also to the Greek [i.e. the gentile]." It is striking that the Jew has a priority in Paul's scheme of salvation. You were born a Jew and the mark of the Jew was that the males were circumcised, this being carried out on the eighth day according to the law (Gen 17:12). But it was also possible to convert to Judaism. Such converts were called proselytes and it was necessary for the males to undergo circumcision. Many interested in Judaism were understandably not prepared to take this step. Instead they were on the fringes of the synagogue, worshipping the God of Israel, and keeping the festivals and food laws. Such people were technically gentiles and were termed "God fearers" and a number were to convert to the Christian faith.

For the Jewish people the land of Israel was clearly central for their identity and I will return to this later. The focus of the land was Jerusalem and it was here that the temple stood. Whereas there was just one temple there were a multiplicity of synagogues and these could be found across the land of Israel and in fact outside of Israel in what we call the diaspora, the dispersion. In the synagogues the language used could be Hebrew and Aramaic or in fact you could have synagogues where just Greek was used.

Although Paul employs the distinction between Jews and gentiles, it was fundamentally eroded because of Christ. But Paul introduced a new distinction: those in the Christian church (i.e. those who believe in Christ) and those outside the church who do not believe. The very first Christians were in fact Jews and in the early years of the church they were seen as a Jewish sect. Among these Jewish Christians were those who spoke Hebrew/Aramaic and a little later those who were Greek-speaking Jews (called the Hellenists). But fairly soon the gospel spread to the gentiles and it was through the church that Jews and gentiles could come to be reconciled.[1]

The Greek term Paul used for church is *ekklēsia* from which we get the word ecclesiastical and in the Septuagint this renders the Hebrew *qāhāl*, the assembly. The word *ekklēsia* can be used in a secular sense in Acts 19:39 but Paul uses it for the congregation of believers. Nearly all instances in the seven letters refer to the local congregation but there are in fact seven texts that could refer to the wider church: Rom 16:23; 1 Cor 6:4; 10:32; 12:28; 15:9; Gal 1:12; Phil 3:6.[2]

The churches were centred around households, where the meetings took place (1 Cor 16:19; Phlm 2). There seems to be relatively little formal leadership; the idea of bishops, priests, and deacons that we now know in the Roman Catholic Church or the Anglican Church are to be found in the Pastoral Epistles, not in Paul.[3]

CHURCH AS BODY OF CHRIST

A key image Paul uses for the church is the body of Christ, two key texts being Rom 12:4–8 and 1 Cor 12:12–31. So Paul explains in Rom 12:4–8:

> [4]For as in one body we have many members, and not all the members have the same function, [5]so we, who are many, are one body in Christ, and individually we are members of one another. [6]We have gifts that differ according to the grace given to us: prophecy, in proportion to faith; [7]ministry, in ministering; the teacher, in teaching; [8]the exhorter, in exhortation; the giver, in generosity; the leader, in diligence; the compassionate, in cheerfulness.

1. This reconciliation is beautifully expressed in Eph 2:11–22.

2. In Ephesians, however, the term *ekklēsia* is always used for the universal church, not "the sum total of a number of local communities" but rather "the sum total of believers" (Best, *Ephesians*, 625).

3. See 1 Tim 3:1–7 (bishop); Titus 1:5–9 (elders or "priests"); 1 Tim 3:8–13 (deacons). Paul does refer to the "bishops" and "deacons" (Phil 1:1), but his "bishops" (plural rather than the singular of 1 Tim 3:1–7) are essentially equivalent to elders.

In this body everyone is a minister and one's ministry is according to the gifts given by the Holy Spirit. So in 1 Cor 12:4–5 Paul writes: "Now there are varieties of gifts, but the same Spirit; [5]there are varieties of service, but the same Lord; and there are varieties of activities but it is the same God, who activates all of them in everyone." Note incidentally the trinitarian structure of what Paul is saying, referring to the Spirit, the Lord (that is Jesus), and God (the Father).[4]

Paul's view on the church was to have some radical implications, although there are texts where he seems to hold to views from his Pharisaic past. So in Gal 3:28 he writes: "There is no longer Jew or Greek, there is no longer slave or free, there is no longer male and female; for all of you are one in Christ Jesus." This is truly inspiring, but the question is whether he saw the full implications of this. He certainly saw the full implications regarding Jews and gentiles since he fought for the full equality of Jews and gentiles in the churches. But there are certain texts that suggest that perhaps he did not see the full implications regarding slave and free and male and female. For example, on the question of slave and free he returned the escaped slave Onesimus back to his master, although one could make the case that Paul "lit the fuse" so to speak in telling Philemon that he is to receive Onesimus no longer as a slave but as a brother (Phlm 16).

On the question of male and female there are also certain texts that do point to the subordination of women either within marriage or in the Christian congregation. So 1 Cor 11:3 speaks of the husband being the head of the wife: "But I want you to understand that Christ is the head of every man, and husband is the head of his wife, and God is the head of Christ." Especially difficult is 1 Cor 14:34–35, which could be a possible interpolation: "Women should be silent in the churches. For they are not permitted to speak, but should be subordinate, as the law also says. [35]If there is anything they desire to know, let them ask the husbands at home. For a shameful for a woman to speak in church." Some have argued that these verses are an interpolation, that is a later insertion by someone other than Paul.[5] My own view is that the arguments for and against an interpolation are fairly evenly balanced but there is much to be said for Fee's proposal that the verses were a marginal gloss by someone other than Paul; this would account for the different placement of the verses in the Western texts (where they appear at the end of the chapter).[6]

4. On the church as the body of Christ, see also chapter 10.

5. E.g., Fee, 1 Corinthians, 699–708, and Empowering Presence, 272–81; but contrast, e.g., Thiselton, 1 Corinthians, 1147–61.

6. This fulfils Bengel's first principle that the reading that best explains how the others came into being is to be preferred as the original (Fee, Empowering Presence, 272, n. 2).

But despite these possible problems Paul can be given credit for being well ahead of many of his contemporaries in relation to the leadership of women. So he commends Phoebe a deacon in Rom 16:1 and in Rom 16:7 refers to what may well be a married couple, Andronicas and Junia, "prominent among the apostles."[7]

ISRAEL I: 1 THESSALONIANS 2:14–16

Since the holocaust the theme of Israel in the New Testament has become a key issue. One of the accusations levelled against the New Testament is that it contains anti-Jewish elements or even that it is inherently anti-Jewish.[8]

In Paul's first letter, 1 Thess 2:14–16, there are clear anti-Jewish sentiments:

> [14]For you, brothers and sisters, became imitators of the churches of God in Christ Jesus that are in Judea, for you suffered the same things from your own compatriots as they did from the Jews, [15]who killed both the Lord Jesus and the prophets, and drove us out; they displease God and oppose everyone [16]by hindering us from speaking to the Gentiles so that they may be saved—so as always to fill up the measure of their sins; but God's wrath has overtaken them at last (*eis telos*).

The phrase *eis telos* most likely means either "finally" or possibly "forever."[9] There is, according to this early letter of Paul (50AD), no hope for Jews who do not believe in Christ in the here and now

---

7. The accusative object is *Iunian*, which gives the possibilities *Iunia* (feminine) or *Iunias* (masculine). The problem with *Iunias* is that the name is otherwise not attested but could be a contraction of the known name *Iunianus* (*Iunia(nu)s*) (Lampe, *Christen*, 140, 147). The Authorised Version has Junia, the Revised Version Junias (Junia in the footnote), the RSV has Junias, and the NRSV Junia (Junias in the footnote). The NRSV adds that some ancient authorities read Julia; this comes from the accusative *Iulian*, a reading found in the oldest text, P46 (date around 200AD). The name Iulia, like Iunia, is well attested (Lampe, *Christen*, 139, 146–47).

8. Ruether, *Faith and Fratricide*.

9. *BAG* give the following meanings for *eis telos*: 1. in the end, finally; 2. to the end, until the end; 3. forever; 4. decisively, fully. Of these possibilities I think the first is the most appropriate (cf. Best, *Thessalonians*, 121). Dodd, "The Mind of Paul: II," 120, writes that according to 1 Thess 2:16, "'the Wrath' has fallen *finally* on the Jews" and so *eis telos* implies "that this sentence of reprobation cannot ever be reversed." Two attempts to harmonize Rom 11:25–32 (discussed below) with 1 Thess 2:16 are: (i) to adopt solution 2 and argue that the Jews are under God's wrath "until the end" (Hahn, *Mission*, 90 n. 1); however, the context implies a certain finality about what takes place (Best, *Thessalonians*, 122). (ii) Holtz, *Der erste Brief an die Thessalonicher*, 110, adopts a

This passage cannot be dismissed as an interpolation (that is, an insertion into the text by someone other than Paul)[10] as some have done; nor can it simply be described as "an unreflected traditional statement."[11] Although Paul is clearly anti-Jewish here, what he writes is perhaps understandable. Paul had been constantly hindered by the Jews in his mission. The Acts of the Apostles, which I believe is fairly historically accurate for the later part of Paul's career, certainly portrays Paul's problems with the Jews, and Acts 17:1–15 specifically portrays the problems Paul faced with the Jews in Thessalonica.

So in this first letter of Paul, dated around AD 50, he clearly believed that the Jews who do not now believe in Jesus or who will not believe in Jesus before their death or the second coming (the parousia) have no chance of salvation. A similar view is probably held in Galatians.[12] It may be that Paul in these earlier letters had a substitution theory: the church has substituted the Jews as the people of God.

Such a substitution model is not unique to Paul in the New Testament. It is found also for example in Matt 8:11–12: Jesus is reported to have said, "I tell you, many will come from east and west and sit at table with Abraham, Isaac and Jacob in the kingdom of heaven, [12]while the sons of the kingdom (i.e., the Jews) will be thrown into the outer darkness; there men will weep and gnash their teeth." Matthew has the view that Israel has been disinherited; Israel is no longer the people of God. A similar view is put forward in Matt 21:43: "Therefore I tell you, the kingdom of God will be taken away from you and given to a people that produces the fruits of the kingdom."

Paul probably shared this substitution view in his early years as a Christian. But he changed his mind. First we have 2 Cor 3:16, which we

---

particular interpretation of solution 4 ("fully"; "gänzlich") and writes that Rom 11:25–32 does not contradict 1 Thess 2:16 since *eis telos* does not apply to the judgement of the Jews at the end of time. However, *eis telos* should have a temporal element since v. 16c parallels 16b ("so as always to fill up the measure of their sins").

10. See Pearson, "1 Thessalonians 2:13–16," who supports Baur's thesis (*Paulus* 2:97), that 2:16c refers to the destruction of Jerusalem in 70 AD (Baur considered the whole letter un-Pauline). Pearson's arguments have been criticized by Hurd, "1 Thess. 2:13–16," 35, who warns against assuming that 1 Thess 2:16c must refer to the events of 70 AD. In fact, Paul is probably not referring to any historical event but is asserting that "judgement is about to overtake the Jews" (Best, *Thessalonians*, 120). To this may be added that there is no textual evidence that 1 Thess 2:13–16 is an interpolation. (See the first of Kurt and Barbara Aland's "Twelve basic rules for textual criticism," in *Text*, 275: "Textual difficulties cannot be solved by conjecture, or by positing glosses or interpolations, etc., where the textual tradition itself shows no break; such attempts amount to capitulation before the difficulties and are themselves violations of the text.")

11. Luz, *Geschichtsverständnis*, 290–91.

12. See Bell, *Irrevocable Call*, 160–80.

have studied before: "But when an Israelite turns to the Lord, the veil is removed." Paul here envisages the conversion of an Israelite when the veil, which is preventing them from understanding the gospel, is removed. Then in Rom 9–11 we have a complete change, as we shall see in Rom 11:26.

ISRAEL II: ROMANS 9:1–29

In Romans, probably Paul's last letter, we have the most positive statements concerning Israel. But such statements do not come immediately; indeed, the very first chapter of the section, Rom 9:1–29, sounds particular harsh on Israel.

At the end of Romans 8 Paul declares that nothing can separate us from the love of God (Rom 8:31–39); but then a problem immediately crops up. If nothing will separate us from the love of God, what about Israel? God made promises to Abraham but if the vast majority of Jews do not believe in Christ and if there is salvation only in Christ, the Jews are damned: they are separated from the love of God. Paul admits that the Jews are separated from the love of God in that they are separated from Christ: "For I could wish that I myself were cursed and cut off from Christ for the sake of my own people, my kindred according to the flesh" (Rom 9:3). Paul is employing a euphemism here in that rather than saying directly that Israel is cut off from Christ he says he is prepared to be cut off from Christ for the sake of Israel. Paul then goes on to argue that Israel do not believe because a hardening has come upon Israel.

I now follow his argument in Rom 9:1–29. Paul begins in Rom 9:1 by mourning over Israel and in v. 2 writes: "I have great sorrow and unceasing anguish in my heart." The Jews, he implies, are separated from Christ (Rom 9:3). But although Israel is cut off from Christ, Israel still has her privileges. He lists six in v. 4: the adoption as sons, the glory, the covenants, the giving of the law, the worship, and the promises. It is particularly striking that he begins with the adoption as sons, the very privilege Christians enjoy (see Rom 8:15). Then in v. 5 he says that theirs are the patriarchs and from them has come the Christ, something considered in the previous chapter on the person of Christ. These privileges Paul lists *still hold*. Note that the promise of the land is missing. This may be because Israel was then under Roman occupation. But it may be worth adding that Paul certainly thought the Jews had the right to live there and they would need the temple in Jerusalem in order to carry out the worship.

Paul then goes on to ask why Israel does not believe in Jesus. His answer is: because God has predestined them so. Looking at the history of

Israel he notes that some were predestined to salvation, other to damnation. So Abraham had two sons: Isaac was accepted and Ishmael was rejected. Isaac had two sons: Jacob was accepted and Esau was rejected. In Rom 9:13 he quotes Mal 1:2–3 in a condensed and devastating form: "I have loved Jacob, but I have hated Esau."

Paul then argues that there has been a narrowing of Israel even within Jacob (that is within Israel). Some God accepted and others he rejected. Rom 9:18: "So then he (God) has mercy upon whomever he wills, and he hardens the heart of whomever he wills." This process of narrowing goes to such an extent that only a remnant will be saved. So Paul in Rom 9:27 quotes Isa 10:22: "Though the number of the children of Israel were like the sand of the sea, only a remnant of them will be saved."[13] If we were to stop at this point in the argument we would have the overwhelming impression that only a remnant will be saved and the vast majority of Jews will be damned.

ISRAEL III: ROMANS 9:30—10:21 AND 11:1–36

Romans 9:30—10:21 concerns the unbelief of Israel and the acceptance of the gentiles. There is much one could say about the passage but I mention just the final heart-breaking words, where Paul quotes from Isa 65:2 and applies the words to the Israel of his day: "All day long I have held out my hands to a disobedient and contrary people." Again if you were to end the Israel discussion at this point, the news is grim. But in chapter 11 everything begins to change.

He asks in v. 1: "has God rejected his people?" The somewhat surprising answer is: "by no means! I myself am an Israelite." So the fact that God has chosen Paul is an indication that God has not rejected his people. Paul then explains that God's purpose in hardening Israel was so that the salvation goes to the gentiles. Romans 11:11b: "through their trespass salvation has come to the Gentiles, so as to make Israel jealous." Only by Israel rejecting Christ could the gentiles come into the community of salvation, the church. If all Israel had believed in Jesus the gentiles would never consider joining the church. So Israel's disobedience led to the salvation of the gentiles. The gentiles then in turn make Israel jealous. This provoking to jealousy then prepares Israel for her final conversion when Jesus comes again.

13. Note that Isa 10:22 in turn alludes to Gen 22:17a where are the angel of the LORD says to Abraham: "I will indeed bless you, and I will make your offspring as numerous as the stars of heaven and as the sand that is on the seashore." See Olson, *Gospel*, 154–55.

And so we come to those crucial verses, Rom 11:25–26, which I translate thus:

> [25]For I want you to know
> this mystery, brothers and sisters,
> so that you may not be wise in your own eyes,
> that a partial hardening has come upon Israel
> until the goal is reached, that
> the fullness of the gentiles
> will have come in,
> [26]and so
> all Israel will be saved,
> as it is written,
> "The deliverer will come from Zion,
> he will turn away ungodliness from Jacob,
> [27]and this is my covenant with them,
> when I take away their sins."

And so the hardening of Israel will come to an end when the full number of the gentiles will have come in. Paul may have in mind his mission to Spain which he hoped to accomplish (Rom 15:24) but in fact never did. He explains that when the full number of the gentiles will have come in the conditions are there for the salvation of all Israel.

The fundamental question is the meaning of "all Israel." I offer four possibilities:

First, Calvin thought it meant the church of Jews and gentiles.[14] But throughout Rom 9–11 Israel has referred to the Jews. Romans 9–11 is about the contrasting roles of Jews (referred to as Israel) and gentiles. Some argue for "all Israel" referring to the church because of Gal 6:16 which talks about the "Israel of God." Israel of God in Gal 6:16 may refer to the church, but in 11:26 Israel must I think refer to Jews.

The second view is that it means the remnants of Israel, as in Rom 9:27.[15] But if Paul wanted to refer to a remnants of Israel why did he use the expression "*all* Israel"?

The third view is that "all Israel" means simply every single Israelite. There are Old Testament texts where "all Israel" is used in this sense (Deut 27:9; Josh 3:17; 8:33). But there are also texts where "all Israel" means a representative part of Israel (1 Kgs 12:1) or Israel as a whole (Dan 9:11; 2 Chr 12:1).

---

14. Calvin, *Romans*, 255.

15. Bengel, *Gnomon*, 602.

This leads to a fourth view: "all Israel" means Israel as a whole but not necessarily including every single member.[16] Mishnah Sanhedrin 10:1 is seen as a parallel: it opens with the words "all Israel has a share in the world to come" but this is then is followed by a long list of exceptions.

Of these views I think the third and the fourth are the strongest and I myself have argued for the third view.[17] One reason for holding to this is that Paul declares in v. 29 that the God's gifts and call are irrevocable. If they are irrevocable it would seem odd that certain Israelite are excluded from salvation.

One reason Paul writes these chapters is because he has to work out in his own mind God's purpose concerning Israel and the gospel. The early Christians in Rome tended to live in the Jewish areas[18] and one of the questions that perhaps bothered these Christians was that if God had not been faithful to the Jews, how are they to know whether he is going to be faithful to them? So one of his key messages in Rom 9–11 is the "perseverance of the saints"! Paul's message in Rom 9–11 is that God will keep to his promises to the gentile Christians just as he will keep to his promises to the Jewish people.

Now one of the key questions that divides scholars is *how* Israel will be saved. As I understand v. 26, Israel will be saved by receiving the gospel directly from Christ at his second coming. They can only be saved through faith in Christ, as Rom 11:23 suggests ("And even those of Israel, *if they do not persist in unbelief,* will be grafted in, for God has the power to graft them in again"). And just as Paul came to faith in Christ through a direct encounter with him so he believed it will be for the Jewish people.

A final question: will it be only those Jews alive at the second coming who will be saved through faith in Christ or it will it be Jews from every single age. If Paul is insistent that God's call and gifts are irrevocable (see v. 29) I think Paul must be referring to every single Jew who has ever lived.

IS THERE NO DISTINCTION BETWEEN JEW AND GENTILE?

Paul throughout his letter to the Romans stresses that God is no respecter of persons and he says this in respect to the Jew-gentile issue. See 3:22b: "For there is no distinction (*diastole*)." See also 10:12: "For there is no distinction (*diastolē*) between Jew and Greek." But in Rom 9–11 we read "All Israel will

16. E.g., Kühl, *Römer*, 392–93.
17. Bell, *Provoked to Jealousy*, 136–45.
18. Lampe, *Christen*, 26–28.

be saved" but only "the fullness of the Gentiles" will be saved. The fullness of the gentiles does not necessarily mean the totality of gentiles and probably means the number God wishes to save. Is not God favouring Israel? Israel has a second chance; the gentiles do not.

Dodd argued that Paul's premises "All Israel will be saved" and "there is no distinction between Jew and Gentile" must imply a universal salvation.[19] Paul in a number of texts was certainly not a universalist. See 1 Cor 1:18: "For the word of the cross in folly to those who are perishing." See also 2 Cor 2:15: "For we are the aroma of God among those who are being saved and among those who are perishing." But are there other texts that imply universalism? Romans 11:32 is often taken as a text for universal salvation: "God has consigned all to disobedience that he may have mercy on all." But Paul is here most likely referring to two *groups:* God has salvation on all, i.e., Jews and gentiles. Another text that may appear to support universalism is 1 Cor 15:22: "For as in Adam all die, so also in Christ shall all be made alive." However "all" in the second half means only "all who are in Christ" as 1 Cor 15:23 suggests.

A parallel text to 1 Cor 15:22 is Rom 5:18: "Just as one man's trespass led to condemnation for all men, so one man's act of righteousness leads to acquittal and life for all men." One way of understanding this is to say "all those on Adam's side will be condemned, all on Christ's side will be acquitted." However, I find this a rather unnatural way to understand the verse. A better understanding is that there are two ways of viewing human beings, "in Adam" and "in Christ." "In Adam" all will be condemned, but "in Christ" all will be acquitted. Of all the Pauline texts this is perhaps the one that points most clearly to universalism. It is particularly interesting (and comforting!) that there is a form of double predestination not in the Calvinist sense that one group is damned and one group is acquitted. This was the sense in the texts I quoted above from 1 Cor 1:18 and 2 Cor 2:15. Rather we have a double predestination in the sense that *all are damned* in that they are in Adam, and *all are acquitted* in that they are in Christ.[20]

The reason Paul comes to a universalist conclusion here in Rom 5 is that he is dealing with a mythical scheme and not one that deals with how the word reaches human beings in order to save them. Another "mythical" scenario is presented in 2 Cor 5:19: "God was in Christ reconciling the world to himself." Here he speaks of the world as a "cosmic whole": "The world as one whole; not a person here and there, snatched as brands from

19. Dodd, *Romans*, 183–84.
20. For the detailed argument see Bell, "Universal Salvation."

the burning; not a group here and a group there; but the reconciliation of the whole world."[21]

Romans 5:18–19 and 2 Cor 5:19 do not address the issue of how the reconciling word reaches human beings. However, Phil 2:11 does address this in that "every tongue will confess 'Jesus Christ is Lord.'" The one who confesses "Jesus Christ is Lord" is the one who will be saved (Rom 10:9) and such a confession can only be made through the power of the Holy Spirit (1 Cor 12:3).

UNIVERSAL SALVATION, DOUBLE EXIT, AND MISSION

The two basic options for salvation of humankind are the double-exit (some are saved, the rest are damned) or universalism. The latter can then be subdivided into those who believe salvation can only be through faith in Christ (hence all must come to faith) or all will be saved on some other basis (e.g., on the basis of their own religion).

If one believes in the double-exit then there is clearly a strong motive for mission. Some indeed have lived and acted as Christians in conformity with such a belief. For example, the missionary zeal of James Hudson Taylor (1832–1905) was motivated by the idea of Chinese people going to a Christless eternity. This drove him to evangelize China, which entailed the tragic sacrifices of the lives of his wife, new born baby, and his six-year-old, Samuel.[22] However, many who claim to hold to this belief appear not to actually believe it. If they did, would they be watching soap operas or playing sport?

It is often said that the universalist has no motive whatsoever for evangelism. It is interesting though that Paul, although believing in the universal salvation for Jews, continued to evangelize Jews. He wanted them to enjoy Christ in the here and now and, perhaps more importantly, to see Christ glorified in the here and now. The same logic can hold for a universalism for gentiles.

21. Forsyth, *Work of Christ*, 84.
22. Yates, "Taylor, J. H.," 659.

CONTEMPORARY QUESTIONS CONCERNING ISRAEL

I have addressed these issues elsewhere,[23] but I will outline briefly the relevance of Paul for the issues of the election of Israel, the land of Israel, and mission to Israel (i.e., to Jewish people).

In Romans Paul holds to the abiding election of Israel (although he did not do so earlier).[24] In Paul's time the definition of who was a Jew was relatively clear: one was a Jew by matrilinear descent or by conversion. This idea goes back to the mid-fifth century BC and was precipitated by the experience of the Babylonian exile. Before that Israel was a land-related national identity but afterwards Israel was not simply defined by attachment to the land and so the issue of genealogy became important.[25] But even in Paul's time the question of who belongs to "Israel"—and therefore to whom the promise of Rom 11:26 ("All Israel will be saved") applies—was not entirely clear. The well-known case of a "half-Jew" is Herod the Great, whose father Antipater was a descendant of Idumeans converted to Judaism but whose mother was Nabatean.[26]

Today the idea of a clearly defined Israel is even more problematic. There is a core who are clearly "Jews" but there are so many who are half, quarter, eighth Jews, etc. So even if one wished to apply Rom 11:26 today there would be certain problems in doing so. Perhaps one has to work with an "Israel in the mind of God"!

The election of Israel may seem at first glance to be an affirming idea for the Jewish people. But an important question is, *for what* are they elected? In Romans Paul applies the election of Israel in what can be called a dialectical pattern. This is in fact set out by Gutbrod in an article on "Israel."[27] Paul highlights the disobedience of Israel (Rom 10:21; 11:2) in seeking their own righteousness (Rom 9:31–32) which is a *result* of God hardening their hearts.[28] But "all Israel" will be saved (Rom 11:26)[29] because of God's promise to the patriarchs (11:28) and Israel's abiding election (Rom 11:29). Israel's election therefore has both a negative and positive aspect for Israel.

23. Bell, *Irrevocable Call*, 338–407.

24. On the earlier letters see Bell, *Irrevocable Call*, 160–90.

25. Schiffman, *Who Was a Jew?* 16.

26. Schiffman, *Who Was a Jew?* 12.

27. Other contributors to this article are Gerhard von Rad and K. G. Kuhn.

28. Cf. Gutbrod in von Rad, Kuhn, and Gutbrod, "Ἰσραήλ," 387, who thinks the hardening is a result of their disobedience.

29. Gutbrod, "Ἰσραήλ," 387, understands "all Israel" to mean Israel as a whole, not every single Israelite.

Gutbrod's article appeared in volume 3 of *Theological Dictionary of the New Testament*, edited by Gerhard Kittel, which appeared in 1938. This fine German scholar, Walter Gutbrod, died on the Russian front in 1941 at the age of twenty-nine. Volume 4 of Kittel's *Dictionary* has a dedication to his memory and to three others who fell in the war and also worked on the *Dictionary*.[30] Kittel himself would appear to share Gutbrod's understanding of the basic elements of Rom 9–11.[31] The frightening aspect of Kittel's work, though, was applying this to the current political situation in Germany. Kittel applied the idea of the election of Israel to argue that Jews should not be assimilated in German society and must remain universal strangers.[32] It may appear positive that he wishes the Jews to retain their traditions and customs (a view that angered the Nazi authorities) but he wished them to be so identified so it was clear that God's judgement had come down upon them![33] Although Kittel opposed many of the Nazi policies and was often a thorn in their side, his antisemitism was serious enough for him to be interred by the French authorities at the end of the Second World War.[34] Although he showed personal kindness to individual Jews, some views expressed in his writings are abhorrent. He held that no Jew should teach in schools or universities or hold a position in any of the professions; marriages between Jews and non-Jews should be forbidden; no Jew should be an ordained pastor or elder of a German congregation but rather Jewish Christians should form their own congregations. He is reported to have said during his internment at Balingen: "My position in the Jewish question is based on Holy Scripture and the tradition of the primitive Christian

---

30. See the dedication to his memory in *ThWNT* 4:III (published 1942). The three others are Albrecht Stumpff (died in France, aged thirty-one), Hermann Fritzsch (died in Russia, aged twenty-eight), and Hermann Hanse (died in Russia, aged thirty-one). This dedication is missing in the English translation, *TDNT*.

31. See Kittel, "Neutestamentliche Gedanken zur Judenfrage." Note, however, that he makes the odd comment that "so you may not claim to be proud" applies to *Jewish* Christians (906); Paul is clearly addressing *gentile* Christians. Further although Kittel refers to the grafting back of the natural olive branches (i.e., Jews) into the olive tree (Rom 11:24), the "lifting the curse" ("Aufhebung des Fluches"), and mercy on Israel (Rom 11:31) he refrains from referring to Rom 11:26 that "all Israel will be saved" (906). The same pattern can be found in his "Judenfrage im Lichte der Bibel."

32. Bell, *Irrevocable Call*, 413.

33. Bell, *Irrevocable Call*, 394.

34. It should also be added that Kittel, like Kuhn (who contributed to the article on "Israel," see the note above), joined the Nazi party and took part in Walter Frank's "Reichsinstitut für Geschichte des neuen Deutschlands" ("Imperial Institute for the History of the New Germany").

Church."[35] This is a warning to all who attempt to apply any New Testament theology to political and social realities.[36]

Just as Israel's election has its positive and negative sides for Jewish people so it has this double nature for gentiles. The negative side is the idea that gentiles are second class, an idea expressed in Rom 1:16 (the gospel of for the Jews first) and in a text such as Mark 7:24–30. But Israel's election has an overwhelmingly positive aspect: for according to Paul's logic, only by Israel being set aside could salvation come to the gentiles (Rom 11:11–14).

The election of Israel is related to the question of the land. Paul's texts have little support for a state of Israel as we now know it. The most we can glean from his letters is that Jewish people have the right to live in Israel for the temple worship (Rom 9:4). But since the temple no longer exists this hardly has any relevance. The question of the land has to be settled by other arguments. One is the protection of Jewish people from persecution. But the other is justice for Palestinians. On both these issues it is worth emphasizing that views among Jewish people themselves vary enormously.

Another controversial issue is the question of a Christian mission to Jewish people. Paul engaged in such a mission, even after he came to the conclusion of Rom 11:26 that all Israel will be saved. The issue of a mission to Israel has become extremely sensitive with the growing awareness of the history of Christian antisemitism and especially our living in the shadow of the holocaust. In some quarters the narrative has been developed that a "Christian" nation (Germany) attempted to eradicate the Jewish people. What right then have Christians to engage in mission to the Jewish people? Further, mission erodes the culture of the Jewish people since any converts are under no obligation to keep the law or any Jewish customs and festivals. The problem of eroding culture applies, of course, to evangelizing any other religious group. However, despite these issues, which one should always bear in mind, I see no problem is sharing the Christian message with Jewish people or indeed with any who belong to other religions or none. I think the best evangelism is low-key evangelism and a fine example is the one I gave in chapter 3 of the Jerusalem shop that displayed an open New Testament, turning a page each day, so someone such that the young man I mentioned could "hear" the gospel and come to faith in Jesus Christ. He was eternally grateful for that opportunity to read the New Testament. It is refreshing to speak with Christian Jews, a neglected group in Jewish–Christian dialogue,

---

35. Porter, "Kittel," 401.

36. Kittel died in 1948 at the age of 59. The *Dictionary* then was edited by Gerhard Friedrich. Despite the antisemitism of Kittel and some of the other early contributors, this *Dictionary* remains a valuable resource for study of the New Testament.

who rejoice in their faith in Christ and who are thankful to those who had the courage to share the Christian faith with them.

FROM "EAST SIDE STORY" TO "WEST SIDE STORY"

Much of the music I include at the end of a chapter is fairly obviously connected to the chapter theme. But for the music for this chapter I do need to explain some things. The music I've chosen is not in the stratosphere of Bach or Mozart but I think is nevertheless from a fine artwork: "West Side Story," the creation of a Jewish composer (Leonard Bernstein) and a Jewish librettist (Stephen Sondheim). In the second clip Bernstein himself is rehearsing for a recording of the musical using the voices one hears in musicals; but for the main parts, Tony and Maria, he uses operatic voices.

The reason this musical is especially fitting is that when it was first conceived it was set in the East part of Manhattan, New York City and was to concern two gangs, one Jewish and one Catholic. As Sondheim and Bernstein worked further on the musical it was decided to move the action over to the West Side and certain changes were made. But one can still discern I think the Jewish–Catholic theme.

The story is an updated version of Shakespeare's *Romeo and Juliet*, but rather than having Montagues and Capulets it is about these two gangs, the white gang of Jets and the gang from Puerto Rico, the Sharks. And it was at a dance that across the crowded room Tony and Maria fall in love. Tragically, as in Shakespeare's drama, things do not work out and at the end Tony is killed. But there is a hint that the two gangs are going to be reconciled. At the end Tony's body is picked up by his gang mates (Jews) but quickly they are helped by the rival gang, the Sharks. The first clip is from earlier in the musical: the balcony scene where Maria and Tony express their love and their hopes that they will be able to come together despite the warfare between their respective gangs.

Paul likewise had a vision in Romans that Israel and the church will one day be reconciled, but only on the day of the second coming of Christ. Reflecting on this reconciliation one could say it is the final stage in the ecumenical progress. In the ecumenical vision Protestant groups (e.g., Lutherans, Anglicans, Methodists, Baptists) come together, then Protestants and Catholics come together, and then this whole Western church is reconciled to the Eastern churches (Greek, Russian, Armenian orthodox, etc.), and then finally those churches that do not recognize the Council of Chalcedon will be brought in. And then the final stage is reached at the parousia for the church and Israel to be brought together as one people of God.

FURTHER READING

Romans 11:25–32.

10

Anthropology

INTRODUCTION AND PAUL'S PESSIMISM

THIS CHAPTER CONSIDERS PAUL's understanding of the human person. His letters do not give a neat outline of his anthropology; and perhaps we should hardly expect him to do that. In his letters he was primarily concerned with reminding his readers of matters of salvation and conduct. It is also worth reflecting on the fact that the human person is so mysterious that a neat understanding of anthropology is impossible anyway. So we will find that Paul's use of anthropological terms such as body, soul, and flesh, is untidy. But we can, nevertheless, glean something of his understanding of the human person and I think it is possible to form a relatively coherent view of his anthropology.

The first thing to say about his anthropology is that it is pessimistic in that without Jesus Christ and the transforming power that comes from him there is no hope for humanity. On many occasions already we have seen how he stresses the sinful nature of humanity. He has an ontological view of sin, i.e., sin is something that affects the person's very being. Further as we have seen in chapter 4 a text such as Rom 3:23 ("all have sinned and fall short of the glory of God") could even imply that the image of God has been lost after the fall. Or to take another example, in Rom 1:28 he speaks of giving people up to a corrupt mind (*nous*). But we have also seen how his anthropology is also filled with hope, for the problems I just mentioned can be resolved. The lost image can be regained. So in Rom 8:29 he talks about being conformed to the image of Jesus, and Jesus bears the image of God. Further, the corrupt mind of Rom 1:28 can be renewed (see Rom 12:2). And in fact, according to Paul, the human being who has faith in Christ has a future of the greatest glory and this glory is anticipated already in the present time. So justification by faith says that the Christian already has received God's verdict of "not guilty."

But all this raises serious questions as to whether Paul's pessimism regarding the human person is at all realistic. Do we not know many who are fine human beings without Jesus Christ? And do we not know Christians who are supposed to be recreated and conformed to Christ's image who are some of the worst human beings on the planet? I think Paul's pessimism can be largely explained by the fact that he was not a very nice person as a Pharisee; and his ideas of transformation may well reflect the radical change that took place in his life after the Damascus Road experience. But this does not correspond to what we find in many human beings. Many without Christ are not as corrupt as Paul suggests and many Christians are not very nice people.[1] Nevertheless, Paul I think has important things to say about human beings.

FLESH (SARX)

The sinful nature of the human being is often expressed by using the word "flesh" (sarx). Sometimes it can be used in a neutral sense, as when Paul speaks of Christ according to the flesh (Rom 9:5). But often "flesh" can be translated as "fallen human nature." In Rom 8:7 Paul writes that "the mind that is set on the flesh is hostile to God." And in Rom 8:8 he says "those who are in the flesh cannot please God." The phrase "works of the flesh" includes sexual sins, but is by no means restricted to them; rather, they encompass all types of sin of fallen humanity, as is clear in Gal 5:19–21: "Now the works of the flesh are obvious: fornication, impurity, licentiousness, [20]idolatry, sorcery, enmities, strife, jealousy, anger, quarrels, dissensions, factions, [21]envy, drunkenness, carousing, and things like these."

Now the basis of humanity being fallen is not so much that they commit sins but they are fallen, they are sinners. This goes back to Paul's view

---

1. Lewis, "Nice People," raises the problem of the nice non-Christian and the unkind Christian. Saying that the nice non-Christian can thank God for his niceness (176) obviously does not address the problem Paul's pessimistic anthropology raises. Further, his point that "any man who becomes a Christian will be nicer than he was before" (174) does not always stand. Becoming a Christian does not necessarily entail any moral improvement. Indeed, one suspects cases of regression (e.g., hypocrisy, sexism, and homophobia).

that all have participated in the fall of Adam. A key text is Rom 5:12–21[2] and the ideas there are anticipated in an earlier letter, 1 Cor 15:21–22: "For since death came through a human being, the resurrection of the dead has also come through a human being; [22]for as all die in Adam, so all will be made alive in Christ." Romans 5:12 was the fundamental text for the development of the doctrine of original sin and the towering figure here was Augustine.[3] His translation was not correct but his interpretation was! The translation in the NRSV is: "Therefore, just as sin came into the world through one man, and death came through sin, and so death spread to all because all have sinned (*eph hō pantes hēmarton*)." Augustine mistranslated this last part as "in whom (*in quo*, a reference to Adam) all sinned."[4] So according to Augustine, Paul had the view that all sinned in Adam.[5] Although Augustine did not translate Rom 5:12 correctly, he nevertheless rightly understood Paul: just as human beings have participated in Christ, so they have participated in Adam.

"SOUL" (*PSYCHE*)

One of the things I have attempted in an earlier work is to derive some of Paul's anthropology from participation in Christ.[6] I understood Paul's language of participation in an ontological sense and not just as a figure of speech. But how can one participate in Christ's death in Jerusalem in AD 30? This is clearly a problem even for those who may have been alive in Jerusalem at the time of Jesus' crucifixion and for someone not actually alive at the time of Jesus' crucifixion it could be said to be an even greater problem! My suggestion was that Paul may have understood participation to occur through the "soul," a supra-temporal entity. The soul could be understood as the "body in itself";[7] or another way of putting it is that the body is the manifestation of the soul.[8]

---

2. Also important is the difficult text Rom 7:7–25.

3. Note however that he did not originate this view. See Bonner, "Augustine on Romans 5,12," 243.

4. *eph hō pantes hēmarton* is rendered *in quo omnes peccaverunt*.

5. See "Against Two Letters of the Pelagians" 4.4.7 (*NPNF1* 5:419): "all men are understood to have sinned in that first 'man,' because all men were in him when he sinned."

6. Bell, *Deliver Us from Evil*, 189–229.

7. I am here alluding the Kant's concept of the "thing in itself."

8. Cf. Pedersen, *Israel I-II*, 170–76.

Paul does not often employ the term "soul" (psyche). It often means person[9] or it can mean life[10] and in one text it means "mind."[11] 1 Thess 5:23 may suggest a tripartite view of the human person: "May the God of peace himself sanctify you entirely; and may your spirit (pneuma) and soul (psychē) and body (sōma) be kept sound and blameless at the coming of our Lord Jesus Christ." Paul may be using a liturgical formula or if he has composed this himself he may be using the terms loosely.[12] However, I would not wish to exclude the idea of his distinguishing between "soul" and "spirit." But however psychē is understood in these texts, I think the best way of understanding Paul's view of the essence of the human person is not by fixating on anthropological terms (which are untidy) but, as I indicated above, considering his view of participation. If "soul" can be understood in the sense of the body in itself (which only God can destroy) then I think some sense can be made of Paul's fundamental anthropology. Further, it makes sense of Matt 10:28 where Jesus is reported to say: "Do not fear those who kill the body (sōma) but cannot kill the soul (psyche); rather see him can destroy both soul and body in hell."[13] Using Kantian ideas, the soul belongs to the noumenal world whereas the body belongs to the phenomenal world. If the soul is understood as a supra-temporal entity then it makes sense of his ideas of participation. This is especially so since in Lev 17:11 the element that joins the animal and the Israelite in atoning sacrifice is the nephesh. Although nephesh is often translated "life," the term can also be translated and understood in the sense of "soul." See Lev 17:11: "The soul of the flesh [of the bodily animal being] is in the blood. I [God] give it to you on/for the altar to atone for your souls; for the blood atones through the soul."[14] Understanding nephesh and psychē as "soul" rather than just "life" may also illumine Mark 10:45, where Jesus is reported to declare: "For the son of man came not to be served but to serve, and to give his life (psychē) a ransom for many." Although psyche is translated "life" I think the idea of "soul" is also present, as suggested by words of Jesus in Mark 8:35–37: "For those who want to save their life (psychē) will lose it, and those who lose their life (psychē) for my sake, and for the sake of the gospel, will save it. [36]For what will it profit them to gain the whole world and forfeit their life (psychē)? [37]Indeed, what can they give in return for their life (psychē)?"

9. Rom 2:9; 13:1; 16:4; 1 Cor 15:45 (Gen 2:7); 2 Cor 1:23; 12:15; 1 Thess 2:8.

10. Rom 11:3 (1 Kgs 19:10, 14); Phil 3:20.

11. Phil 1:27.

12. Best, Thessalonians, 244.

13. Bell, Deliver Us from Evil, 203–6.

14. Cf. Bell, Deliver Us from Evil, 194, and the discussion in 202–11.

Behind v. 37 is Ps 49:7–8: "Surely, no ransom avails for one's life, there is no price one can give to God for it. For the ransom of life is costly, and can never suffice." Do these texts not suggest that something more than physical life is at stake?

If I am on the right lines in my understanding of "soul" then in Christ's sacrifice the soul of the human being is knit with that of Christ and so comes to participate in this event. This is possible since the soul is a supra-temporal entity. If one thinks in these terms one can make sense of what Paul was saying about participation in Christ and in Adam. Such participation could be understood in a mythical sense. It is worth emphasizing that a myth is not necessarily untrue. So even if Adam, for example, was not a historical figure (which actually I do not think he was) one could nevertheless speak of the myth of Adam and of such a myth having a claim to truth.

BODY (SŌMA)

As I mentioned earlier, Paul tends to use the term *sarx*, flesh, in a negative sense. Body, *sōma*, though tends to be used in a more neutral sense and it is qualified by various terms that can then specify the meaning.[15] So in Rom 6:6 he talks of the "body of sin"; in Rom 8:11 he speaks of the "mortal body." But it can take on a positive sense, as in 1 Cor 15:35–50: so whereas "flesh and blood" cannot inherit the kingdom of God, the body can be transformed. Paul makes a distinction between a physical body and a spiritual body. The body is sown as a physical body (*sōma psychikon*) but it is raised a spiritual body (*sōma pneumatikon*). See 1 Cor 15:42b-44:

> [42b] What is sown is perishable; what is raised is imperishable. [43]It is sown in dishonor; it is raised in glory. It is sown in weakness; it is raised in power. [44]It is sown a physical body; it is raised a spiritual body. If there is a physical body, there is also a spiritual body.

I suggest that the element of continuity between the mortal body and the resurrection body is the "soul." The resurrection of the body does not have to conflict with the idea of the immortality of the soul.[16] But whereas

---

15. Whereas the Greek word *sarx* ("flesh") corresponds to the Hebrew term *bāśār*, the Greek word *sōma* ("body") has no Hebrew equivalent.

16. Cullmann, *Immortality*, finds such a conflict, one that is rightly criticized by Barr, *Eden*, 94–116.

the Greeks saw salvation as being freed from the body, Paul's eschatology is remarkably "physical."[17]

Dunn understands *sōma* as "embodiment". It is a "relational concept" and "denotes the person embodied in a particular environment." "It is the means by which the person relates to that environment, and vice versa."[18] But *sōma* as embodiment can mean more than just the physical body.[19] For although the term "body" can take on a relatively prosaic sense as the physical body (e.g., Gal 6:17: "I carry the marks of Jesus branded on my body"), often the term body becomes for Paul an overarching theological concept. So he can write of "the body of sin" from which humans need to be redeemed (Rom 6:6) and the body of Christ into which believers are incorporated (1 Cor 12:13). Christians are called upon to present their bodies as a living sacrifice (Rom 12:1) and it is through Christ's body in the Eucharist that they are sustained (1 Cor 10:16–17; 11:23–26). Finally, Christians are destined to bear the image of Christ, "the man of heaven" (1 Cor 15:49) in the resurrection of the body (1 Cor 15:35–58).[20]

For the remainder of this section on the "body," I focus on the believer and the "body of Christ." As I have just noted, Paul speaks of Christians being incorporated into the body of Christ: "For in the one Spirit we were all baptized into one body—Jews or Greeks, slaves or free—and we were all made to drink of one Spirit" (1 Cor 12:13). Paul's idea of being incorporated into Christ is best understood mythically. He is dealing with a certain reality that he is not just trying to depict (as in a metaphor) but is dealing with reality itself. So when Paul writes about the church as the body of Christ (Rom

---

17. Dunn, *Theology*, 61, writes: "It is [. . .] this somatic character of Paul's anthropology which prevents Paul's theology from falling into any real dualism between creation and salvation. For it is precisely as part of creation and with creation that Paul the individual and his fellow believers share in the birth pangs of creation, groaning with the rest of creation as they await the redemption of their bodies (Rom 8:22–23)." This is true but it is also the Christology that prevents a creation–salvation dualism. It is worth noting Dunn's low Christology (so Christ's role in creation is minimized); hence, he has to find anthropology as the factor that prevents dualism between creation and salvation.

18. Dunn, *Theology*, 56.

19. Gundry, *Sôma*, 159–244, argues that *sōma* always means physical body in Paul. He does this to counter Bultmann's claim that *sōma* means "the whole person." Note also Robinson, *Body*, 28, who claims *sōma* "is the nearest equivalent to our word 'personality.'"

20. Cf. Robinson, *Body*, 9, who comments: "Here, with the exception of the doctrine of God, are represented all the main tenets of the Christian Faith—the doctrines of Man, Sin, the Incarnation and Atonement, the Church, the Sacraments, Sanctification, and Eschatology." I offer a correction to Robinson by saying that "body" does in fact include the doctrine of God, for God [i.e. Christ] has a body!

12:4–8; 1 Cor 12:12–31) he is not *likening* the church to the body of Christ. The church actually *is* the body of Christ.[21] In this connection it is worth considering 1 Cor 12:27, for which the NRSV which may give a misleading impression: "Now you are the body of Christ and individually members of it." This may suggest that one is a member of the church as one is the member of the Labour Party, a member of the golf club, or whatever. Robinson, I think, captures the sense (even in his archaic language): "Ye are the body of Christ and severally membranes thereof."[22] Robinson then quotes these arresting words of Thornton: "We are members of that body which was nailed to the Cross, laid in the tomb and raised to life on the third day. There is only one organism of the new creation; and we are members of that one organism which is Christ."[23] Robinson adds: "Paul knows no distinction between the ascended body of Christ and His 'mystical body.'"[24] My own view is that the "body of Christ" is best understood as a mythical entity.

Just as through baptism the Christian is incorporated into Christ, so in the eucharist one participates in Christ: "The cup of blessing that we bless, is it not a sharing in the blood of Christ? The bread that we break, is it not a sharing in the body of Christ?" (1 Cor 10:16). So in both baptism and the Eucharist it is not simply bringing before us a re-enactment of the Christ event but it is enabling an existential displacement for the believer.[25] But Paul also expects to see the fruit of such an existential displacement. So Paul says in Rom 12:1, "present your bodies as a living sacrifice, holy and acceptable to God, which is your spiritual worship." The body is a temple of the Holy Spirit (1 Cor 6:19) and Paul writes one should therefore live accordingly.

21. Cf. Fischer, "Mythos," 306–7, who argues that what Paul describes in 1 Cor 12:12–31 is the not empirical "is" situation of conflict and competition in the Corinthian church. Neither is it a description of what things should be like. Paul's words, rather, are words to be held in faith, words that bring to the congregation a new reality. This is what Fischer calls "practical knowing" ("praktische Erkenntnis").

22. Robinson, *Body*, 51, who adds: "The body that he has in mind is as concrete and as singular as the body of the Incarnation. His underlying conception is not of a supra-personal collective, but of a specific personal organism."

23. Thornton, *Common Life*, 298, having just referred to 1 Cor 6:15; 12:12.

24. Robinson, *Body*, 52, appealing to Eph 1:20–23; 2:6 (which I judge to be deutero-Pauline).

25. Cf. Hofius, "Herrenmahl," 235; Bell, *Deliver Us from Evil*, 279.

MIND (*NOUS*) AND HEART (*KARDIA*) I

The ancient Greeks had an exalted view of reason and the mind. Plato understood mind (*nous*) to be the highest part of the soul. The mind is the ruling principle of pure thought and he describes it as the pilot of the soul. Plato writes this in *Phaedrus* 247C: "For the colourless, formless, and intangible truly existing essence, with which all true knowledge is concerned, holds this region [above the heaven] and is visible only to the mind, the pilot of the soul (*psychēs kybernētē*)."[26] Moreover, the Greeks postulated a fundamental relationship between mind and God.[27] For Aristotle, the *nous* is immortal and divine; it is the most important part of the human being and the embodiment of the divine.[28] The link between *nous* and the divine is also characteristic of Stoicism. See Epictetus: "What then is the true nature of God (*tis oun ousia theou*)? [. . .] It is intelligence (*nous*), knowledge (*epistēmē*), right reason (*logos orthos*)."[29]

Together with *nous* there are a whole series of words derived from the same root, one of the most important for our purposes being *dianoia*, the act or faculty of thinking. But when we move from pagan writers to the Septuagint, we discover that words with the root *nous* are used sparingly. So *nous* ("mind") and its cognate *noeō* ("I perceive", "I understand") are used just thirty-five times; *dianoia* ("understanding") is used more frequently, seventy-five times. The sparing use of these words can be partly explained by the fact that Hebrew has no substantive corresponding to *nous*.[30]

In the Hebrew Bible the seat of the intellect is the "heart," *lēb*, *lēbāb*; this is related to the "will" and right conduct.[31] It is nearly always translated into Greek with *kardia*, but in six instances it is rendered *nous*[32] and on

26. Fowler, *Plato I*, 475–77. He goes on to speak of the "divine intelligence" (*theou dianoia*), which is nurtured on mind (*nous*) and pure knowledge (*epistēmē akēratos*) and the "intelligence of every soul which is capable of receiving that which befits it."

27. See Harder, "Reason, Mind, Understanding," 122–23.

28. Aristotle, *Nicomachean Ethics* 1177a 14–15 (10.7.1; Rackham, *Aristotle XIX*, 612–13). Note also that Aristotle distinguished between a theoretical mind (*nous theōrētikos*) and a practical mind (*nous praktikos*). See *De anima* 432B-433A (Hett, *Aristotle VII*, 184–87); *Nicomachean Ethics* 1139a27–28 (6.2.3; Rackham, *Aristotle XIX*, 328–29).

29. Oldfather, *Epictetus I*, 258–59 (*Discourses*, 2.8.2).

30. The closest is *bînāh*, "understanding."

31. One could say that there is no clear distinction between theoretical and practical reason. Contrast Aristotle.

32. On one occasion in the Septuagint *nous* renders the Hebrew word "spirit" (*rûaḥ*). This we shall see is highly significant for Paul's understanding of the Christian mind.

thirty-eight occasions by *dianoia*. The intellectual faculty in the Old Testament is most clearly seen in the use of the verb *noeō*, which renders *bîn* ("to understand"). The Old Testament emphasizes that understanding is a gift of God and is not an independent achievement of human beings. This is related to the striking distinction the biblical witnesses make between God and humans. We have seen that much pagan Greek thought sees reason as the link between God and humans. The biblical witnesses say something rather different. It is the case that reason is rooted in God and indeed in Christ.[33] But already the Old Testament witnesses make it clear that there is a fundamental distinction between God (who is "spirit") and humanity (which is "flesh").[34]

There is, in addition to what one can call this ontological distinction between God and human beings, the distinction between a holy God and a sinful humanity. This is found throughout the Bible but is particularly strong in the writings of Paul, and it to his writings that I now turn.

MIND (*NOUS*) AND HEART (*KARDIA*) II

I now turn to look at what Paul writes about heart, mind, and reason, and I have already touched on this in an earlier chapter. In Romans 1 he makes some arresting statements about the human mind but the chapter, like much of the letter, is not straightforward, and I must put Paul's comments in context. In v. 18 Paul speaks of the eschatological judgement[35] that is coming upon humankind, who "suppress the truth in unrighteousness." This truth is the "revealed reality of God" and the suppression of this is seen by Paul as a *deliberate* as opposed to an *unconscious* act. Paul continues in 1:19–20a: "For *God in his knowability* (*to gnōston tou theou*) *is manifest* to them, because *God has revealed himself* to them. [20]For since the creation of the world *God in his invisibility* (*ta aorata autou*), namely, his eternal power and deity, has been clearly perceived (*noumena kathoratai*) in the things that have been made."[36] The crucial point to emphasize here is that God takes the initiative in making himself known. And it is here that the root "mind" (*nous*) appears in the participle *nooumena*, which modifies the verb *kathoratai* (*kath-oraō* = to discern clearly). The sense is "to see with the

---

33. Ratzinger (Pope Benedict XVI) points to John 1:1, where Christ is identified with the *Logos*, translated as "Word" but having associations with reason. See McDermott, "Ratzinger on Faith and Reason," 369.

34. Cf. Lang, *Korinther*, 46, who points to Gen 2:7 and Isa 31:3.

35. See chapter 4 above and Bell, *No one seeks for God*, 12–18.

36. My translation (see Bell, *No one seeks for God*, 37).

understanding." Paul can then conclude that since this knowledge of God is available, humankind are without excuse.

Before proceeding it is worth emphasizing that this knowledge of God that is available to human beings is *personal* knowledge; it is not merely a knowledge of God's attributes.[37] Further, this knowledge does *not* come about by means of a process of logical deduction. Rather than seeing God "out of the things that have been made" (*ek tōn poiēmatōn*) he is seen "in the things that have been made" (*en tois poiēmasin*).[38] In comparison to much Hellenistic thought, Paul says little in Rom 1:19–20 about the mechanism of coming to a knowledge of God.[39]

Many theologians who attempt to develop a "natural theology" (that is an ability to seek God unaided by special revelation) from this passage make the mistake of stopping here in Paul's argument. But the next stage in the argument, the fall of humankind, is crucial. In Rom 1:21 Paul argues that although human beings had a knowledge of God, this knowledge was not retained for they failed to acknowledge him: they failed to glorify God and failed to give thanks to him. Rather "they became empty in their thoughts" (*alla emataiōthēsan en tois dialogismois autōn*) "and their senseless hearts became darkened" (*kai eskotisthē hē asynetos autōn kardia*). By speaking of the "thoughts" (*dialogismoi*) and the "heart" (*kardia*)[40] Paul is emphasizing the "intellectual" dimension of the fall. So because there was no acknowledgement of God or giving thanks to God, knowledge of God was essential lost. (Again one sees that in Paul, as in much of the Old Testament, the "mind" is very much tied up with the "will.")

One of the consequences of this fall is that God gives up humankind to all forms of idolatry, immorality, and, above all, a corrupt mind (*eis adokimon noun*) (Rom 1:28). We have here this crucial word *nous* and there

---

37. One of the problems with some inter-religious dialogue is that views of God in different religions are said to be "close" or "distant" to each other according to whether they agree on the attributes of God. So "monotheistic religions" are put together and opposed to "polytheistic" religions.

38. Wilckens, *Römer I*, 106.

39. Bell, *No one seeks for God*, 79–80. Compare Philo *On Rewards and Punishments* (*De praemis et poenis* 43), who speaks of "truly admirable persons" who have "advanced from down to up by a sort of heavenly ladder and by reason and reflection happily inferred the Creator from His works" (Colson et al, *Philo*, 8:337).

40. The precise nature of the type of "intellectual" element is not clear. Behm, "καρδία D," 612–13, classifies "heart" in Rom 1:21 as *both* "the seat of understanding, the source of thought and reflection" and "the one centre in man to which God turns, in which the religious life is rooted, which determines moral conduct." The meaning in Rom 1:24 is ascribed solely to the latter (which could be described as "practical reason").

has been considerable disagreement among New Testament scholars as to the meaning of this term in the various occurrences in Paul's epistles.[41] The tendency has been to argue that Paul is speaking of a way of thinking rather than an organ of thought. In particular, Gutbrod understands *nous* as that which sets the will in motion and guides it; like his teacher, Adolf Schlatter, he understands it as *practical* rather than *theoretical* reason.[42] I wonder whether this distinction is helpful in understanding Paul and I will return to the precise nature of *nous* later on. But for now I will simply say that one cannot easily exclude this element of "organ of thought." Therefore, *nous* should not simply be reduced to a constellation of thoughts and assumptions.[43]

Returning to Rom 1, we see that although knowledge of God is essentially lost, there remains some residual knowledge of God's demand and the principle of retribution. Romans 1:32 says that human beings know of God's decree, namely that those who practice immorality deserve to be condemned.[44] The significance of this "residue" is that it points to the limited role fallen reason can have; namely, it can be applied to "things below" (and even here there are problems). But as far as knowledge of "things above" is concerned, human beings create idols.[45] They create images of God that are essentially human constructions.[46]

But this bad news of the corrupt mind is not the last word by any means since Paul calls upon the Christians in Rome to renew their minds: "Do not be conformed to this world, but be transformed by the renewing of your minds, is so that you may discern what is the will of God—what is good and acceptable and perfect" (Rom 12:2).

The second text to consider is 1 Cor 2:6–16, focussing on v. 16, where Paul quotes Isa 40:13: "'For who was known the mind of the Lord so as to instruct him?' But we have the mind of Christ." Many commentators think that mind here simply means "mindset," but "mindset" is too narrow an understanding of *nous*. In the Old Testament quotation Isa 40:13 "mind of

---

41. The term is only used in Luke 24:45; Rev 13:18; 17:9 outside the Pauline corpus.

42. Gutbrod, *Anthropologie*, 49. On Schlatter's (and Gutbrod's) approach, see Jewett, *Anthropological Terms*, 365.

43. This may be one aspect of *nous* but as Jewett, *Anthropological Terms*, 450, writes, *nous* also "acts as the agent of rational discernment and communication."

44. Bell, *No one seeks for God*, 61.

45. See again Luther's view of "free will" in *The Bondage of the Will*: "free choice is allowed to man only with respect to what is beneath him and not what is above him" (*LW* 33:70).

46. Cf. Feuerbach, *Essence of Christianity*.

God" is something more like "an organ of thought."[47] So Elliger writes that the "mind" of Yahweh is like the "heart" of Yahweh and is that which defines the *person* of Yahweh.[48] Duhm writes that in Isa 40:13 it is the organ of divine perception and decision.[49] That Paul shared a similar view is suggested by the context of 1 Cor 2:6–16, for v. 11 speaks of knowing the human being through his spirit and likewise knowing God through God's Spirit. This is not, as many now recognize, suggesting that the human spirit is the link to the divine.[50] Rather, Paul is simply arguing that the essence of the human being can only be known through the spirit of the human being. Likewise, the essence of God can only be known through the Spirit of God.[51] Then in v. 15 he says that those who are spiritual discern all things, and they are themselves subject to no one else's scrutiny. This extraordinary idea is then established in v. 16. This can be paraphrased thus: *Just as no one has known the mind of the Lord so as to instruct him (Isa 40:13c), so no one has the known the mind of the spiritual person so as to instruct him either.* Paul is speaking of the privilege of the "spiritual" Christians. They have the mind of Christ in some ontological sense.[52] They have this "organ of thought."

The logic from 15b–16a is therefore as follows: because no one can access God's mind, no one can make a judgement about the "spiritual person" who has received God's Spirit.[53] Or considering the logic from 15b–16c Knox writes: "No man knows the mind of the Lord, so as to be able to instruct Him; but the natural man who criticises the spiritual man is in effect

47. In the Hebrew the word is *rûah*. This is usually translated as "spirit" but here the Septuagint renders it as *nous*, mind. See Bell, "Mind of Christ," 180–85.

48. Elliger, *Deuterojesaja I*, 50.

49. Duhm, *Jesaia*, 294, commenting on the specific use of the word *rûah* here.

50. Stuhlmacher, "1 Cor 2:6–16," 330, points to Semler's equation of Calvin's *testimonium Spiritus Sancti internum* with "man's inner conviction of rational, moral truths" thereby eliminating "the distinction between the Holy Spirit and rational insight that was characteristic of Paul and the Reformers." Such a view was bolstered by Hegel's idealism. So Baur writes that in Christian consciousness God's Spirit and human spirit become identical. Such a view was "permanently shattered" by Gunkel who wrote that for the early church "the relationship between divine and human activity is that of mutually exclusive opposition. The activity of the Spirit is thus not an intensifying of what is native to all. It is the absolutely supernatural and hence divine" (*Influence of the Holy Spirit*, 34; *Wirkungen des heiligen Geistes*, 22).

51. Paul is therefore arguing that like things can only be known through like things, an ancient philosophical maxim. See, e.g., Merklein, *I Korinther, Kapitel 1–4*, 236–37.

52. Cf. Weiß, *Der erste Korintherbrief*, 67.

53. Cf. Schrage, *1 Korinther*, 1:266–67: "Weil kein Mensch in Gottes Denken eindringen kann, kann auch niemanden ein Urteil über die zukommen, die Gottes Geist empfangen haben."

trying to do so, for he is criticising the mind of Christ, as possessed by the spiritual Christian."[54]

If my understanding of 1 Cor 2:16 is correct then we have a case where *nous* means "organ of thought." What Paul writes here chimes in with passages such as 2 Cor 5:17 which speaks of the Christian having undergone an ontological change. In 1 Cor 2:16 this change in being is indicated by the fact that the Christian shares Christ's mind or that the mind of Christ is formed in them. There are various ways of understanding how this occurs but one is though participation, a key theme in 1 Corinthians (10:16–22; 12:12–31; 15:20–58). Participation in Christ can also be seen as participation in the "Trinity" and the very argument of 1 Cor 2:6–16 could suggest this. Hodgson's comments on Rom 8:15 and Gal 4:4–6 equally apply to 1 Cor 2:16: "there is a social life in the godhead, into the current of which life the Christian is taken up, so that his life is that of a member of the divine society, *looking out on the world from within it*."[55] One may not be aware of the point from which one looks out at the world since the greater part of our personhood in unknown to us, a point recognized by the Hebrew prophets, the ancient Greeks, and Paul himself.[56] And whether one is looking out on the world from within the Trinity cannot be proven but can only be held in faith.

THE MYSTERY OF THE HUMAN PERSON

As I have already indicated, the human person is mysterious and that is one reason why it is so difficult to grasp this mystery simply by looking at anthropological terms such as flesh, soul, body, etc. Paul was not writing philosophy, but it is worth reflecting on this: one way to judge the best philosophy is to ask whether it can address the key issues in human experience. Iris Murdoch said that the writings of Gilbert Ryle describe a world in which no one would fall in love or join the Communist Party.[57] This cannot be said of Paul in that he did address many issues of human existence. However, there is one that is absent in his extant works: one of the most powerful of human emotions, namely falling in love.

54. Knox, *Church of the Gentiles*, 116. The "natural person" is often translated as the "unspiritual" person (*psychikos*) who does not receive the Spirit of God. Such a person is contrasted to the "spiritual" person (*pneumatikos*). This contrast is very unusual for Greek anthropology where "soul" (*psychē*) and "spirit" (*pneuma*; see also *nous*) were closely linked and stand in contrast to the material body (*sōma*).

55. Hodgson, *Trinity*, 49 (my emphasis).

56. On this see Bell, "Mind of Christ," 193.

57. Magee, *Confessions*, 452.

I do wonder whether he ever understood anything of falling in love. His discussion of homosexuality in Rom 1:26–28 simply lives in the world of what people do with their genitalia and has given rise to an unfortunate tradition of an obsession with the mechanics of sex. Paul was single and one could say he had a pragmatic approach to questions of love and sexuality. So in 1 Corinthians 7 he tells the unmarried and widows in the Corinthian church that they should remain unmarried as Paul himself is. But he says if they are not practising self-control, they should marry. "For us is better to marry than to be aflame with passion" (1 Cor 7:9b).

HANDEL'S *ARIODANTE*; PUCCINI'S *MADAME BUTTERFLY*

Paul's pragmatic view contrasts with what we often find in the world of literature, drama, and opera. Such works presents a wonderful world of adventure in love, but sadly such adventures often end in despair and tragedy.

To illustrate the mystery of the human person I present two opera extracts, both sung in Italian, one from the eighteenth century and one from the twentieth. Handel's Aria from his opera *Ariodante*[58] presents remarkable pathos. Ariodante, although sung by a soprano, is actually a man. He believes himself to be betrayed by Ginevra. Happily this is not true and he finally marries her.

The second extract is the love duet at the end of Act I of Puccini's *Madame Butterfly*.[59] Here everything moves in the opposite direction to what we find in *Ariodante*. The vulnerable Japanese Butterfly, very much in love with the American Pinkerton, is later cruelly abandoned by him. In experiencing this duet one is transported into a world of the enchantment of romantic love. Sadly though, their love does not work out and Butterfly in her despair takes her own life. Perhaps Paul did after all understand something of romantic love, its power and its dangers, and hence emphasizes the priority of being "in Christ" and that there is a dimension of love that transcends the fragile world of romantic love, namely "the love of God in Christ Jesus our Lord" from whose love nothing can separate (Rom 8:38–39). But despite the Christian tradition where this has been affirmed, I imagine that many find romantic love the most powerful.[60]

58. This was first performed in 1735 in London.

59. First performed in 1904 in Milan.

60. It is surely no accident that expressions of spiritual love have employed images (consciously or unconsciously) of sexual love. A celebrated example is the vision of St. Teresa of Avila in her autobiography (chapter 29.13; Kavanaugh/Rodrigues, *Teresa of*

The words of *Ariodante* are as follows:[61]

Recitative:

Do I still live?	E vivo ancora?
And without a sword,	E senza il ferro,
O gods! what shall I do?	oh, Dei! che farò?
What do you say, o my troubles?	Che mi dite, o affanni miei?

Aria:

Enjoy yourself, o faithless one, in the arms of your lover.	Scherza, infida, in grembo al drudo,
Betrayed by you,	io tradito a morte in braccio
I will now give myself up to death's embrace.	per tua colpa ora men vo.

Madame Butterfly (after the violin solo):[62]

Butterfly:

Ah, love me a little,	Vogliatemi bene,
Oh just a very little.	un bene piccolino,
As you would love a baby.	un bene da bambino
It's all that I ask for.	quale a me si conviene.
I come of a people	Noi siamo gente avvezza
Accustomed to little;	alle piccolo cose
Grateful for love that's silent;	umili e silenziose,
Light as a blossom	ad una tenerezza
And yet everlasting	sfiorante e pur profonda
As the sky, as the fathomless ocean.	come il ciel, come l'onda del mare.

Pinkerton:

Give me your hands that I may softly kiss them.	Dammi ch'io baci le tue mani care.

(*He exclaims tenderly*)

My butterfly! What a good name they gave you,	Mia Butterfly! . . . come t'han ben nomata
Fragile thing of beauty.	tenue farfalla . . .

Avila, 252) and the depiction by Bernini in the Cornaro Chapel, Rome (Zeki, *Slendors*, 162–63).

61. The music may be found in Köhs, *Ariodante*, 103–7.

62. Translation of Elkin, "Madam Butterfly," 94–95.

Butterfly:

Ah, but in your country	Dicon cho oltre mare
If a butterfly is caught by man	se cade in man dell'uom, ogni farfalla
(*with an expression of fear*)	
He'll pierce its heart with a needle	da uno spillo è trafitta
(*with anguish*)	
And then leave it to perish!	ed in tavola infitta!

Pinkerton:

(*taking her hands again gently and	
smiling*)	
In that there is some truth	Un po' di vero c'è.
And shall I tell you why?	E lo sai tu perchè?
It never can escape.	Perchè non fugga più.
(*with ardor, caressing her affectionately*)	
See I have caught you . . .	Io t'ho ghermita . . .
I hold you as you flutter.	Ti serro palpitante.
You're mine.	Sei mia.

Butterfly:

(*She throws herself into his arms*)	
Yea, yours for ever.	Si, per la vita.

Pinkerton:

Come then, come then . . .	Vieni, vieni.
(*Butterfly draws back, as though	
ashamed of having been too bold*)	
Love what fear holds you trembling?	Via dall'amina in pena
Have done with all misgivings	l'angoscia paurosa.
(*he points to the starlit sky*)	
The star light is shining	È note serena!
And the world lies a-sleeping!	Guarda: dorme ogni cosa!

Butterfly:

(*looking at the sky, enraptured*)	
Ah! Night of wonder! Stars unending!	Ah! Dolce note! Quante stelle!
I have never seen such glory!	Non le vidi mai si belle!
Throbbing, sparkling, each star in	Trema, brilla ogni favilla
heaven,	
Like a fiery eye is flashing.	col baglior d'una pupilla.
Oh! How shining are the heavens;	Oh! quanit occhi fissi, attenti

Every star that shines afar	d'ogni parte a riguardar!
Is gazing on us,	Pei firmamenti,
Lighting the future for us . . .	via pei lidi, via pel mare . . .
See the stars!	Quanti sguardi!
Thy perfect calm is breathing	Tutto estatico d'amor
Love near and far.	ride il ciel . . .
Pinkerton:	
(*with passionate longing*)	
Ah, come beloved!	Vieni, vieni!
(*They go up from the garden into the house. The curtain falls*)	

FURTHER READING

Romans 5:12–21.

11

The Last Things

ESCHATOLOGY

IN THIS CHAPTER I consider Paul's eschatology, a word is derived from two Greek words *eschatos* ("last") and *logos* ("word"). Eschatology is therefore the doctrine of "the last things."[1] The phrase "the last things" (*ta eschata*) is not in Paul but is found in Isa 41:22; 46:9–10; Dan 2:28; 8:19; Sirach 7:36. In the old systematic theologies such as that of the presbyterian Charles Hodge (1823–86) or the baptist Augustus Strong (1836–1921), eschatology, the treatment of the last things, came at the end. So in these systematic theologies from the nineteenth century, after discussing the doctrine of God, creation, salvation, etc., came the final section on the so-called four last things: death, judgement, heaven, and hell. It was New Testament scholarship in the nineteenth century that placed eschatology "at the centre of its own interests and those of theology generally."[2] In opposition to Ritschl, who stressed the moral character of the kingdom of God as something humans could bring about, Johannes Weiß stressed that this kingdom was not an ethical ideal but solely a religious entity that God alone could bring about.[3] His approach was also followed and developed by Albert Schweitzer. If such eschatology is at the center of the message of Jesus and of Paul and entailed the view that

---

1. The term was first used by Abraham Calovius (1612–86) and then later taken up in the nineteenth century (Fahlbusch, "Eschatologie," 1107).

2. Rowland, "Eschatology," 161–62.

3. See Weiß, *Predigt Jesu* (1892), 63–64.

the second coming was imminent then theological problems were to arise and occupy much of twentieth-century theology.

For Paul the coming of Jesus and the preaching of the gospel mean the last days have already come and this colors his theology through and through. By putting Paul's eschatology almost at the end of this book, it may be suggested that I am reverting to this old system. Well, I will be looking at issues such as death and judgement, and putting such themes of traditional eschatology at the end is a good way of summing up some remaining aspects of Paul's theology.

THE SECOND COMING

One of the most important aspects in Paul's understanding of eschatology is that with the coming of Jesus the last times have already arrived. The last crucial things have been achieved in the history of the world. Jesus has come, he has died and been exalted, and now the gospel is being preached to the whole world. The next crucial thing to happen is the second coming of Jesus together with the conversion of Israel, the resurrection of the dead, and judgement.

So from where did Paul get the idea that Jesus will come again? The answer is: most likely from the teaching of Jesus himself, which had been passed on to him by other apostles. Paul rarely refers to the teaching of Jesus but one striking example is 1 Thess 5:2: "For you yourselves know very well that the day of the Lord will come like a thief in the night." Compare Matt 24:36, 42–44. Jesus is reported to tell his disciples:

> [36]But about that day and hour no one knows, neither the angels of heaven, nor the Son, but only the Father. . . . [42]Keep awake therefore, for you do not know what day your Lord is coming. [43]But understand this: if the owner of the house had known in what part of the night the thief was coming, he would have stayed awake and would not let his house be broken into. [44]Therefore you also must be ready, for the Son of Man is coming at an unexpected hour.

Although Matthew was most likely written after 70 AD, some of this text follows Mark (most likely the first gospel, composed around 65–70 AD), and in particular in Matt 24:43–44 there is a parallel in Luke 12:39–40. These verses common to Matthew and Luke (and not to Mark) are assigned to the so-called "Q" material, some of the earliest in the Gospels, and is often dated around 50 AD (which happens to be the date of 1 Thessalonians).

So Paul shared the view of the Jesus of the Synoptic Gospels that he would come again as judge.[4]

Paul speaks of this coming using the Greek word *parousia* (1 Cor 15:23; 1 Thess 2:19; 3:13; 4:15; 5:23). One can compare the use of the word *parousia* in Matt 24:3, 27, 37, 39. So Paul shared the view that Jesus could come anytime, indeed at an unexpected hour. He could come in five years time, in five days time, or in five minutes time.

This idea that Jesus and Paul taught a coming at an unexpected hour is fairly undisputed. But what is disputed is that Paul, like Jesus, expected the second coming within a generation. My own view is that Jesus did expect to return within a generation. See Mark 9:1, where Jesus tells his disciples and the crowd: "Truly I tell you, there are some standing here who not taste death until they see that the kingdom of God has come with power." The kingdom of God coming with power is not the transfiguration that follows in the text (Mark 9:2–8).[5] The immediately preceding words make it clear that it is the second coming: "Those who are ashamed of me and my words in this adulterous and sinful generation, of them the Son of Man will also be ashamed when he comes in the glory of his Father with the holy angels" (Mark 8:38). Mark 9:1, therefore, belongs to Mark 8:34–38 (culminating in the second coming, v. 38) and not to Mark 9:2–8 (the transfiguration). This is an instance where the chapter division is misleading![6]

It seems that the early Christians, including Paul, believed both that the second coming could happen at any time and that it would happen within a generation. Some, usually conservative scholars, have been unhappy about the second thesis, one key reason being of course that Jesus did not come within a generation! But it is not always just the conservative scholars who have objected to the idea that the early Christians expected the second coming within a generation. Two of the liberal evangelical wing, who have argued against the idea that Jesus and the early church believed Jesus' return is so delimited, are Cranfield and Moore.[7]

---

4. It is also possible that Paul's ideas fed into the gospel tradition.

5. This is the view of Cranfield, *Mark*, 287–88.

6. Chapter divisions were introduced into the Latin Vulgate first by Stephen Langton in the twelfth century AD. Robert Estienne (Stephanus) added verse divisions to the fourth edition (1551) of his Greek New Testament (Elliott and Moir, *Manuscripts*, 78).

7. Cranfield, *Mark*, 287–88; Moore, *Parousia*, 108–218. So Moore's conclusion concerning the parousia in the New Testament is thus: "The End will be regarded indeed as near, as ready to break in at any moment, as held back only by the merciful patience of God who wills that men should repent whilst there is time; but the End's coming will not be delimited either, either by our calculations or by our imagining that its coming is determined by our success and witnessing his for God only to decide (Mk. 13.32)."

There are many texts in Paul that suggest that the parousia will occur soon. In fact, in several letters Paul probably thought he would himself experience the parousia. In what is probably Paul's first letter there is an important section on eschatology, 1 Thess 4:13—5:11. The problem in Thessalonica was that Christians were dying, but how could this be for Jesus has not yet returned. So Paul says that "we who are alive, who are left until the coming of the Lord, will by no means precede those who have died" (1 Thess 4:15). So Paul assumes here that he will experience the parousia. He then describes what will happen: "For the Lord himself, with a cry of command, with the archangels call and with the sound of God's trumpet, will descend from heaven, and the dead in Christ will rise first. Then we who are alive, who are left, will be caught up in the clouds together with them to meet the Lord in the air; and so we will be with the Lord forever" (1 Thess 4:16–17).

The second text which indicates the end if near is 1 Cor 7:29–31. In 1 Cor 7 Paul advises against marriage on account of persecution and on account of the nearness of the end: "[29]I mean, brothers and sisters, the appointed time has grown short; from now on, let even those who have wives be as though they had none, [30]and those who mourn as though they were not mourning, and those who rejoice as though they were not rejoicing, and those who buy as though they had no possessions, [31]and those who deal with the world as though they had no dealings with it. For the present form of the world is passing away" (1 Cor 7:29–31). This final sentence is a clear reference to the fact that the end is near.

A third text is 1 Cor 15:51–52 towards the end of a chapter concerning the resurrection of the body: "Listen, I will tell you a mystery! We will not all die, but we will all be changed, [52]in a moment, in the twinkling of an eye, at the last trumpet." So not all will die before the *parousia*; as to whether Paul included himself here among those who would experience the *parousia* is an open question.

It is only in Philippians that Paul questions whether he will live to see the *parousia*, not surprising as he was writing from prison and was not sure of his future. "[21]For to me, living is Christ and dying his gain. [22]If I am to live in the flesh, that means fruitful labor for me; and I do not know which I prefer. [23]I am hard pressed between the two: my desire is to depart and be with Christ, for that is far better; [24]but to remain in the flesh is more necessary for you" (Phil 1.21–24). But even here the belief that Jesus will soon come is still there, for he writes in Phil 4:5b: "The Lord is [nevertheless] near."

Then in Romans, which I take to be Paul's last letter, we find that Paul may have reverted to his previous idea that he will see the *parousia*. This is implied in Rom 11:25–26, which we looked at in the chapter 9. I think that Paul believed that the fullness of the gentiles will have come in when the Spanish mission is complete. Spain was at the Western extremity of the Roman Empire and for Paul, the world was essentially equivalent to the Roman Empire. Later in the letter Paul expressed his hope to go to Spain to evangelize (Rom 15:24). He most likely believed that once the fullness of the gentiles had been brought in, Jesus would come and then Israel on seeing the coming Messiah would believe in him.

A final text to consider pointing to the near expectation is Rom 13:11–12a: "[11]Besides this, you know what time it is, how it is now the moment for you to wake from sleep. For salvation is nearer to us now than when we first became believers; [12]the night is far gone, the day is near."

JUDGEMENT ACCORDING TO WORKS

Paul understood that at the coming of Jesus everyone would be judged. First there is the judgement concerning salvation: those believing in Christ will be acquitted; those not believing in Jesus will be condemned. But I should also add that at the second coming Paul believed that there was a second chance for Israel (Rom 11:26) and perhaps he also believed in a second chance for all, Jews and gentiles (Phil 2:11).[8]

But what about judgement according to works? I argued in chapter 7 that a corollary of salvation by grace alone (*sola gratia*) is the "perseverance of the saints." God's call and gift are irrevocable (Rom 11:29). But what then do we make of the judgement according to works? Was not James right after all: justification is by faith and works? Are works after all a condition of salvation?

The idea of judgement according to works has been frequently misunderstood. Most texts concerning the judgement according to works concern not the *salvation* of the person; rather they concern the judging of his or her works and the *reward received*. See 1 Cor 3:12–15:

> [12]Now if anyone builds on the foundation with gold, silver, precious stones, wood, hey, straw—[13]the work of each builder will become visible, for the day will disclose it, because it will be revealed with fire, and the fire will test what sorts of work each has done. [14]If what has been built on the foundation survives, the builder will receive a reward. [15]If the work is burned up, the builder will suffer loss; the builder will be saved, but only as through fire.

8. See chapter 9 above.

According to this text, even if the Christian's work is worthless, he or she will be saved, but as through fire. This, by the way, has been a text used to support purgatory, the place Christians go to, to refine them for paradise. I read these verses in 1 Cor to suggest that the day of judgement will be an uncomfortable and painful experience for all. But it is a gross mistake to develop medieval views of purgatory and the system of indulgences (whereby one's time in purgatory could be reduced by giving money to the church). If there is an afterlife, concepts of time do not really make much sense and if one speaks of time then I suggest that purgatory could be understood as an infinitesimal instant whereby Christians are cleansed and, as Pope Benedict XVI puts it, such an encounter with Christ as judge and saviour "transforms and frees us, allowing us to become truly ourselves."[9] So the judgement of 1 Cor 3:12–15 concerns the *reward, not salvation.*

I suggest the same situation is seen in text like 2 Cor 5:10 and Rom 14:10. 2 Corinthians 5.10: "For all of us must appear before the judgement seat of Christ, so that each may receive recompense for what has been done in the body, where the good or evil." Romans 14:10–11: "Why do you pass judgement on your brother or sister? Or you, why do you despise your brother or sister? For we will all stand before the judgement seat of God. [11]For it is written 'As I live, says the Lord, every knee shall bow to me, and every tongue shall give praise to God'. So then, each will be accountable to God." These texts are not suggesting that Christians may be condemned on the day of judgement. Again, they concern *rewards.*

There is one text left that does speak of a judgement according to works and that has relevance for salvation: Rom 2:1–16. See Rom 2:5–6: "But by your hard and impenitent heart you are storing up wrath for yourself on the day of wrath, when God's righteous judgement will be revealed. [6]For he will repay according to everyone's deeds." See also Rom 2:9–10: "There will be anguish and distress for everyone who does evil, the Jew first and also the Greek, [10]but glory and honor and peace for everyone who does the good, the Jew first and also the Greek." To understand these texts it is essential to consider the context. Paul in 1:18—3:20 is wishing to stress that every person, Jew and gentile, is living under the power of sin. There is no one who will be acquitted on the last day on the basis of his or her works. It is then clear to me that for Paul the teaching on judgement according to works does not mean that believers can be condemned on the day of wrath. For "there is no condemnation for those who are in Christ Jesus" (Rom 8:1).

---

9. Encyclical *Spe Salvi* of 30 November 2007. The title *Spe Salvi* ("saved in hope") is taken from the Vulgate of Rom 8:24.

Now it could be that salvation is ultimately independent of sanctification. A text to suggest this is 1 Thess 5:9–10: "For God has destined us not for wrath but for obtaining salvation through our Lord Jesus Christ, [10]who died for us, so that whether we are awake or asleep we may live with him." That is the translation from the NRSV. I now offer my own translation of v. 10: "so that whether we are morally awake (*grēgorōmen*) or morally asleep (*katheudōmen*) we might live with him." The verb here for sleep is *katheudō*, which can mean morally asleep. The verb for "to fall asleep" in the sense of "to have passed away" is a different verb, *koimaō* (see 1 Thess 4:13). So perhaps even if one is going backwards in terms of sanctification, one will live with Christ.[10]

DEATH

We have seen in Rom 5:12 that Paul believed death came into the world with the sin of Adam. He describes death in 1 Cor 15:26 as the "last enemy." But it an enemy he believes that has been destroyed by Christ and he can say: "'Death has been swallowed up in victory.' [55]'Where, O death, is your victory? Where, O death, is your sting?'" (1 Cor 15:54b-55).[11]

I outline three ways of understanding the removal of the sting of death. Paul's own view is that Jesus has overcome death with his own death and resurrection and that this is an anticipation of the general resurrection of the dead. I can understand why some see Paul as overreaching himself here.[12] But one thing to consider carefully is that there are grounds for believing that *one* person was brought to new life, namely Jesus Christ. I find it difficult to discount Paul's Damascus Road experience: he must have experienced *something* and this something is most likely the "resurrected life" of Jesus Christ.

How then can one make sense of Paul's view? The first possibility is to take what he says at face value and add that such a view of resurrection can also accompany the idea of the immortality of the soul.[13] The immortal soul then provides the element of continuity between the old body and the resurrection body; each body is a different manifestation of the same soul.

---

10. See Lautenschlager, "Heiligung und Heil."

11. He quotes from Isa 25:7 (25:8 LXX); Hos 13.14.

12. See, e.g., Harris, *Hegel's Ladder*, 2:701 n. 16: "When we refer the 'resurrection of the body' to the supersensible world of Faith's 'pure thinking,' it becomes (as pagan critics always recognised) the most intolerable of all the absurdities in the Christian Creed."

13. As noted in chapter 10, Cullmann, *Immortality*, places the resurrection of the dead in opposition to immorality of the soul. For critique of this, see Barr, *Eden*, 94–116.

A second interpretation of Jesus overcoming death is that death is no longer to be feared, even though there may be no "life after death." Such views are influenced by figures such as Hegel who speaks little about a "life after death."[14] Hegel's reconstruction of the events of Jesus in his early book *Life of Jesus* (1795) ends with his burial.[15] There are some texts in Hegel that may point to a life after death,[16] but generally speaking his whole philosophical scheme is usually seen as denying the usual idea of immortality.[17] Houlgate agrees with Hegel's understanding of "eternity": it does not mean "duration" ("Dauer") but rather "a quality of life which we enjoy now [. . .] through our faith in and knowledge of God."[18]

Such an approach contradicts Paul's stark statement in 1 Cor 15:19: "If for this life only we have hoped in Christ, we are of all people most to be pitied." However, we need to ask whether Paul's comment is reasonable. Wedderburn comments that before we assent too readily to such a sentiment

> . . . we need to note the implications of what Paul is saying. For what he says surely implies that a Christian life is worthless, not worth living, if there is no continuation of that life beyond the grave in a resurrection with Christ. But would *we* be prepared to say that of Paul himself? Is it really the case that all he did, all that he struggled to bring about, all that he has left behind in the shape of his churches and his writings, for us above all his writings, are simply pointless if he did not in fact survive his death to live on in another world? Or what of Jesus himself? Have his ministry and his teaching no value or point or worth unless he rose bodily from the dead?[19]

---

14. He does, however, speak about "immortality," although this is radically interpreted. Inwood, "Death, Hegel, and Kojève," 76, writes that for Hegel "belief in immortality and belief in God go together." He quotes his *Lectures on the Philosophy of Religion*, 1:79–80 (Speirs/Sanderson): "The ideas of God and of immortality have a necessary relation to each other; when a man knows true about God, he knows truly about himself too." But Hegel drastically revises his conceptions of both God and immortality. "Immortality dwindles from endless duration to durationless 'eternity,' while God is no longer transcendent, but immanent; God not an entity distinct from the world, but the unfolding 'logical' structure of the world" (Inwood, "Death, Hegel, and Kojève," 76).

15. Hegel, *Leben Jesu*, 74.

16. In Hegel, *Philosophy of History*, 326–30, he quotes (and does not appear to question) New Testament texts that refer to a future life.

17. See Hegel, *Philosophy of Religion*, 3:208–9. My own view is that Hegel's views on immortality are not unambiguous.

18. Houlgate, *Introduction to Hegel*, 265.

19. Wedderburn, *Beyond Resurrection*, 153–54.

Wedderburn has a point here and so despite what Paul writes in 1 Cor 15:19 such an approach to death is not to be dismissed out of hand.

A third interpretation is one that lies somewhere between the two. Jüngel speaks of the resurrection of the dead but denies the immortality of the soul. Quoting Luther ("It was through his death that death itself was put to death") he declares that through the death of Christ "death is deprived of its power in the name of God."[20] But time is a servant of human beings that enables them to fulfil their history[21] and "the Christian resurrection hope should not be allowed to obscure the fact that this human life of ours is temporally limited."[22] There is no immortality of the soul and "the hope of resurrection must be something quite different from hope in endless continuity."[23] The Christian hope is not an egoistic conception;[24] rather, the objective is "that God may be everything to everyone" (1 Cor 15:28).[25] I confess I am somewhat unsure as to how the human "I" relates to such a view of the resurrection of the dead in Jüngel's 1971 work entitled *Death*. A clearer picture is given in "theses on eschatology" where, although still opposing the immortality of the soul (as presented by Plato), he affirms the future life of the resurrection of the body.[26] This is also found in his 1990 article "Meine Theologie" ("My Theology"): "The believer has a foundation for hope, hope in his or her own resurrection from the dead and an eternal life in communion with God."[27]

Of these three approaches I would tend to follow the first: taking Paul at face value and making sense of what he says by holding together the immortality of the soul and the resurrection of the dead. The physical body is a manifestation of the soul and the resurrection body is also a manifestation of the same soul. I therefore know that the resurrected "I" is in fact myself. But although it may be possible through the immortality of the soul

20. Jüngel, *Death*, 116.

21. Jüngel, *Death*, 118.

22. Jüngel, *Death*, 119.

23. Jüngel, *Death*, 120.

24. Jüngel, *Death*, 120. He does not mention Feuerbach, but this is one of his key concerns in *Thoughts on Death and Immortality*.

25. Jüngel, *Death*, 120. Many translations render this "that God may be all in all (*panta en pasin*)." I suggest "in all" (*pasin*) is neither exclusively neuter ("all things") nor exclusively masculine ("all people") but "*the totality* of the world experienced by human beings" (de Boer, *Defeat of Death*, 125–26).

26. These theses were distributed to students at the end of a series of lectures in Tübingen on eschatology in summer semester 1987. At various points in this chapter I am indebted to some of the details given in those theses.

27. Jüngel, "My Theology," 15.

to clarify that it is *I* who am resurrected in the new heaven and new earth, Paul's language of the future life is that of "picture language" which cannot be taken literally (just as the "picture language" of the beginnings of the cosmos cannot be taken literally).[28]

I can fully understand why many wish to deny a future life and I have had many questions in my mind at funeral services. But if this life is the only one we have there is an insuperable problem when faced with those who die hungry, in war, or are seriously ill and disabled from a young age. Arguments against any "life after death" include Hegelian arguments (such as that put forward by Houlgate), which are to be taken seriously, but also others that suffer from a "simple lack of imagination."[29] An example of the latter is that of Bernard Williams who claims that an "endless life would be a meaningless one," entailing perpetual boredom.[30] But the problem with his approach is that he is working with our usual concepts of time and experience.[31] The New Testament writers clearly had a more imaginative view of the afterlife.

One aspect of Paul's theology is that the future life is seen as a compensation for the present life. Romans 8:18: "I consider that the sufferings of this present time are not worth comparing with the glory about to be revealed to us." A somewhat different complexion of this is found Schiller's poem "Resignation," where the one who has renounced so much in the earthly life demands compensation in the future life.[32]

I also was born in Arcadia (1)	Auch ich war in Arkadien geboren
[...]	[...]
but the prime of life brought only tears. (5) [...]	Doch Tränen gab der kurze Lenz mir nur. [...]

28. That such language cannot be taken literally is clear from a sober reading of 1 Thess 4:15–17 (quoted above).

29. Ward, *Holding Fast*, 120–21.

30. Williams, "Makropulos Case," 89.

31. Williams, "Makropulos Case," considers the case of Elina Makropulos (of the play by Karel Čapek and made into an opera by Janáček), who is 342 because for 300 years she had been forty-two. Although he considers variations on this sort of scenario, for example "an eternal existence as occupied in something like intense intellectual enquiry" (96), he nevertheless remains in the confines of the normal experience of time.

32. See Jüngel, *Death*, 120. Schiller's poem of 1786 was also discussed at the beginning of Jüngel's lecture series on eschatology in summer semester 1987. The German text of can be found in *FSSW* 1:130–33, which gives a twenty-verse version, each verse having five lines; originally there were eighteen verses (Hoffmann, "Resignation," 261). The two versions are given in *SWNA* 1:166–69 and *SWNA* 2/I:401–3. For the translation, I have adopted that in Jüngel, *Death*, 120.

I have sacrificed all my joys to you,	Alle meine Freuden hab ich dir geschlachtet,
Now I cast myself before your judgement throne (81–82).	Jetzt werf ich mich vor deinen Richterthron
[. . .]	[. . .]
From you, the rewarder, I demand requittal" (85).	Vergelterin, ich fodre meinen Lohn.
[. . .]	[. . .]
That which you omit in the moment,	Was man von der Minute ausgeschlagen,
All eternity cannot bring back (99–100)	Gibt keine Ewigkeit zurück.

The poem sets out two flowers that bloom for the wise seeker, hope (*Hoffnung*) and pleasure (*Genuß*). They are set out as (false) alternatives (lines 89–92). But the final two lines (99–100) make clear that life must be lived to the full in the here and now, even though there may be an eternity beyond this life.

Many quite naturally worry about the existential threat of death. Paul's message is that death is not to be feared. Commenting on Rom 6:14 in lectures on Romans, Luther declared: "He who fears death more than Christ and loves life more than Christ does not yet possess Christ through true faith."[33] Then towards the end of the section concerning Rom 8:5–13, he relates what Paul there write to 1 Cor 15:55:

> None has vanquished this fear but Christ alone. He has overcome death in all temporal evils and even eternal death. Those who believe in him have absolutely nothing more to fear, but with a blessed feeling of pride, they can despise all those evils and laugh at them and rejoice in them, knowing that they will not perish and be swallowed up but that they will experience and live to see even with their own eyes the victory that Christ has won over those evils. So they can say: "O death, where is thy sting?"[34]

Perhaps one can laugh at death, but the death of loved ones brings sorrows from which one can never fully recover. Luther, as he peered into the coffin of his daughter Magdalena, who had died at the age of fourteen, is recorded to have said this: "Darling, Lena, you will rise and shine like a star, yea like the sun. [. . .] In spirit I am happy, but the flesh sorrows and

33. Pauck, *Romans*, 189; WA 56:331 (Scholien).

34. Pauck, *Romans*, 230; WA 56:366 (Scholien). This text is also quoted in Whale, *Protestant Tradition*, 101.

will not be comforted; the parting grieves me beyond measure. [. . .] I have sent a saint to heaven."[35]

RICHARD STRAUSS, *FOUR LAST SONGS*; RICHARD WAGNER, *TRISTAN AND ISOLDE*

I find that one of the best ways of reflecting on death is through music; and music offers the solace we desperately need when we lose loved ones. I have chosen two pieces of music that present death in very different ways but which in their own way offer solace.

The first is the last of Richard Strauss's four last songs, which were composed in 1947 just two years before the composer's death at the age of eighty-five. Strauss had a long and productive life and at eighty-five he felt that he was ready to leave this world. I find the music of this song to be beautiful but painful at the same time. In the last of *Four Last Songs, At Sunset* (*Im Abendrot*) he sets words by Joseph von Eichendorf (1788–1857):[36]

Here both in need and gladness	Wir sind durch Not und Freude
we wandered hand in hand;	gegangen Hand in Hand;
Now let us pause at last	vom Wandern ruhen wir
above the silent land.	nun überm stillen Land.
Around us, the valleys bow	Rings sich die Täler neigen,
as the sun goes down.	es dunkelt schon die Luft,
Two sky-larks soar upwards	zwei Lerchen nur noch steigen
dreamily into the light air.	nach träumen in den Duft.
Draw close, and let them fly.	Tritt her und lass sie schwirren,
Soon it will be time for sleep.	bald ist es Schlafenszeit,
Let us not lose our way	dass wir uns nicht verirren
in this solitude.	in dieser Einsamkeit.
O vast, tranquil peace!	O weiter, stiller Friede!
So deep in the evening's glow!	So tief im Abendrot.
Now we are tired, how tired!	Wie sind wir wandermüde
Can this perhaps be death?	ist dies etwa der Tod?

The second piece is from the close of Wagner's *Tristan and Isolde*. Wagner described the work not as an opera but as a "Handlung," which

---

35. Quoted in Atkinson, *Luther*, 248.
36. This translation is largely indebted to that of Michael Hamburger.

literally means "action." Such "action" could be understood as a translation of the Greek "drama" = "action" represented on stage.[37] Alternatively,
"Handlung" could be a translation of the Spanish "auto," a term Calderón
used for his plays on spiritual themes modelled on the medieval mystery
plays. Hence, for Wagner's work "Handlung" indicated that a transcendent
truth lay behind the "action."[38] He completed the work in 1859 and it was
first performed in 1865 under Hans von Bülow. Later Richard Strauss himself conducted the work with his wife, Pauline, singing the part of Isolde.
Here the young lovers, Tristan and Isolde, die in their prime. The music
is strangely optimistic as we hear Isolde reflect on the death of her lover,
believing that he lives on in another realm, a realm she herself will shortly
enter. Isolde begins her "transfiguration" with these words: "How gently and
quietly / he [Tristan] smiles, / how fondly / he opens his eyes! / Do you not
see, friends? / Do you not see? / How he shines / ever brighter, / soaring
on high, / stars sparkling around him?" Just one of the remarkable aspects
of this final scene is that the music tells you that death is nothing to fear.
Isolde's final words are:[39]

Isolde:

How gently and quietly	Mild und leise
he [Tristan] smiles,	wie er lächelt,
how fondly	wie das Auge
he opens his eyes!	hold er öffnet—
Do you see, friends?	Säht ihr's, Freunde?
Do you not see?	Säht ihr's nicht?
How he shines	Immer lichter
ever brighter,	wie er leuchtet,
soaring on high,	sternumstrahlet
stars sparkling around him?	hoch sich hebt?
Do you not see?	Seht ihr's nicht?
How his heart	Wie das Herz ihm
proudly swells	mutig schwillt,
and, brave and full,	voll und hehr,
pulses in his breast?	im Busen ihm quilt?
How softly and gently	Wie den Lippen
from his lips	wonnig mild,

37. Ewans, *Aeschylus*, 11.
38. Carnegy, *Theatre*, 58.
39. The translation into English is by Lionel Salter.

sweet breath	süßer Atem
flutters—	sanft entweht—
see, friends!	Freunde! Seht!
Do you not feel and see it?	Fühlt und seht ihr's nicht?
Do I alone	Hör' ich nur
hear this melody	diese Weise,
which, so wondrous	die so wundervoll
and tender	und leise,
in its blissful lament,	Wonne klagend,
all-revealing,	alles sagend,
gently pardoning,	mild versöhnend
sounding from him,	aus ihm tönend,
pierces me through,	in mich dringet,
rises above,	auf sich schwinget,
blessedly echoing	hold erhallend
and ringing round me?	um mich klinget?
Resounding yet more clearly,	Heller schallend,
wafting about me,	mich umwallend,
are they waves	sind es Wellen
of refreshing breezes?	sanfter Lüfte?
Are they billows	Sind es Wogen
of heavenly fragrance?	wonniger Düfte?
As they swell	Wie sie schwellen
and roar around me,	mich umrauschen,
shall I breathe them,	soll ich atmen,
shall I listen to them?	soll ich lauschen?
Shall I sip them,	Soll ich schlürfen
plunge beneath them,	untertauchen?
to expire	Süß in Düften
in sweet perfume?	mich verhauchen?
In the surging swell,	In dem wogenden Schwall,
in the ringing sound,	in dem tönenden Schall,
in the vast wave	in des Welt-Atems
of the world's breath—	wehendem All—
to drown,	ertrinken—
to sink	versinken—

| unconscious— | unbewußt— |
| supreme bliss! | höchste Lust! |

*(Isolde, as if transfigured, sinks
    gently on to Tristan's body:
    Deep emotion and sense of
    exaltation among those pres-
    ent. Marke blesses the bodies.)*

FURTHER READING

1 Corinthians 15:35–58.

12

Critical Reflections

EVALUATING PAUL

I FIND STUDYING PAUL enormously enriching, one reason being that he offers an invigorating theology with Christ at the center. Further, he is comprehensive in what he covers, addressing issues such as natural revelation, revealed theology, doctrine of God, the human person, redemption, and eschatology. But, of course, we only see things from the perspective of one human being, even though he may be considered "inspired" in his thinking and writing.

As I said at the beginning of the first chapter, Paul has had immense influence and if you were to ask somebody about the essence of the Christian message, especially someone from the evangelical tradition, you may well find that they summarize much of Paul's theology.

I conclude with some personal reflections, considering how Paul may need to be reinterpreted today and, to put it bluntly, what I think he got right and what I think he got wrong. This may sound somewhat arrogant to some who hold that our mind should always be in submission to Scripture. Such an evangelical position of holding to everything Scripture "affirms"[1] is rarely held to consistently, in my experience. Most conservative evangelicals I know engage in a *selective* fundamentalism. Although there is some inconsistency here it is certainly better than a consistent fundamentalism,

---

1. The Lausanne Covenant for example states the Bible "is without error in all that it affirms" (cf. Stott, *Authority*, 6).

which would entail supporting the death penalty, having a subordinate view of women, and considering slavery to be morally justified.

But if Paul is to be questioned, what criteria can be employed? One criterion is to seek *a core to Paul's theology* and then critique what may be at variance with this. For example, in view of Gal 3:28, it could be argued that since issues of race are irrelevant (i.e., there is neither Jew nor genitle) so should issues of male and female and of master and slave. A second criterion is to critique Paul on the basis of *scientific advances* made since he penned his letters. An obvious case here is evolution and another is the question of homosexuality. A third criterion is through *philosophical enquiry*. There are of course so many approaches in philosophy, but it is worth bearing in mind that much of Western philosophy has grown out the Christian tradition to which Paul himself contributed and may then be a perfectly legitimate means of critiquing Paul. Last of all, and in fact the most crucial criterion, is *judging his teaching by Jesus Christ*. There are two aspects to this. The first is questioning Paul on the basis of what we can discern from the teaching of Jesus. This can be slightly involved since one has to ask to what extent the Gospels reflect Jesus' teaching.[2] The second is the principle Luther enunciated of "what urges Christ" ("was Christum treibet"). In the "Preface to Epistles of James and Jude," Luther questions James' view of justification and that "he teaches nothing about [Christ], but only speaks of general faith in God."[3] He then enunciates his principle of judging books of the New Testament:[4]

> All the genuine sacred books agree in this, that all of them preach and inculcate (*treiben*) Christ. And that is the true test by which to judge all books, when we see whether or not they inculcate Christ. For all the scriptures show us Christ, Romans 3[:21] and St Paul knew nothing but Christ, 1 Corinthians 2[:2]. Whatever does not teach Christ is not yet apostolic, even though St. Peter or St. Paul does the teaching. Again, whatever preaches Christ would be apostolic, even if Judas, Annas, Pilate, and Herod were doing it.

I judge Luther's view of Scripture to have many strengths. He rightly emphasized the crucial distinction between God and Scripture: "God and the scripture of God are two things, no less than the creator and the creature

---

2. Each Gospel writer had a particular theological slant and this is something we need to take into account.

3. Luther, "Prefaces to the New Testament," *LW* 35:396.

4. Luther, "Prefaces to the New Testament," *LW* 35:396 (the German is in Bornkamm, *Vorreden*, 216–17).

are two things."[5] He promoted a *Christ-centred* approach to Scripture: "Take Christ out of the scriptures, and what will you find left in them."[6] And a crucial aspect of his thought (not always sufficiently emphasized) is that reality itself is formed by the word of God.[7] But although Luther's approach to Scripture has many strengths, he did not always see the problems in Paul's letters, as I shall later demonstrate.

WHAT PAUL GOT WRONG

The State

The matters that Paul got wrong in my judgement largely center on questions of ethics and anthropology. The first four cases I consider all have a relation to Paul's concept of "order."

My first example is his teaching on the state in Rom 13:1–7. Whilst his teaching on paying taxes (Rom 13:6) has special relevance in many parts of the world at present, the passage has caused some major headaches in the history of its influence.[8] The very opening verse is: "Let every person be subject (*hypotassesthō*) to the governing authorities; for there is no authority except from God, and those authorities that exist have been instituted by God." The verb "be subject" reflects the divine order (*taxis*).[9] Although Paul has in mind the local authorities (magistrates), the "authorities" cannot be confined to such and since the letter was addressed to the capital of the empire, he most likely had in mind also the central authorities rooted in the emperor.

Very few people wish to live in a society in which there is no order. This text, however, teaches a somewhat extreme submission to authority even though Paul no doubt knew that obedience to the state has its limits.[10] As already indicated, Rom 13:1–7 has had an appalling "history of

5. Rupp and Watson, *Luther and Erasmus*, 110. WA 18:606; Delius, *Studienausgabe* 3, 184.

6. Rupp and Watson, *Luther and Erasmus*, 110. WA 18:606; Delius, *Studienausgabe* 3, 185.

7. Ebeling, "Wirklichkeitsverständnis."

8. The German term *"Wirkungsgeschichte"* can be translated as "history of influence." An alternative view is to speak of "reception history" (*"Auslegungsgeschichte"*), which stresses what *recipients do* rather than what *the text does*.

9. Käsemann, *Romans*, 351, contrasts "being subject" to the verb *hypakouein* ("to obey") which can mean free obedience.

10. As Schrage, *Ethics*, 238, points out, Paul "would never have obeyed an order to cease preaching Christ [. . .], nor would he have allowed 'Caesar is Lord' to pass his lips."

influence" ("*Wirkungsgeschichte*"). One key reason so many Christians in Nazi Germany failed to resist Hitler is because of Rom 13:1 and the fact that Luther put his full weight behind this text.[11] Paul Althaus, whose wide theological interests included work on Paul, also appealed to this text in the Third Reich[12] and sadly Althaus realized only a little too late the mistake he had made. One brave Christian who resisted Hitler to the extent of being involved in a plot to assassinate Hitler was Dietrich Bonhoeffer.[13] Bonhoeffer was involved in the resistance but his pleas to get British and American support for this fell on deaf ears;[14] he was arrested (April 5, 1943) and later executed (April 9, 1945). Some of Bonhoeffer's comments on the state are conservative, such as when he writes "According to Holy Scripture, there is no right to revolution."[15] But as Bethge points out,[16] the following words are highly significant and may indicate something of his thoughts on his role in the conspiracy: "but there is a responsibility of every individual for preserving the purity of his office and mission in the *polis*. In this way, in the true sense, every individual serves government with his responsibility. No one, not even government itself, can deprive him of this responsibility or forbid him to discharge it, for it is an integral part of his life in sanctification, and it arises from obedience to the Lord of both church and government."[17]

11. Luther regularly appealed to Rom 13:1. One example is "Instructions for the Visitors of Parish Pastors in Electoral Saxony" (*LW* 40:269–320). He argues that "government is a special ordinance and function of God." Such an ordinance can be abused by a tyrant such as Julian or Nero. Nevertheless "[t]he ordinance, by which peace and justice is maintained, remains a divine creation even if the person who abuses the ordinance does wrong" (284).

12. He together with the Lutheran theologian Werner Elert supported the "Anbacher Ratschlag" ("Ansbach Advice", 1934), which opposed the Barmen declaration, a document highly critical of the Nazi regime. See Bell, *Irrevocable Call*, 362–63.

13. For a summary of his resistance activities, see Bethge, *Exile and Martyr*, 120–27.

14. Bonhoeffer met George Bell (bishop of Chichester) in Sigtuna, Sweden in 1942. He passed on to Bell information about the resistance and asked Bell to pass on an urgent message to Anthony Eden and then to Churchill and Roosevelt, requesting support for the resistance. No reply was received. It is worth adding that Bell castigated the British government for the carpet bombing of German cities. It is widely believed that this prevented him being appointed as archbishop of Canterbury on the death of William Temple in 1944. Instead, Geoffrey Fisher was appointed!

15. Bonhoeffer, *Ethics*, 314; "Staat und Kirche," 532.

16. Bethge, *Exile and Martyr*, 134.

17. Bonhoeffer, *Ethics*, 314–15; "Staat und Kirche," 532. Just as Rom 13:1 discouraged many from opposing Hitler, so it prevented many, especially in the Dutch Reformed Church, in opposing apartheid in South Africa. On the relevance of Bonhoeffer for apartheid South Africa, see Bethge, *Exile and Martyr*, 167–78, and de Gruchy, "Bonhoeffer in South Africa," 26–42.

The text goes on to support the death penalty. Such a penalty is commanded in the Old Testament for a variety of offences (e.g., Exod 21:12–17) and Paul clearly allows it (Rom 13:4). Even if one were to soften the blow by arguing that the death penalty is permissible but not mandatory this raises fundamental questions. Many prominent Christians have appealed to Paul in support of the death penalty, from the apologist C. S. Lewis to the archbishop of Canterbury Geoffrey Fisher to the evangelical leader John Stott.[18] Fortunately, many have advanced theological objections to capital punishment, from human beings usurping the prerogative of God[19] to it being a crime against the sovereignty of God.[20] In particular, the fact that Jesus Christ was executed under the Roman authorities should relativize the power of the state. As Moltmann writes: "If the Christ of God was executed in the name of the politico-religious authorities of his time, then for the believer the higher justification of these and similar authorities is removed. In that case political rule can only be justified 'from below.'"[21] The irony of Rom 13:4 is that Paul himself was executed under the Roman state. It may seem odd that Paul could even pen these verses, especially given the fact that the emperor at the time was Nero. But, as I argued in chapter 2, they can be accounted for by the fact that Paul was a Roman citizen and a political conservative.

One reason Rom 13:1–7 has lost its relevance is that for those countries who now at least enjoy a certain degree of democracy, the citizens choose the government. It is nevertheless possible to glean something from this text. Despite corruption in government circles (and I include my own

18. John Stott had enormous influence, even being treated as a kind of evangelical pope As I understand it, Stott himself was extremely uneasy with being treated in this way; but one has to recognize that he influenced vast numbers of Christians on a whole range of issues. Sometimes his influence was for the better; see, e.g., his writing on global and social issues in *Issues*, 80–232 (much of this being based on sermons give at All Souls, Langham Place, London). But regarding the death penalty, I offer this anecdote. When I was at All Souls Church (1974–79) a lady in the congregation explained to me that she had always had doubts about the death penalty but when John Stott spoke on the issue she then realized that it was acceptable for Christians to support it. Stott's mature view as expressed in *Romans*, 345, is that capital punishment is not mandatory. However, he can make this statement: "The punishment of evil is God's prerogative, and during the present age he exercises it through the lawcourts." On the church's support for the death penalty, see Potter, *Hanging*.

19. See Barth, *Church Dogmatics*, 3.4:445: "in capital punishment the state leaves the human level and acts with usurped divinity."

20. Jüngel, *Death*, 134, writes that "if God has taken death upon himself in order to bind it to himself for ever, then death cannot any longer be regarded as a legal remedy. In the light of this, 'capital punishment' becomes a 'crimen laesae maiestatis', a 'lèse-majesté' against the crucified God."

21. Moltmann, *Crucified God*, 328.

country here), the citizen can (and usually should) keep to the rules. So at a time of tax evasion the exhortation to pay taxes is highly relevant (Rom 13:6–7). For examples beyond Rom 13:1–7, speed limits are imposed for good reason and should be adhered to. Air quality laws should be respected and indeed Christians, as "slaves of righteousness" (Rom 6:18), should go beyond such legal requirements.

Slavery

My second example flows from the first. Just as Paul supported order (*taxis*) in relation to the state so he sees an order in relation to the social order of master and slave. He, along with pretty much everyone else at that time, clearly thought that slavery was morally acceptable. One could argue he placed a time-bomb in telling Philemon that he is to receive Onesimus no longer as a slave but as a brother (Phlm 16), but I think this is special pleading. Paul accepted the institution of slavery to the extent that he thinks Philemon has been wronged because he had been deprived of his slave's labor. "If [Onesimus] has wronged you in any way, or owes you anything, charge that to my account" (Phlm 18).[22] "The Rev. R. Harris" appealed to this text in his notorious 1788 defence of slavery.[23] It is also sobering to read how an evangelical such as Charles Hodge (1797–1878) felt he could not condemn the institution of slavery as evil because of the writings of Paul.[24] Earlier George Whitefield (1714–70) owned slaves and even attempted to reintroduce slavery in Georgia.[25] Jonathan Edwards (1703–58) owned slaves,

22. Some take the view that Onesimus had probably stolen money and this was an added reason why Philemon needed to be recompensed (e.g., Lightfoot, *Colossians and Philemon*, 343; Stuhlmacher, *Philemon*, 49). However, a number have cast doubt on this hypothesis (e.g., Martin, *Colossians and Philemon*, 167; Lohse, *Colossians and Philemon*, 204).

23. Harris, *Scriptural Researches*, 75–76. This supposed Anglican clergyman was in fact a Jesuit priest Raimundo Hormasa, expelled from his Spain by his order and settling in Liverpool. For his efforts to defend the slave trade he was given £100 by the Liverpool Corporation. The Society for the Abolition of the Slave Trade sponsored replies by James Ramsay, William Roscoe, and Henry Dannett.

24. Wallace, "Hodge," 306, explains that although Hodge did condemn American slavery "he opposed the radical abolitionists who insisted that slavery was inherently sinful and that slaveowners should not be allowed in Christian churches. Hodge believed that since the Bible does not condemn slavery, it could not be called inherently sinful." Contrast Hegel who, although coming a little late on the scene (but preceding Hodge by twenty-seven years), was firm in his opposition to slavery (Loy, "Greek Ethical Life," 165–66).

25. Slavery had been banned in 1735, Whitefield campaigned to reintroduce it, and the ban was in fact repealed in 1750. In the next twenty-five years the slave population

defending it on the basis that it was allowed by Paul.[26] I imagine that many of the problems in certain sectors of USA white evangelicalism go back to these two figures.[27]

Down the centuries Christians did condemn slavery. One striking early opponent was Gregory of Nyssa (c. 330–95).[28] Augustine (354–430) departed from Aristotle's teaching that some are by nature born to be slaves. But although Augustine viewed slavery as a consequence of sin, his position was far from being abolitionist.[29] Many of the medieval theologians (including Aquinas) essentially adopted Aristotle's view.[30] Luther's two-kingdoms theory, to some extent indebted to Rom 13:1–7,[31] did little to oppose slavery, but the Anabaptists, stressing the equality of all human beings, opposed any bond service.[32] It was only with the Enlightenment that opposition began in any meaningful sense. The key Enlightenment figure to change views on slavery was Montesquieu.[33] Enlightenment thought was impor-

---

grew to 18,000. Whitefield defended slavery on biblical and economic grounds. On the former, he notes that "some of the servants mentioned by the Apostles were slaves," no doubt having in the mind texts such as Phlm; Eph 6:2–9; Col 3:22–4.1. Regarding the latter he wondered "how many whites [had been] destroyed for want of [slaves] and [how many] thousands of pounds spent to no purpose" (Gilles, *Works of Whitefield*, 2:401–5, quoted in Lambert, *Pedlar*, 204). It is remarkable how many evangelical admirers of Whitefield fail to mention his support for slavery and ownership of slaves. Pollock, *Whitefield*, 221–25, is to be given credit for including in his popular biography a chapter entitled "Whitefield's Black Spot."

26. Even though he had in mind the deutero-Pauline texts Eph 6:2–9; Col 3:22—4:1, such acceptance of slavery can be found not only in Philemon but also in 1 Cor 7:21–22.

27. It is worth adding that every generation of Christians has blind spots. No doubt future generations will judge us for the things we have tolerated.

28. See *Homilies on Ecclesiastes*, Homily IV, where he comments on the biblical text "I bought male and female slaves, and had slaves who were born in my house" (Eccl 2:7).

29. O'Donnell, *Augustine*, 23.

30. Hertz, "Die christliche Lebenswelt," 242.

31. One place where Luther sets out his teaching on church and state is in "Temporal Authority: To What Extent It Should Be Obeyed" (1523). Christians live in two kingdoms, the kingdom of God and the kingdom of the world, simultaneously and the two governments are to be carefully distinguished (*LW* 45:88–94). Although Luther thinks there are occasions when the secular state should be resisted (he refers to the words of Peter and the apostles: "We must obey God rather than any human authority," Acts 5:29; *LW* 45:125) his two realms teaching ultimately leads to a highly submissive attitude to authorities. A key text he cites to support this view is Rom 13:1–7 (e.g., discussion of Rom 13:1, 3–4 in *LW* 45:93, 91).

32. Davis, *Problem of Slavery*, 199–200.

33. See, e.g., Fletcher, "Montesquieu's Influence."

tant for the Christian abolitionists, although it must be said that it was the biblical picture of God's wrath directed towards wrongdoing that became the fundamental force in thinkers such as Anthony Benezet and William Wilberforce.[34]

Gender

A third example of "order" is in relation to the sexes. Although there are some liberating texts for women (e.g., Gal 3:28), Paul also promoted the submission of women, as in 1 Cor 11:3: "But I want you to understand that Christ is the head of every man, and the husband is the head of his wife, and God is the head of Christ" (cf. Eph 5:22–30). Further, 1 Cor 14:34–35 calls upon women to be subordinate and silent in church. As pointed out in chapter 9 a significant number of commentators consider these verses to be an interpolation (texts added by someone other than Paul); I myself consider the arguments for and against the theory of an interpolation to be fairly evenly balanced.

One possible explanation for Paul's views of the subordination of women is his Jewish background. The position of women in the Old Testament legal texts was subordinate, although the social realities did not always conform to legal prescriptions.[35] In Paul's time Judaism was like a rich patchwork quilt. It is therefore not surprising that ideas concerning women varied considerably.[36] But Paul's Pharisaic position, if it in any way reflects the teaching of the Mishnah,[37] may have been at the conservative end of the spectrum.[38] One Jewish "sect" that stands out in promoting women's rights was Jewish Christianity.[39]

34. Coffey, "Tremble, Britannia!"

35. Note the independent position of women in narrative and poetic texts. So we have not only the military leaders such as Deborah (Judges 4–5) but also assertive women such as Rebecca (Gen 27:1–17).

36. Brooten, *Women Leaders*, has argued on the basis of Greek and Latin inscriptions that there were female synagogue leaders in the diaspora, although her understanding of what such a "synagogue leader" entails has been questioned (e.g., Rajak, "Jewish Community," 22–24).

37. The Mishnah was edited around 200 AD but contains material going back to the time of Paul. The material on women is set out in Witherington, *Women in the Ministry of Jesus*, 1–10. Although Witherington's work on women in Judaism and early Christianity has come in for some criticism (Levine, "Yeast of Eden"), his assessment of the Mishnaic material seems balanced.

38. See the overview given in "Women, position of," in *DJBP* 2:673–76.

39. One example is the position of Priscilla who, with her husband, "took [Apollos] aside and explained the Way of God to him more accurately" (Acts 18:26).

Sexuality

A fourth example related to order in creation is sexuality. If one accepts Paul's argument in Rom 1, one would arrive at the conclusion of Richard Hays that "homosexual relations [. . .] represent a tragic distortion of the created order."[40] A number of church leaders have supported such a view and in my opinion this has caused considerable hardship to gay Christians who have either tried to live a celibate life or who have lived with the burden of guilt or even both. As far as leaders with a homosexual orientation are concerned, there have been those who have apparently lived celibate lives with good grace even though this has no doubt caused them personal pain; but there are others who have made not only their own lives a misery but more importantly the lives of others because they denied themselves a stable gay relationship and instead found bizarre and cruel outlets for their sexual feelings.

As I have said, I consider the conservative teaching that gay Christians should lead a celibate life a terrible burden for them. In this connection I should also add that I consider the position of organizations such as Living Out and True Freedom Trust to be incoherent.[41] They offer support to gay people and teach that their "orientation" is not sinful but that homosexual acts are. At the same time they also generally reject conversion therapy. The problem with this approach, which purports to follow the teaching of Scripture, is that it runs counter to Paul's argument in Rom 1, which is psychological.[42] So, for Paul, the sin starts with the "sense of attraction."

I add three further points on the stance taken by conservative evangelicals. First, there are very few who are fitted for celibacy. Luther, whom I find was so often a realist concerning the Christian life, wrote that "Scriptures and experience teach us that there is only one in several thousands to whom God gives the gift to live chastely in a state of virginity."[43] Many, of course, have to live celibate lives for various reasons: those who have not found a partner, or the widowed, etc. But for such people there is always hope that a partner can be found. But gay people having to be celibate removes all such hope; and without hope life can become insufferable.

My second point is that in conservative evangelical circles emphasis is often placed on what one should or should not do with genitalia. This obsession with the mechanics of sex appears to miss the point that sexual

40. Hays, *Moral Vision*, 396.

41. Both organizations are affiliated to the Evangelical Alliance in the UK.

42. Loader, "Homosexuality," 147.

43. Letter to three nuns, 6 August 1524 (Tappert, *Luther's Letters of Spiritual Counsel*, 271).

expression between gay people in good relationships is an expression of their love for each other. Third, and related to this second point, is that Christians should be encouraging good and permanent relationships, including for those of the LGBT+ community. Hence, civil partnerships and gay marriage should be encouraged and not opposed.[44]

I reject Paul's teaching on homosexuality partly because of the devastating consequences of his approach and partly because we now have new insights into human sexuality and the pain Paul's teaching has caused. Simon Calow spoke movingly at the remembrance service of Bryan Magee of how he had experienced years of anxiety and depression as a young gay man. But reading Magee's book *One in Twenty* gave him an enormous sense of release.[45] I think the way forward is to reject Paul's teaching on homosexuality and to foster good loving gay relationships that will serve the wider community.[46]

Denigration of Non-Christians

A fifth instance of Paul getting things wrong is his denigration of non-Christians. He views humanity not only in terms of Jews and gentiles but also with a new division: between Christians and non-Christians. His theology could even imply that it is only Christians who bear the image of God in that they are being conformed to the image of Christ (Rom 8:29). Further, although in 1 Cor 9:9–12 he says he has no business in judging "those outside" (v. 12) he issues this command in 2 Cor 6:14: "Do not be mismatched with unbelievers. For what partnership is there between righteousness and lawlessness? Or what fellowship is there between light and darkness?" Although it is not entirely clear what this "mismatching" involves (it may concern matters of "idolatry" understood literally or metaphorically),[47] he appears to be denigrating non-Christians. The Brexit debate in the UK has taught me many things, and one of them is that my former fundamental allegiance with Christians was misguided. The issue of Brexit sums up so

44. Several bishops in the UK "House of Lords" opposed both!

45. Magee, *One in Twenty*. This book helped in the decriminalising of homosexuality in 1967.

46. A relationship that has borne much fruit in promoting music in the UK is that of Benjamin Britten and Peter Pears.

47. See 2 Cor 6:16. An additional complication is that a number of commentators see 2 Cor 6:14–7:1 as an interpolation. Harris, *2 Corinthians*, 492, considers the passage Pauline but "perhaps composed by Paul previously." Schmeller, *2 Korinther*, 371, 378–82, thinks the most likely explanation is that a redactor has inserted a Pauline text from elsewhere.

many of the values we hold and when I see a good proportion of fellow Christians supporting Brexit,[48] yet at the same time so many secular humanists opposing it, it does make me question any fundamental allegiance I should have with Christians.[49]

WHAT NEEDS RE-INTERPRETING

Paul was a man of his time and many of his utterances have a truth claim but require some degree of re-interpretation. Such matters largely concern questions of beginnings and endings. Paul believed in a historical Adam and would be shocked by Darwinism (as many Christians have been). Darwinism would conflict with his views of a "paradise" of no sin and suffering and for the opportunity for immortality. If one holds to some form of Darwinism his mythological view in Rom 5:12–21, whilst standing on its own feet as myth, needs to be reinterpreted when we move from "mythos" (the narrated world) to "logos" (the discussed world). So we cannot teach in any *literal* sense that death came into the world with sin, even though the myth itself has its own power and truth claim.[50]

Although many would not classify the apocalyptic ends of the world as "myth,"[51] these also, while having their own power, require some form of re-interpretation. So Christ coming "out of Zion" (Rom 11:26) needs to be reinterpreted. The author of Luke-Acts sees the second coming as a reversal of the ascension. Two men in white robes tell the disciples at the ascension: "Men of Galilee, why do you stand looking up toward heaven? This Jesus, who has been taken up from you into heaven, will come in the same way as you saw him go into heaven" (Acts 1:11). Although Paul does not write of an "ascension" as such (he holds to an exaltation at the resurrection, Phil 2:9–11) his idea of the second coming would appear to correspond to what we

48. One such supporter is Michael Nazir-Ali, former bishop of Rochester, who has now converted to the Roman Catholic Church. Among his achievements is to make UKIP respectable (see, e.g., his address to the UKIP conference on September 29, 2017). Another supporter is Steve Baker, a vocal Christian and MP for High Wycombe, who promoted a hard Brexit. As I write Baker is also a trustee of the Global Warming Policy Foundation, an organization set up by Nigel Lawson aimed at challenging claims that humans are exacerbating climate change, and receiving support from a former bishop of Chester.

49. One of the complicating factors in weighing up the value of a humanist world view is that many "humanists" have been influenced by the Christian tradition, including that of Paul.

50. On the role of myth in theology, see Bell, *Deliver Us from Evil*, 23–65.

51. See Bell, *Deliver Us from Evil*, 56–59. Sellin, "Mythologeme," 215–16, rightly argues that in apocalyptic myth moves over into allegory.

find in Acts 1:11. As far as "out of Zion" (Rom 11:26) is concerned, there has been debate as to whether Paul is referring to the earthly or heavenly Zion. This is a false antithesis. In view of the probable importance Paul places on Isa 2:2, where "in days to come" Zion "will be established as the highest of mountains" Paul most likely viewed the earthly and heavenly Jerusalem as corresponding at the end of time.[52] Can we envisage Christ returning from such a Jerusalem in the last days? I suggest it can only be so envisaged in the realm of our imagination.

WHAT PAUL (ROUGHLY) GOT RIGHT

Christianity as Absolute Religion

For me Paul's greatest insights regard the person of Jesus Christ and salvation through him. He believed that Jesus was fully divine and that salvation is through faith in him. Paul's message fully supports Hegel's claim that Christianity is the "absolute religion" in view of the incarnation.[53] This could appear to be an arrogant claim and certainly goes against the grain in today's culture of religious tolerance and inter-religious dialogue. However, understanding Christianity as the absolute religion does not necessarily mean there is no truth in other religions.[54]

Related to this first point regarding the person of Jesus and salvation through him, I think he was also right in his understanding of God, which I am happy to describe as proto-trinitarian. Although I have not devoted a separate chapter to "God" the question of God has cropped up constantly in the discussion. Paul did not simply accept a Jewish view of God;[55] the very meaning of the word "God" changed for him as a result of his Damascus Road experience. Proto-trinitarian language is not confined to the prayer

---

52. Cf. the vision of Rev 21:10: "And in the Spirit [the angel] carried me away to a great, high mountain and showed me the holy city Jerusalem coming down out of heaven from God."

53. See, e.g., Miller, *Phenomenology*, 459 (§759).

54. Paul tends to be somewhat negative towards the religions of which he knows. Hegel by contrast finds truth in many religions. See Macquarrie, *Jesus Christ*, 220, who quotes Hegel's *Philosophy of Religion* (translated by Speirs and Sanderson), 1:77: "The thought of the Incarnation pervades every religion." Thereby Macquarrie thinks Hegel reduces the "scandal of particularity." See the discussion below.

55. Hence I reject the view of Dunn, *Theology*, 28, who writes that the problem of saying anything about Paul's understanding of God is that his "convictions about God are all too axiomatic." Further, "Paul did not need to explain his beliefs about God because they were already common to and shared with his readers." Such "shared beliefs were Jewish through and through" (29).

at the end of 2 Corinthians: "The grace of our Lord Jesus Christ, the love of God, and the communion of the Holy Spirit be with all of you" (2 Cor 13:13). His whole system of thought is proto-trinitarian, a fine example being 1 Cor 2:6–16.[56]

In chapter 8 on the person of Christ I commented on the value of Hegel's philosophy for understanding the incarnation. He can also be called upon for elucidating the Trinity. Trinitarianism is written into the very structure of Hegel's thought and to a great extent he is indebted here to Paul (and to John).[57]

Paul's thinking on predestination, although appearing non-trinitarian in that he can speak of a God in more simple monotheistic terms (Rom 9:6–29), is nevertheless largely proto-trinitarian. The appearance of a simple monotheistic predestination may be because of a superficial reading of Calvin's doctrine and his concept of a decree made before the foundation of the world concerning those to be saved and those to be damned. This wording is *partly* indebted to Eph 1:4 but the actual wording is that God chose us "in Christ," something Calvin rightly emphasizes in his commentary.[58] Whereas Calvin writes of this eternal decree, Paul has a dynamic view of predestination in that it occurs as the gospel is preached. Christ is the content of the gospel and, with the Spirit, is active in the preaching of the gospel.[59] Even in Rom 9–11 there is a central section Rom 9:30–10:21 where Christ has a central role and in Rom 11:26 "all Israel" comes to salvation in that they will receive the gospel from Christ at his second coming.

We are left with a problem though that at times predestination presents a capricious God. This is especially so in Rom 9:6–29 where God chooses

56. See Bell, "Mind of Christ," 188–89.

57. To give an idea of how trinitarian thought is written in to the very fabric of Hegel's philosophy, consider the *Phenomenology of Spirit*, which contains a long chapter on "Spirit" (§§438–671) with an extended section on "Culture" (§§484–595) in which he writes this about faith (§§532–33): [J]ust as in the world of culture state power, or the Good, was primary, so here, too, the first is the *Absolute Being*, Spirit that is in and for itself in so far as it is the simple eternal *substance*. But in the actualization of its concept, in being Spirit, it passes over into *being-for-another*, its self-identity becomes an *actual*, self-*sacrificing* absolute Being; it becomes a *self*, but a mortal, perishable self. Consequently, the third moment is the return of this alienated self and of the humiliated substance into their original simplicity; only in this way is substance represented as Spirit. These distinct Beings, when brought back to themselves by thought, out of the flux of the actual world, are immutable eternal Spirits, whose being lies in thinking the unity which they constitute" (Miller, *Phenomenology*, 325). As Macquarrie, *Jesus Christ*, 219, notes, "[e]ven a superficial reading of this passage suggests the Christian teaching about the triune God."

58. Calvin, *Ephesians*, 125–26.

59. See chapter 7 above.

Jacob and rejects Esau (v. 13). Taking Romans 9 out of context does indeed present what may appear a capricious God[60] and even within Rom 9–11 there are problems: "all Israel" comes to salvation but there is no similar hope for "all gentiles"! One way of solving this problem is to appeal to the universalist texts in Paul. Although there are not many of them, they are nevertheless highly significant: Rom 5:18–19; 2 Cor 5:19; Phil 2:10–11.[61]

An advantage of affirming God's sovereignty is that if he is good and desires the good of his creatures then there is hope that evil will be one day overcome. The problem though is that he has allowed horrendous suffering throughout the ages. Again Hegel may offer a way forward. "*Absolute Being, Spirit that is in and for itself*", or in another translation "Absolute Being, Spirit absolutely self-contained,"[62] is for Hegel, "only a hypothesis, that is to say, a hypothetical beginning or ground." Such an absolute Monarch "has never existed"[63] for "the absolute Being must have from the start *implicitly* sacrificed *itself*."[64] Macquarrie explains: "The Son is the historical Other in whom the Absolute Spirit has imaged itself, in whom the implicit sacrifice which that Absolute has been making since the beginning receives its actual historical realisation."[65] Hence Hegel can write of the "speculative Good Friday" as distinct from the "historical Good Friday." Such a speculative Good Friday is the sacrifice that has always been there in the Absolute Spirit.[66] Although Hegel can see incarnation in a variety of religions[67] it is shown in its most profound form in the cross of Christ when one can say "God himself lies dead." This is a line from a hymn by Johann Rist:

---

60. Although Piper, *Justification*, ix, can write that "[t]he God of Romans 9 took me captive while I was yet in seminary. No other picture of God ever commended itself to me as more true to what the Creator must be." Note that this study covers Rom 9:1–23 and can therefore present a somewhat skewed view of Paul's understanding of God since his argument takes a radical turn in Rom 11:1.

61. See chapter 7 above.

62. Baillie, *Phenomenology of Mind*, 554.

63. Macquarrie, *Jesus Christ*, 220.

64. Baillie, *Phenomenology of Mind*, 722 (cf. Miller, *Phenomenology*, 434, §718).

65. Macquarrie, *Jesus Christ*, 220.

66. Macquarrie, *Jesus Christ*, 220, points to the reflection of this idea in the Lamb "that was slaughtered from the foundation of the world" (Rev 13:8).

67. Hegel, *Philosophy of Religion*, 1:194: "The human form, the incarnation of God, must appear as an essential element of religion in the definition of its object—in the lower religions may be just *this* being, this immediate determinate being, a unity with a finite in base forms [such as] stars <and animals>—so-called anthropomorphisms."

O Great woe!	O grosse Not!
God himself lies dead.	Gott selbst liegt tot.
On the cross he has died;	Am Kreuz ist er gestorben;
And thus he has gained for us	hat dadurch das Himmelreich
By love the kingdom of heaven.	uns aus Lieb' erworben.

Anthropology

As we saw in chapter 9 Paul's anthropology is inherently pessimistic. Although this reflects Paul's own inner experience, I think a case can be made that he roughly got this right even though his view may be too extreme. Reinhold Niebuhr claimed that original sin is "the only empirically verifiable doctrine of the Christian faith."[68] An alternative is that this is something that can only be affirmed in the light of the cross of Christ and through faith. As Luther said:[69]

> But now God has revealed to us what he thinks of us and what he judges us to be, namely, that we are all sinners. We must, therefore, yield to this, his revelation and his words, and believe them and thus acknowledge them as just and true in order in their light to confess ourselves sinners, which is something that we could not learn from ourselves.

One problem I have found with the application of Paul's approach is that some who publicly proclaim such pessimistic anthropology seem remarkably immune from the teaching itself and appear to be unaware of the damaging psychological effect such teaching can have, especially for those with a fragile self-image. Another possible anomaly in applying Paul's teaching on sin is that one can easily get hardened to it such that when recounting the "general confession" of the Holy Communion service of *The Book of Common Prayer* these words can easily flow off the tongue: "We acknowledge and bewail our manifold sins and wickedness, Which we from time to time most grievously have committed, By thought, word and deed [. . .] We do earnestly repent and are heartily sorry for these our misdoing; The remembrance of them is grievous unto us; The burden of them is intolerable." Likewise I imagine I am not alone in hearing so many sermons about sin that one can become immune to the message, crucial though it is.

---

68. See also Wilckens, *Römer*, 1:178–79.
69. Pauck, *Luther: Romans*, 79–80; WA 56:231 (Scholion to Rom 3:5).

Justification by Faith

Related to anthropology is the question of justification. A pessimistic anthropology requires justification by grace alone and by faith alone. Hence, whatever one may say about Paul's doctrines on justification there is an inner consistency; and in fact his whole theology demonstrates a remarkable cohesion. Paul boldly and courageously claimed that Abraham was justified by faith and not by works, this going completely against the Jewish tradition. The issue of justification by faith alone has traditionally divided Protestants and Roman Catholics (and divided Protestants from the Orthodox tradition). Ironically many Protestants do not seem to believe it and some Catholic theologians hold to it and consider Luther correct on the issue.[70]

One of the ironies of teaching Paul's theology in a university setting is that a fair amount of time is spent marking student's essays (for which students have invested much time). Further, teachers are also subject to student evaluation of teaching as well as being evaluated in all aspects of their work by their university. Hence, one's mindset is constantly on "justification by works." While wishing students to do well and endeavoring to give the best lectures I can within the constraints of time, there is this problem of self-justification; and such self-justification is evident in wider society with the desire for worldly success. Justification by faith liberates one from such pressures and demonstrates that our value depends not on what we may achieve but on being accepted by God. As Klaiber writes, justification by faith means "being set free to live. It is the gift of a new life, a life that finds its place and its goal in fellowship with God, a fellowship that becomes possible through God's word of judgement that deems us righteous."[71]

Salvation by Grace

Related to justification by faith is salvation by grace. As we have seen, Paul presents a liberating gospel and this has profound pastoral and psychological implications. In many respects I think he got the balance correct. The idea of salvation by grace from beginning to end, which is found in a number of key passages, avoids the fear of losing salvation. The place to find the best theological toilet graffiti is probably in Tübingen. In the gents' toilet in the Protestant faculty someone had scribbled (here translated): "Those in the Tübingen psychiatric clinic would like to thank the Württemberg

---

70. It was noted in chapter 7 that Schlier, *Römer*, 117, considered Luther correct on Rom 3:28, namely that a person is justified by faith *alone*.

71. Klaiber, *Justified before God*, 153.

pietism." Württemberg pietism essentially had a pattern of religion rather like that of E. P. Sanders that one "gets in" by grace and "stays in" by works; and if you fail to produce the works you can lose your salvation. The writer of the graffiti may have had something like this in mind.

One danger of a cavalier attitude to salvation by grace is that you could argue that works do not really matter. Works *do* matter though and this is something that Paul constantly emphasized. So it is not as though you need James to offer a correction to Paul since Paul offers his own correction. Paul understands works as issuing from faith. Galatians 5:6: "For in Christ Jesus neither circumcision not on circumcision counts for anything; the only thing that counts is *faith working through love.*" Christians are free from law but nevertheless they are expected to love their neighbor. Luther's idea of works issuing from faith fairly represents Paul's view. Houlgate points out that Hegel shared this view too. Kant understood religion as "the recognition of all our duties as divine commands."[72] So for Kant faith makes us aware of what we ought to do; such a moral consciousness "understands itself to be bound by laws (albeit determined by its own free, self-determining reason) that constrain its ever reluctant will."[73] By contrast, for Hegel "[f]aith [. . .] does not feel bound by laws and obligations or by the burden of duty because it is the consciousness of been reconciled with God, of being filled with the spirit of love, and thus is actually having been transformed and reconstructed in accordance with God's will, with what is right."[74]

Although usually Christians have opportunities to allow their faith to issue in good works there are cases where some come to faith at the end of their life. An example of the scandal of Paul's gospel of grace is the case of Joachim von Ribbentrop, Hitler's foreign minister. At the Nuremberg Trials he was found guilty of all four charges made against him.[75] He was sentenced to death by hanging; it took him some time to die, some accounts saying it took ten minutes, others almost twenty minutes. Among his last words on the scaffold were "God have mercy on my soul." This was sincerely meant for in his last days he spent time with the prison chaplain, Pastor Gerecke, and had studied the Bible and catechism. Finally, turning to Gerecke

---

72. Kant, *Religion within the Boundaries of Mere Reason*, 153.

73. Houlgate, *Introduction to Hegel*, 264. For Hegel this is "unhappy consciousness."

74. Houlgate, *Introduction to Hegel*, 264. See also Westphal, "Hegel's Critique."

75. The four charges were conspiracy, crimes against peace, war crimes, and crimes against humanity. Many questions arise about the legitimacy of the Nuremberg trials. All that matters here in my argument is that Ribbentrop was responsible for horrendous suffering.

he said: "I'll see you again."[76] According to Paul's gospel, he is now enjoying fellowship with God.

Mission

Given Paul's new understanding of God and salvation it was natural that he was to engage in his adventurous mission. He went to the point of saying that an obligation is laid on him to preach the gospel "and woe to me if I do not proclaim the gospel" (1 Cor 9:16). He believed that everyone should hear the gospel and in fact such a gospel was for the Jew *first*. Hence, he held the view that Judaism has been superseded.

Someone coming to faith in Jesus Christ is certainly a gain in my eyes. There is of course the problem that becoming a Christian can lead to self-righteousness. But despite the weaknesses of Christians and the atrocities some have perpetrated, generally speaking coming to faith actually makes a human being more complete. This completion is viewed by Paul, using his mythical language, as a rebirth and a union with Jesus Christ.

Mission is a controversial issue. But if done sensitively I see no problem. And if Christians feel they have a message to give the world, why not just go ahead and share the good news, but share it as the issue of faith naturally arises as they interact with friends, family, and colleagues.[77]

CAN YOU TRUST THE WORD OF GOD? J. S. BACH CANTATA 18 "JUST AS THE RAIN AND SNOW FROM HEAVEN FALLS"

For this final chapter I have chosen a piece to stress the preciousness of the "word of God": J. S. Bach's Cantata 18.[78] By "word of God" I mean not so much the "things that you're liable to read in the Bible"[79] but rather the

76. Bloch, *Ribbentrop*, 455–56.

77. In my student days I did engage in door-to-door evangelism and I hope that was of some help to those I visited; but I was essentially invading people's privacy!

78. See Melvin, *Cantata Texts*, 58–62.

79. These words are taken from "It ain't necessarily so," a song of Sportin' Life in the folk opera *Porgy and Bess* (first performed in New York, 1935), the music being composed by George Gershwin and the words by DuBose Heyward and Ira Gershwin. The first verse runs as follows: "It ain't necessarily so / It ain't necessarily so / The things that you're liable / To read in the Bible / It ain't necessarily so." He then goes on to mock the stories of David killing Goliath, Jonah who "made his home / In that fish's abdomen," Moses being found on water by "old Pharaoh's daughter," and Methuselah who lived to nine hundred years (precisely 969 years, Gen 5:27). On a more theological level

transcendent word that comes to us and is witnessed to in the Bible! This is the word that issues from the mouth of God. The cantata is in five movements, the first being purely orchestral (Sinfonia). The key text for the second movement (a Bass recitative) is Isa 55:10–11 and the parable of the sower is central for the third (my Catholic friends will have to excuse the three anti-pope sentiments), involving tenor and bass soloists and the choir. The fourth movement (soprano aria) focuses on the word of God as a true treasure and the final chorale is a prayer that God's word not be taken away. The libretto is by Erdmann Neumeister.

The words for the second movement are:

Just as the rain and snow from heaven falls	Gleichwie der Regen und Schnee vom Himmel fällt
and returns not empty, but rather moistens the Earth	und nicht wieder dahin kommet, sondern feuchtet die Erde
and makes it fruitful and fertile	und macht sie fruchtbar und wachsend,
so that it gives seed for sowing and bread for eating	daß sie gibt Samen zu säen und Brot zu essen;
so shall the word, which goes out of my mouth also be;	Also soll das Wort, so aus meinem Munde gehet, auch sein;
it shall not return to me empty	es soll nicht wieder zu mir leer kommen,
but rather do what pleases me and shall succeed for that for which I send it.	sondern tun, das mir gefället, und soll ihm gelingen, dazu ich's sende.

---

he explains that the devil may not be a villain and that one should take "that gospel, / Wherever it's possible, / But with a grain a salt."

Further Reading

THE MOST IMPORTANT TEXTS to read are the seven letters of Paul that are generally considered authentic (Romans, 1 and 2 Corinthians, Galatians, Philippians, 1 Thessalonians, and Philemon). Hence at the end of chapters 2–11 I have suggested a passage from one of his letters to read. It is also a good idea to read the letters that many today consider pseudonymous: Ephesians, Colossians, 2 Thessalonians, 1 and 2 Timothy, and Titus.

Below is a selection of works of secondary literature, some of which are referred to in the above chapters, but some are not. This is a personal selection and is not intended to reflect the current state of scholarship on Paul.

I. ENGLISH WORKS

1. Paul (General)

John M.G. Barclay, *Paul and the Gift*. Grand Rapids: Eerdmans, 2015.
Günther Bornkamm, *Paul*. Translated by D.M.G. Stalker. London: Hodder and Stoughton, 1975.
Francis Watson, *Paul and the Hermeneutics of Faith*. London: T. & T. Clark, 2005.
N.T. Wright, *Paul and the Faithfulness of God*. 2 vols. London: SPCK, 2013.

2. Pseudonymous literature

David G. Meade, *Pseudonymity and Canon: An Investigation into the Relationship and Authority in Jewish and Earliest Christian Tradition*. Grand Rapids: Eerdmans, 1986.

3. Paul and the law; Justification by faith

F. F. Bruce, "What the Law Could Not Do." In *Paul Apostle of the Free Spirit*, 188–202. Exeter, UK: Paternoster, 1977.

Hans Hübner, *Law in Paul's Thought*. Translated by James C. G. Greig; edited by John Riches. Edinburgh: T. & T. Clark, 1984.

Eberhard Jüngel, *Justification: The Heart of the Christian Faith*. Translated by Jeffrey F. Cayzer. London: T. & T. Clark, 2006.

Ernst Käsemann, "'The Righteousness of God' in Paul." In *New Testament Questions of Today*, 168–82. Translated by W. J. Montague. NTL. London: SCM, 1969.

Mark A. Seifrid, *Christ, Our Righteousness: Paul's Theology of Justification*. New Studies in Biblical Theology. Downers Grove, IL: IVP, 2000.

Peter Stuhlmacher, *Re-visiting Paul's Doctrine of Justification*. With an essay by Donald A. Hagner. Downers Grove, IL: IVP, 2001.

4. Sacrifice of Christ

Daniel P. Bailey, "Biblical and Greco-Roman Uses of *Hilastērion* in Romans 3:25 and 4 Maccabees 17:22 (Codex S)." In Peter Stuhlmacher, *Biblical theology of the New Testament*, edited by Daniel P. Bailey, 824–68. Grand Rapids: Eerdmans, 2018.

Richard H. Bell, "Sacrifice and Christology in Paul." *Journal of Theological Studies* 53 (2002) 1–27.

5. Christology

F. F. Bruce, "Paul and the Exalted Christ." In *Paul Apostle of the Free Spirit*, 113–25. Exeter, UK: Paternoster, 1977.

Robert Morgan, "Christ." In *The Oxford Handbook of Nineteenth-Century Christian Thought*, edited by Joel D. S. Rasmussen, Judith Wolfe, and Johannes Zachhuber, 591–609. Oxford: Oxford University Press, 2017.

N. T. Wright, "Jesus Christ Is Lord: Philippians 2.5–11." In *The Climax of the Covenant: Christ and the Law in Pauline Theology*, 56–98. Edinburgh: T. & T. Clark, 1991.

6. Israel and the Gospel

Otfried Hofius, "'All Israel Will be Saved': Divine Salvation and Israel's Deliverance in Romans 9–11." Translated by Judith M. Gundry. *Princeton Seminary Bulletin* (1990) 19–39.

7. Anthropology

James D. G. Dunn, *The Theology of Paul the Apostle*, 51–78. Reprint, London: T. & T. Clark, 2003.

Susan Grove Eastman, *Paul and the Person: Reframing Paul's Anthropology*. Grand Rapids: Eerdmans, 2017.

8. The authority of Paul's letters

Martin Luther, "Prefaces to the New Testament." Translated by Charles M. Jacobs and E. Theodore Bachmann. *Luther's Works, Volume 35: Word and Sacrament I*, 355–411. Philadelphia: Fortress, 1960.

9. Paul and Freedom

Martin Luther, "The Freedom of a Christian." Translated by W. A. Lambert and Harold J. Grimm. *Luther's Works, Volume 31: Career of the Reformer I*, 327–77. Philadelphia: Fortress, 1957.

II UNTRANSLATED GERMAN WORKS

Georg Eichholz, *Die Theologie des Paulus im Umriß*. 5th ed. Neukirchen-Vlyn: Neukirchner, 1985.

Otfried Hofius, *Paulusstudien*, 203–40. WUNT 51. Tübingen: J.C.B. Mohr (Paul Siebeck), 1989.

Otfried Hofius, *Paulusstudien II*. WUNT 143. Tübingen: Mohr Siebeck, 2002.

Bibliography

SOURCES

Bible

Aland, Barbara, et al., eds. *Novum Testamentum Graece*. 28th ed. Stuttgart: Deutsche Bibelgesellschaft, 2014.

Aland, Barbara, et al., eds. *The Greek New Testament*. 5th ed. New York: United Bible Societies, 2014.

Luther, Martin. *Die gantze Heilige Schrifft Deudsch (Wittenberg 1545)*. Edited by Heinz Blanke and Han Volz. 3 vols. Munich: Rogner & Bernhard, 1972.

Rahlfs, Alfred, ed. *Septuaginta: Id est Vetus Testamentum graece iuxta LXX interpretes*, 2 vols. Stuttgart: Württembergische Bibelanstalt, 1935.

The Holy Bible: New Revised Standard Version. Oxford: Oxford University Press, 1995.

Tyndale Commemoration Volume, Reproducing substantial parts of Tyndale's Revised Testament of 1534. Edited by R. Mercer Wilson. London: Lutterworth, 1939.

Ancient Jewish Sources

Charlesworth, James H., ed. *The Old Testament Pseudepigrapha*. 2 vols. London: Darton, Longman & Todd, 1983–1985.

Colson, F. H., and G. H. Whitaker, R. Marcus, J. W. Earp, eds. *Philo*. LCL. 10 vols. with 2 supplements. Cambridge: Harvard University Press, 1929–62.

Danby, Herbert. *The Mishnah*. Reprint, Oxford: Oxford University Press, 1985.

Neusner, Jacob, ed. *Sifre to Deuteronomy: An Analytical Translation*. BJS 98, 101. 2 vols. Atlanta: Scholars, 1987.

Vermes, Geza, ed. *The Complete Dead Sea Scrolls in English*. 4th ed. Harmondsworth, UK: Penguin, 1998.

Early Christian Writings

Diekamp, Franz, ed. *Hippolytos von Theben: Texte und Untersuchungen*. Münster: Verlag der Aschendorff'schen Buchhandlung, 1898.

Hennecke, E., and W. Schneemelcher, eds. *New Testament Apocrypha*. English translation edited by R. Mc.L. Wilson. 2 vols. London: SCM, 1973–74.

Lake, Kirsopp, ed. *Eusebius: The Ecclesiastical History* 2 vols. LCL 153, 265. Cambridge: Harvard University Press, 1964–65.

Roberts, A, J. Donaldson, and A.C. Coxe, eds. *Ante-Nicene Fathers*. 10 vols, Reprint, Peabody, MA: Hendrickson, 1994.

Schaff, Philip, ed. *Nicene and Post-Nicene Fathers: First Series*. 14 vols. Reprint, Peabody, MA: Hendrickson, 1994.

Schaff, Philip, and H. Wace, eds. *Nicene and Post-Nicene Fathers: Second Series*, 14 vols. Reprint, Peabody, MA: Hendrickson, 1994.

Scherer, Jean. *Le commentaire d'Origène sur Rom. III.5-V.7*. Le Caire, 1957.

Stählin, Otto, ed. *Clemens Alexandrinus, Band 2*. GCS. Leipzig: Hinrichs'sche Buchhandlung, 1906.

Classical Sources

Collard, Christopher, and Martin Cropp. *Euripides VIII: Fragments*. LCL 506. Cambridge: Harvard University Press, 2008.

Fowler, Harold North, ed. *Plato I: Euthyphro; Apology; Crito; Phaedo; Phaedrus*, LCL 36. Reprint, Cambridge: Harvard University Press, 1995.

Hett, W. S., ed. *Aristotle VII: On the Soul; Parva Naturalia; On Breath*. LCL 146. Reprint, Cambridge: Harvard University Press, 2000.

Oldfather, W. A. *Epictetus I: Discourses Books I and II*. LCL 131. Reprint, Cambridge: Harvard University Press, 1989.

Rackham, H. *Aristotle XIX: Nicomachean Ethics*. LCL 73. Reprint, Cambridge: Harvard University Press, 1938.

Sommerstein, Alan, ed. *Aeschylus II: Oresteia*. LCL 146. Cambridge: Harvard University Press, 2008.

Way, Arthur S., ed. *Euripides I: Iphigeneia at Aulis; Rhesus; Hecuba; Daughters of Troy; Helen*. LCL 9. Reprint, Cambridge: Harvard University Press, 1988.

Confessions and Liturgy

The Book of Common Prayer. Cambridge: Cambridge University Press, n.d.

Schaff, Philip, and David S. Schaff. *The Creeds of Christendom: With a History and Critical Notes*. 3 vols. Reprint, Grand Rapids: Baker, 1983.

REFERENCE WORKS

Blass, F., and A. Debrunner. *A Greek Grammar of the New Testament*. Translated and revised by R. W. Funk, Chicago: University of Chicago Press, 1961.

Cremer-Kögel. *Biblisch-theologisches Wörterbuch des neutestamentlichen Griechisch.* 11th ed. Gotha: Klotz, 1923.

Kittel, G., and G. Friedrich, eds. *Theological Dictionary of the New Testament.* ET. 10 vols. Grand Rapids: Eerdmans, 1964–76.

Kittel, G., and G. Friedrich, eds. *Theologisches Wörterbuch zum Neuen Testament.* 10 vols. Stuttgart: Kohlhammer Verlag 1933–78.

Radermacher, Ludwig. *Neutestamentliche Grammatik: Das Griechisch des Neuen Testaments im Zusammenhang mit der Volkssprache.* HzNT 1. 2nd. ed. Tübingen: J.C.B. Mohr (Paul Siebeck), 1925.

Schwyzer, Eduard. *Griechische Grammatik.* Handbuch der Altertumswissenschaft, 2. Abteilung, 1. Teil. 4 vols. Munich: Beck, 1939–71.

SECONDARY LITERATURE.

Aland, Kurt, and Barbara Aland. *The Text of the New Testament: An Introduction to the Critical Editions and to the Theory and Practice of Modern Textual Criticism.* Translated by Erroll F. Rhodes. Grand Rapids: Eerdmans, 1987.

Alexander, P. S. "Review of E. P. Sanders, Jesus and Judaism." *Journal of Jewish Studies* 37 (1986) 103–5.

Althaus, Paul. *Die Christliche Wahrheit: Lehrbuch der Dogmatik.* 3rd ed. Gütersloh: Bertelsmann, 1952.

Anderson, A. A. *2 Samuel.* WBC 11. Dallas, TX: Word, 1989.

Arnott, William G. "Menander." *OCD³*, 956–57.

Artinian, Robert G. "Luther after the Stendahl/Sanders Revolution; A Responsive Evaulation of Luther's View of First-Century Judaism in his 1535 Commentary on Galatians." *Trinity Journal 27* (2006) 77–99.

Atkinson, James. *Martin Luther and the Birth of Protestantism.* London: Marshall, Morgan & Scott, 1982.

Aulén, Gustaf. *Christus Victor: An Historical Study of the Three Main Types of the Idea of the Atonement.* Translated by A. G. Herbert. London: SPCK, 1070.

Avemarie, Friedrich. "Erwählung und Vergeltung. Zur optionalen Struktur rabbinischer Soteriologie." *New Testament Studies* 45 (1999) 108–26.

———. *Tora und Leben: Untersuchungen zur Heilsbedeutung der Tora in der frühen rabbinischen Literatur.* TSAJ 55. Tübingen: J.C.B. Mohr (Paul Siebeck), 1996.

———. "Die Werke des Gesetzes im Spiegel des Jakobusbrief: A Very Old Perspective on Paul." *Zeitschrift für Theologie und Kirche* 98 (2001) 282–309.

Badenas, Robert. *Christ the End of the Law: Romans 10.4 in Pauline Perspective.* JSNTSup 10. Sheffield, UK: JSOT, 1985.

Bailey, Daniel P. "Biblical and Greco-Roman Uses of *Hilastērion* in Romans 3:25 and 4 Maccabees 17:22 (Codex S)." In Peter Stuhlmacher, *Biblical theology of the New Testament,* edited by Daniel P. Bailey, 824–68. Grand Rapids: Eerdmans, 2018.

———. "Jesus as the Mercy Seat: The Semantics and Theology of Paul's Use of *Hilastērion* in Romans 3:25." PhD diss., Cambridge University, 1999.

Baillie, D. M. *God Was in Christ: An Essay on Incarnation and Atonement.* Reprint, London: Faber and Faber, 1973.

Baillie, J. B., ed. *The Phenomenology of Mind.* 2nd ed. London: George Allen & Unwin, 1949.

Barr, James. *The Garden of Eden and the Hope of Immortality*. London: SCM, 1992.

Barrett, C. K. *A Commentary on the First Epistle to the Corinthians*. BNTC. 2nd ed. London: A. & C. Black, 1971.

Barth, Karl. *Church Dogmatics*. Edited by G. W. Bromiley and T. F. Torrance. 4 vols. Edinburgh: T. & T. Clark, 1936–60.

Bauckham, Richard. "Pseudo-Apostolic Letters." *Journal of Biblical Literature* 107 (1988) 469–94.

Bauer, Willam A., and Otto Erich Deutsch, eds. *Mozart: Briefe und Aufzeichnungen. Gesamtausgabe*. 8 vols. Kassel: Bärenreuter, 2005.

Baur, Ferdinand Christian. *Paulus, der Apostel Jesu Christi*. 2nd ed. 2 vols. Leipzig: Fues's Verlag (L.W. Reisland), 1866–67.

Behm, Johannes. "καρδία D: καρδία in the New Testament." *TDNT* 3: 611–14.

Bell, Richard H., "'But we have the Mind of Christ': Some Theological and Anthropological Reflections on 1 Corinthians 2:16." In *Horizons in Hermeneutics: A Festschrift in Honor of Anthony C. Thiselton*, edited by Stanley E. Porter and Matthew R. Malcolm, 175–97. Grand Rapids: Eerdmans, 2013.

———. *Deliver Us from Evil: Interpreting the Redemption from the Power of Satan in New Testament Theology*. WUNT 216. Tübingen: Mohr Siebeck, 2007.

———. *The Irrevocable Call of God: An Inquiry into Paul's Theology of Israel*. WUNT 184. Tübingen: Mohr Siebeck, 2005.

———. *No one seeks for God: An Exegetical and Theological Study of Romans 1.18—3.20*. WUNT 106. Tübingen: Mohr Siebeck, 1998.

———. *Provoked to Jealousy: The Origin and Purpose of the Jealousy Motif in Romans 9–11*. WUNT 2.63. Tübingen: J.C.B. Mohr (Paul Siebeck), 1994.

———. "Reading Romans with Arthur Schopenhauer: Some First Steps toward a Theology of Mind." *Journal for the Study of Paul and His Letters* 1.1 (2011) 41–56.

———. "Rom 5.18–19 and Universal Salvation." *New Testament Studies* 48 (2002) 417–32.

———. "Sacrifice and Christology in Paul." *Journal of Theological Studies* 53 (2002) 1–27.

———. *Wagner's Parsifal: An Appreciation in the Light of His Theological Journey*. Eugene, OR: Cascade, 2013.

Bengel, Johann Albrecht. *Gnomon Novi Testamenti*. 3rd ed. Berlin: Schlawitz 1855.

Best, Ernest. *A Commentary on the First and Second Epistles to the Thessalonians*. BNTC. Reprint, London: A. & C. Black, 1979.

Bethge, Eberhard. *Bonhoeffer: Exile and Martyr*. Edited and with an Essay by John W. de Gruchy. London: Collins, 1975.

Beutel, Albrecht. "Thomasius, Gottfried." *TRE* 33: 488–92.

Bird, Michael F., and Preston M. Sprinkle, eds. *The Faith of Jesus Christ: Exegetical, Biblical, and Theological Studies*. Milton Keynes, UK: Paternoster, 2009.

Bloch, Michael. *Ribbentrop*. London: Bantam, 1994.

de Boer, Martinus C. *The Defeat of Death: Apocalyptic Eschatology in 1 Corinthians 15 and Romans 5*. JSNTSup 22. Sheffield, UK: Sheffield Academic Press, 1988.

Bonhoeffer, Dietrich. *Ethics*. Edited by Eberhard Bethge. Translated by Neville Horton Smith. London SCM, 1998.

———. "Staat und Kirche." In *Konspiration und Haft, 1940–45*, edited by Jørgen Glenthøj, Ulrich Kabitz, and Wolf Krötke, 506–35. Dietrich Bonhoeffer Werke, 16. Munich: Chr. Kaiser, 1996.

Bonner, G. "Augustine on Romans 5,12." In *Studia Evangelica Vol. V*, edited by F. L. Cross, 242–47. Berlin: Akademie, 1968.

Bornkamm, Günther. "The Letter to the Romans as Paul's Last Will and Testament." In *The Romans Debate*, edited by Karl P. Donfried, 16–28. 2nd ed. Peabody, MA: Hendrickson, 1991.

Bornkamm, Heinrich, ed. *Luthers Vorreden zur Bibel*. 3rd ed. Göttingen: Vandenhoeck & Ruprecht, 1989.

Breuning, Wilhelm. "Wie kann man heute von Sühne reden?" *Bibel und Kirche* 41 (1986) 76–82.

Brian, Rustin E. *Jacob Arminius: The Man from Oudewater*. Cascade Companions. Eugene, OR: Cascade, 2015.

Brooten, Bernadette. *Women Leaders in the Ancient Synagogue*. Brown Judaic Studies 36. Atlanta: Scholars, 1982.

Bruce, F. F. *The Book of the Acts*. NICNT. 2nd ed. Grand Rapids: Eerdmans, 1988.

———. *Paul: Apostle of the Free Spirit*. Exeter, UK: Paternoster, 1977.

Bryan, Christopher. *A Preface to Romans: Note on the Epistle in Its Literary and Cultural Setting*. Oxford: Oxford University Press, 2000.

Bultmann, Rudolf. *Theology of the New Testament*. Translated Kendrick Grobel. 2 vols. London: SCM, 1952–55.

———. *Theologie des Neuen Testaments*. 9th ed. (durchgesehen und ergänzt von Otto Merk). UTB 630. Tübingen: J.C.B. Mohr (Paul Siebeck), 1984.

Calvin, John. *Galatians, Ephesians, Philippians and Colossians*. Translated by T. H. L. Parker. Grand Rapids: Eerdmans, 1965.

Capes, David B. *Old Testament Yahweh Texts in Paul's Christology*. WUNT 2.47. Tübingen: J.C.B. Mohr (Paul Siebeck), 1992.

Carnegy, Patrick. *Wagner and the Art of the Theatre*. New Haven, CT: Yale University Press, 2006.

Carr, Jonathan. *Mahler: A Life*. New York: Overlook, 1997.

Coffey, John. "'Tremble Britannia!': Fear, Providence and the Abolition of the Slave Trade, 1758–1807." *English Historical Review* 127.527 (2012) 852–53.

Conzelmann, Hans. *Die Apostelgeschichte*. HzNT 7. 2nd ed. Tübingen: J.C.B. Mohr (Paul Siebeck), 1972.

———. *1 Corinthians: A Commentary on the First Epistle to the Corinthians*. Hermeneia. Translated by James W. Leitch. Bibliography and references by James W. Dunkly. Edited by George W. MacRae. Philadelphia: Fortress, 1975.

———. *Der erste Brief an die Korinther*. KEK 5. 2nd ed. Göttingen: Vandenhoeck & Ruprecht, 1981.

Cranfield, C. E. B. *A Critical and Exegetical Commentary on the Epistle to the Romans*. ICC. 2 vols. Edinburgh: T. & T. Clark, 1977–79.

———. *The Gospel according to St Mark*. CGTC. Reprint, Cambridge: Cambridge University Press, 1979.

Cremer, Hermann. *Biblisch-theologisches Wörterbuch des neutestamentlichen Griechisch. Mit Nachträgen und Berichigungen, herausgegeben von Julius Kögel*. 11th ed. Stuttgart/Gotha: Perthes, 1923.

Cullmann, Oscar. *The Christology of the New Testament*. Translated by Shirley C. Guthrie and Charles A. M. Hall. 2nd ed. London: SCM, 1963.

———. *Immortality of the Soul or Resurrection of the Dead? The Witness of the New Testament*. London: Epworth, 1958.

Davis, David Brion. *The Problem of Slavery in Western Culture.* Ithaca, NY: Cornell University Press, 1966.

Deane, Sidney Norton. *St. Anselm: Proslogion; Monologium; An Appendix in Behalf of the Fool by Gaunilon; and Cur Deus Homo.* Reprint, La Salle, IL: Open Court, 1954.

Deathridge, John. "Postmortem on Isolde." In *Wagner Beyond Good and Evil*, 133–55. Berkeley: University of California Press, 2008.

Deissmann, Adolf. *Paul: A Study in Social and Religious History.* Translated by William E. Wilson. Harper Torchbooks. New York: Harper & Brothers, 1957.

Delius, Hans-Ulrich, ed. *Martin Luther: Studienausgabe Band 3.* Berlin: Evangelische Verlagsanstalt, 1983.

Denzinger, Heinrich. *Enchiridion symbolorum definitionum et declarationum de rebus fidei et morum.* Edited by Peter Hünermann. Freiburg: Herder, 1991.

Dodd, C. H. *The Epistle of Paul to the Romans.* MNTC. Reprint, London: Hodder and Stoughton, 1949.

———. "The Mind of Paul: I." In *New Testament Studies*, 67–82. Manchester: Manchester University Press, 1953.

———. "The Mind of Paul: II." In *New Testament Studies*, 83–128. Manchester: Manchester University Press, 1953.

Duhm, Bernard. *Das Buch Jesaja.* GHKNT 3.1. 4th ed. Göttingen: Vandenhoeck & Ruprecht, 1922.

Dunn, James D. G. *Christology in the Making: An Inquiry into the Origins of the Doctrine of the Incarnation.* 2nd ed. London: SCM, 1989.

———. *Romans.* WBC 38. 2 vols. Dallas: Word, 1988.

———. *The Theology of Paul the Apostle.* Reprint, London: T. & T. Clark, 2003.

Ebeling Gerhard. "Luthers Wirklichkeitsverständnis." *Zeitschrift für Theologie und Kirche* 90 (1993) 409–24.

Eckstein, Hans-Joachim. "'Denn Gottes Zorn wird vom Himmel her offerbar werden.' Exegetische Erwägungen zu Röm 118." *Zeitschrift für die neutestamentliche Wissenschaft* 78 (1987) 74–89.

Eichholz, Georg. *Die Theologie des Paulus im Umriß.* 5th ed. Neukirchen-Vlyn: Neukirchner, 1985.

Elkin, R. H. "Madam Butterfly: Libretto with Translation." In *Madam Butterfly/Madama Butterfly*, 67–125. Opera Guide 26. London: John Calder, 1984.

Elliger, Karl. *Deuterojesaja I: Teilband Jesaja 40,1–45,7.* BKAT 11.1. Neukirchen-Vluyn: Neukirchener, 1978.

Elliott, Keith, and Ian Moir. *Manuscripts and the Text of the New Testament: An Introduction for English Readers.* Reprint, London: T. & T. Clark, 2003.

Ewans, Michael. *Wagner and Aeschylus: The Ring and the Oresteia.* London: Faber and Faber, 1982.

Fahlbusch, Erwin. "Eschatologie." *EKL* 1:1107–8.

Fee, Gordon. *The First Epistle to the Corinthians.* NICNT. Grand Rapids: Eerdmans, 1987.

———. *God's Empowering Presence: The Holy Spirit in the Letters of Paul.* Peabody, MA: Hendrickson, 1994.

Feuerbach, Ludwig. *The Essence of Christianity.* Translated by George Eliot. Reprint, New York: Harper & Row, 1957.

———. *Thoughts on Death and Immortality.* Translated, with introduction and notes, by James A. Massey. Berkeley: University of California Press, 1980.

Fischer, Johannes. "Über die Beziehung von Glaube und Mythos." *Zeitschrift für Theologie und Kirche* 85 (1988) 303–28.

Fletcher, F. T. H. "Montesquieu's Influence on Anti-Slavery Opinion in England." *The Journal of Negro History* 18 (1933) 414–25.

Forsyth, P. T. *The Work of Christ.* With a Foreword by J. S. Whale and a Memoir of the author by Jessie Forsyth Andrews. London: Collins, 1965.

Frank, Franz Hermann Reinhold von. *Geschichte und Kritik der neueren Theologie, insbesonders der systematische, seit Schleiermacher. Bearbeitet und bis zur Gegenwart fortgeführt von R. H. Grützmacher.* 4th ed. Leipzig: Deichert, 1908.

Fuchs, Ernst. "Das Sprachereignis in der Verkündigung Jesu, in der Theologie und im Ostergeschehen." In *Zum hermeneutischen Problem in der Theologie: Die exstentiale Interpretation, Gesammelte Aufsätze I*, 281–305. 2nd ed. Tübingen: J.C.B. Mohr (Paul Siebeck), 1965.

———. "Was ist ein Sprachereignis? Ein Brief." In *Zur Frage nach dem historischen Jesus: Gesammelte Aufsätze II*, 424–30. 2nd ed. Tübingen: J.C.B. Mohr (Paul Siebeck), 1965.

———. "What Is a 'Language-Event'? A Letter." In *Studies of the Historical Jesus*, 207–12. Studies in Biblical Theology 42. London: SCM, 1964.

Fung, Ronald Y. K. *The Epistle to the Galatians.* NICNT. Grand Rapids: Eerdmans, 1988.

Gager, John G. "Some Notes on Paul's Conversion." *New Testament Studies* 27 (1981) 697–703.

Gerrish, B. A. *The Prince of the Church: Schleiermacher and the Beginnings of Modern Theology.* London: SCM, 1984.

Gese, Hartmut, "Der Dekalog als Ganzheit betrachtet." In *Vom Sinai zum Zion: Alttestamentliche Beiträge zur biblischen Theologie*, 63–80. BEvTh 64. 3rd ed. Munich: Kaiser Verlag, 1990.

———. "Die dreifache Gestaltwerdung des Alten Testaments." In *Alttestamentliche Studien*, 1–28. Tübingen: J.C.B. Mohr (Paul Siebeck), 1991.

———. "Die Sühne." In *Zur biblischen Theologie: Alttestamentliche Vorträge*, 85–106. 3rd ed. Tübingen: J.C.B. Mohr (Paul Siebeck), 1989. ET: "The Atonement." In *Essays on Biblical Theology*, 93–116. Translated by Keith Crim. Minneapolis: Augsburg, 1981.

Gese, Michael, *Das Vermächtnis des Apostels: Die Rezeption der paulinischen Theologie im Epheserbrief.* WUNT 2.99. Tübingen: Mohr Siebeck, 1997.

Gillies, John. *The Works of Rev. George Whitefield.* 6 vols. London, 1771.

Gore, Charles. "The Holy Spirit and Inspiration." In *Lux Mundi: A Series of Studies in the Religion of the Incarnation*, edited by Charles Gore, 315–62. 7th ed. London: John Murray, 1890.

Graves, Robert. *The Greek Myths.* 2 vols. Reprint, Harmondsworth, UK: Penguin, 1974–75.

Gregor-Dellin, Martin, and Dietrich Mack, eds. *Cosima Wagner's Diaries.* 2 vols. Translated by Geoffrey Skelton. New York: Harcourt Brace, 1978–80.

Gruchy, John W. de. "Bonhoeffer in South Africa." In Eberhard Bethge, *Bonhoeffer: Exile and Martyr*, 26–42; edited and with an essay by John W. de Gruchy. London: Collins, 1975.

Gundry, Robert H. "Grace, Works and Staying Saved in Paul." *Biblica* 66 (1985) 1–38.

————. *Sôma in Biblical theology: with Emphasis on Pauline Anthropology.* SNTSMS. Cambridge: Cambridge University Press, 1976.

Gundry-Volf, Judith. "Gender and Creation in 1 Corinthians 11:2–16: A Study in Paul's Theological Method." In *Evangelium–Schriftauslegung–Kirche: Festschrift für Peter Stuhlmacher zum 65. Geburtstag,* edited by J. Ådna, S. J. Hafemann, O. Hofius, and G. Feine, 151–71. Göttingen: Vandenhoeck & Ruprecht, 1997.

————. *Paul and Perseverance: Staying in and Falling Away.* WUNT 2.37. Tübingen: J.C.B. Mohr (Paul Siebeck), 1990.

Gunkel, Hermann. *The Influence of the Holy Spirit: The Popular View of the Apostolic Age and the Teaching of the Apostle Paul.* Translated by Roy A. Harrisville and Philip A. Quanbeck II. Philadelphia: Fortress, 1979.

————. *Die Wirkungen des heiligen Geistes nach der populären Anschauung der apostolischen Zeit und der Lehre des Apostels Paulus.* 2nd ed. Göttingen: Vandenhoeck & Ruprecht, 1899.

Gutbrod, Walter. *Die paulinische Anthropologie.* Stuttgart: Kohlhammer, 1934.

Hahn, Ferdinand. *Mission in the New Testament.* Translated by Frank Clark. SBT 47. London: SCM 1965.

Harder, Günther. "Reason, Mind, Understanding." *NIDNTT* 3: 122–30.

Hardy, Thomas. *Jude the Obscure.* Harmondsworth, UK: Penguin, 1978.

Harnack, Adolf von. *Die Chronologie der altchristlichen Litteratur bis Eusebius.* 2 vols. Leipzig: Hinrichs'sche Buchhandlung, 1897–1904.

————. *Die Mission und Ausbreitung des Christentums in den ersten drei Jahrhunderten.* 2 vols. Leipzig: Hinrichs'sche Buchhandlung, 1924.

Harris, H. S. *Hegel's Ladder II: The Odyssey of Spirit.* Indianapolis: Hackett, 1997.

Harris, Murray J. *Jesus as God: The New Testament Use of Theos in Reference to Jesus.* Grand Rapids. Baker, 1992.

————. *The Second Epistle to the Corinthians.* NIGTC. Grand Rapids: Eerdmans, 2005.

Harris, Raymund (Raimundo Hormasa). *Scriptural Researches on the Licitness of the Slave Trade, shewing is Conformity with the Principles of Natural and Revealed Religion, delineated in the Sacred Writings of the Word of God.* London: John Stockdale, 1788.

Hays, Richard B. *The Moral Vision of the New Testament: A Contemporary Introduction to New Testament Ethics.* Edinburgh T. & T. Clark, 1996.

Heckel, Ulrich. *Kraft in Schwachheit: Untersuchungen zu 2. Kor 10–13.* WUNT 2.56. Tübingen: J.C.B. Mohr (Paul Siebeck), 1993.

Hegel, G. W. F. *Das Leben Jesu: Harmonie der Evangelien nach eigener Übersetzung.* Jena: Diederich, 1906.

————. *Lectures on the Philosophy of History.* Preface by Charles Hegel. Translated by J. Sibree. 1861. Reprint, Meneola, NY: Dover 1956.

————. *Lectures on the Philosophy of Religion.* Edited by Peter C. Hodgson. 3 vols. 2007. Reprint, Oxford: Oxford University Press, 2011–12.

————. *Lectures on the Philosophy of Religion.* Translated by E. B. Speirs and J. Burdon Sanderson. 3 vols. Reprint, New York: Humanities, 1974.

————. *Science of Logic.* Translated by A. V. Miller. Foreword by J. N. Findlay. London: George Allen & Unwin, 1969.

Heirich, Max. "Change of Heart: A Test of Some Widely Held Theories of Religious Conversion." *American Journal of Sociology* 83 (1977) 653–80.

Hengel, Martin. "Der Jakobusbrief als antipaulinische Polemik." In *Tradition and Interpretation in the New Testament*, edited by Gerald F. Hawthorne and Otto Betz, 248–78. Grand Rapids: Eerdmans, 1987 (expanded version in Hengel, *Paulus und Jakobus. Kleine Schriften III*, 511–48. WUNT 141. Tübingen: Mohr Siebeck, 2002).

———. *Judaism and Hellenism: Studies in their Encounter in Palestine during the Early Hellenistic Period*. Translated by John Bowden. 2 vols. London: SCM, 1974.

———. *The Septuagint as Christian Scripture: Its Prehistory and the Problem of Its Canon*. Translated by Mark E Biddle. Edinburgh: T. & T. Clark, 2002.

———. *The Son of God*. In *The Cross of the Son of God*, 1–90. Translated by John Bowden. London: SCM, 1986. (*The Son of God* was first published separately in 1976 by SCM.)

Hengel, Martin, and Christoph Markschies. *The Hellenisation of Jewish Palestine in the First Century After Christ*. Translated by John Bowden. London: SCM, 1990.

Hengel, Martin, and Anna Maria Schwemer. *Paul between Damascus and Antioch: The Unknown Years*. Translated by John Bowden. London: SCM 1997.

Hengel, Martin, with Roland Deines. *The Pre-Christian Paul*. Translated by John Bowden. London: SCM, 1991.

Hertz, Anselm. "Strukturen christlicher Ethik IV: Die christliche Lebenswelt." *HchE*, 236–42.

Heyworth, Peter. *Otto Klemperer: His Life and Times, Volume 2, 1933–1973*. Cambridge: Cambridge University Press, 1996.

Hodgson, Leonard. *The Doctrine of the Trinity*. Reprint, London: Nisbet, 1946.

Hodgson, Peter C. *Hegel and Christian Theology: A Reading of the Lectures on the Philosophy of Religion*. Oxford: Oxford University Press, 2005.

Hoffmann, Michael. "Resignation (1786)." In *Schiller Handbuch: Leben–Werk–Wirkung*, edited by Matthias Luserk-Jaqui, 261–62. Stuttgart: Metzler, 2005.

Hofius, Otfried. *Der Christushymnus Philipper 2,6–11*. 2nd ed. WUNT 17. Tübingen: J.C.B. Mohr (Paul Siebeck), 1991.

———. "The Fourth Servant Song in the New Testament Letters". In *The Suffering Servant: Isaiah 53 in Jewish and Christian Sources*, edited by Bernd Janowski and Peter Stuhlmacher, 163–88. Grand Rapids: Eerdmans, 2004.

———. "Herrenmahl und Herrenmahlparadosis: Erwägungen zu 1 Kor 11,23b-25." In *Paulusstudien*, 203–40. WUNT 51. Tübingen: J.C.B. Mohr (Paul Siebeck), 1989.

———. "Der Mensch im Schatten Adams. Römer 7,7–25a." In *Paulusstudien II*, 104–54. WUNT 143. Tübingen: Mohr Siebeck, 2002.

———. "'Rechtfertigung des Gottlosen' als Thema biblischer Theologie." In *Paulusstudien*, 121–47. WUNT 51. Tübingen: J.C.B. Mohr (Paul Siebeck), 1989.

———. "Sühne und Versöhnung." In *Paulusstudien*, 33–49. WUNT 51. Tübingen: J.C.B. Mohr (Paul Siebeck), 1989.

———. "Das vierte Gottesknechtlied in den Briefen des Neuen Testaments." In *Der leidende Gottesknecht: Jesaja 53 und seine Wirkungeschichte*, edited by Bernd Janowski and Peter Stuhlmacher, 107–27. FzAT. Tübingen: J.C.B. Mohr (Paul Siebeck), 1996. (= *New Testament Studies* 39 (1993) 414–37).

———. "Wort Gottes und Glaube bei Paulus." In *Paulusstudien*, 148–74. WUNT 51. Tübingen: J.C.B. Mohr (Paul Siebeck), 1989.

Holl, Monika, and Karl-Heinz Köhler. *Mozart: Geistliche Gesangswerke I.5*, Basel: Bärenreiter, 1983.

Holtz, Traugott. "Christliche Interpolationen in 'Joseph and Aseneth.'" *New Testament Studies* 14 (1967–68) 482–97.

———. *Der erste Brief an die Thessalonicher.* EKK 13. Neukirchen-Vluyn: Neukirchener, 1986.

———. "Das Gericht über die Juden und die Rettung ganz Israels. 1. Thess 2,15f. und Röm 11,25f." In *Geschichte und Theologie des Urchristentums. Gesammelte Aufsätze,* 313–25. WUNT 57. Tübingen: J.C.B. Mohr (Paul Siebeck), 1991.

Hoover, R.W. "The Harpagmos Enigma: A Philological Solution." *Harvard Theological Review* 56 (1971) 95–119.

Houlgate, Stephen. *Introduction to Hegel: Freedom, Truth and History.* 2nd ed. Oxford: Blackwell, 2005.

Humphreys, David. "Sacred Music." In *The Mozart Compendium,* edited by H. C. Robbins Landon, 310–20. London: Thames and Hudson, 1990.

Hurd, John C. "Paul Ahead of His Time: 1 Thess. 2:13–16." In *Anti-Judaism in Early Christianity: Volume 1: Paul and the Gospels,* edited by Peter Richardson, 21–36. SCJ 2. Waterloo, ON: Wilfrid Laurier University Press, 1986.

Hurst, L. D. "Re-enter the Pre-existent Christ in Philippians 2.5–11?" *New Testament Studies* 32 (1986) 449–57.

Hurtado, L. W. *How on Earth Did Jesus Become a God?* Grand Rapids: Eerdmans, 2005.

Inwood, Michael J. "Death, Hegel, and Kojève." *Eidos* 2 (2017) 68–76.

Iwand, Hans Joachim. *Nachgelassene Werke, Vierter Band: Gesetz und Evangelium.* Edited by Walter Kreck. Munich: Kaiser, 1964.

Janowski, Bernd. "He Bore Our Sins: Isaiah 53 and the Drama of Taking Another's Place." In *The Suffering Servant: Isaiah 53 in Jewish and Christian Sources,* edited by Bernd Janowski and Peter Stuhlmacher, 48–74. Grand Rapids: Eerdmans, 2004.

———. *Sühne als Heilsgeschehen. Studien zur Sühnetheologie der Priesterschrift und zur Wurzel KPR im Alten Orient und im Alten Testament.* WMANT 55. Neukirchen-Vluyn: Neukirchener, 1982.

Jewett, Paul K. *Infant Baptism and the Covenant of Grace.* Grand Rapids: Eerdmans, 1978.

Jewett, Robert. *Paul's Anthropological Terms.* AGAJU 10. Leiden: Brill, 1971.

Jüngel, Eberhard. *Death: The Riddle and the Mystery.* Translated by Iain and Ute Nicol. Philadelphia: Westminster, 1974.

———. "Das Geheimnis der Stellvertretung: Ein dialogisches Gespräch mit Heinrich Vogel." In *Wertlose Wahrheit. Zur Identität und Relevanz des christlichen Glaubens. Theologische Erörterungen III,* 243–60. BevTh 107. Munich: Kaiser, 1990.

———. *God as the Mystery of the World: On the Foundation of the Theology of the Crucified One in the Dispute between Theism and Atheism.* Translated by Darrell L. Guder. Edinburgh: T. & T. Clark, 1983.

———. "'My Theology'—A Short Summary." In *Theological Essays II,* edited by John Webster, translated by Arnold Neufeldt-Fast and J. B. Webster, 1–19. Edinburgh: T. & T. Clark, 1995.

Kant, Immanuel. *Religion within the Boundaries of Mere Reason and Other Writings.* Edited by Allen Wood and George di Giovanni. Revised with an introduction by Robert Merrihew Adams. CTHP. Cambridge: Cambridge University Press, 2018.

Käsemann, Ernst. "Justification and Salvation History in the Epistle to the Romans." In *Perspectives on Paul,* translated by Margaret Kohl, 60–78. London: SCM, 1971.

———. *An die Römer* (HzNT 8a). 4th ed. Tübingen: J.C.B. Mohr (Paul Siebeck), 1980.

————. *Romans*. ET. London: SCM 1980.

————. "'The Righteousness of God' in Paul." In *New Testament Questions of Today*, 168–82. Translated by W. J. Montague. NTL. London: SCM, 1969.

Kavanaugh, Kieren, and Otilio Rodriguez, ed. *The Autobiography of St Teresa of Avila*. New York: Book of the Month, 1995.

Kelly, J. N. D. *Early Christian Doctrines*. 5th ed. London: A. & C. Black, 1977.

Kennedy, Michael. *Mahler*. The Master Musicians. London: Dent, 1974.

Kim, Seyoon. *The Origin of Paul's Gospel*. WUNT 2.4. Tübingen: J.C.B. Mohr (Paul Siebeck), 1981.

————. *Paul and the New Perspective: Second Thoughts on the Origin of Paul's Gospel*. Grand Rapids: Eerdmans 2002.

Kittel, Gerhard. *Die Judenfrage*, Stuttgart: Kohlhammer, 1933.

————. "Die Judenfrage im Lichte der Bibel." *Glaube und Volk* 2 (1933) 152–55.

————. "Neutestamentliche Gedanken zur Judenfrage." *Allgemeine evangelische-lutherische Kirchenzeitung* 66 (1933) 903–7.

Klaiber, Walter. *Justified before God: A Contemporary Theology*. Nashville: Abingdon, 2006.

Knox, Wilfred L. *St Paul and the Church of the Gentiles*. Cambridge: Cambridge University Press, 1939.

Koch, Dietrich-Alex. *Die Schrift als Zeuge des Evangeliums: Untersuchungen zur Verwendung und zum Verständnis der Schrift bei Paulus*. BHTh 69. Tübingen: J.C.B. Mohr (Paul Siebeck), 1986.

Köhs, Andreas, ed. *Händel: Ariodante (Piano Reduction)*. Basel: Bärenreiter, 2007.

Kraus, W. "Menandros 9." *Der Kleine Pauly* 3:1199–1202.

Kuhn, Thomas. *The Structure of Scientific Revolutions*. With an introductory essay of Ian Hacking. 4th ed. Chicago: University of Chicago Press, 2012.

Kühl, Ernst. *Der Brief des Paulus an die Römer*. Leipzig: Quelle & Meyer, 1913.

Lake, Kirsopp. "Your Own Poets." In *The Beginnings of Christianity, Part I: The Acts of the Apostles*, edited by F. J. Foakes Jackson and Kirsopp Lake, Vol. V (Additional Notes to the Commentary), edited by Kirsopp Lake and Henry J Cadbury, 246–51. London: Macmillan, 1933.

Lambert, Frank. *"Pedlar in Divinity": George Whitefield and the Transatlantic Revivals 1737–1770*. Princeton: NJ: Princeton University Press, 1994.

Lampe, Peter. *Die stadtrömischen Christen in den ersten beiden Jahrhunderten: Untersuchungen zur Sozialgeschichte*. WUNT 2.18. Tübingen: J.C.B. Mohr (Paul Siebeck), 1987.

Lang, Friedrich. *Die Briefe an die Korinther* NTD 7. Göttingen: Vandenhoeck & Ruprecht, 1986.

Lautenschlager, Markus. "Εἴτε γρηγορῶμεν εἴτε καθεύδωμεν: Zum Verhältnis von Heiligung und Heil." *Zeitschrift für die neutestamentliche Wissenschaft* 81 (1990) 39–59.

Leaver, Robin A. *Bachs theologische Bibliothek; eine kritische Bibliographie/Bach's Theological Library: A Critical Bibliography*. Neuhausen-Stuttgart: Hänssler-Verlag, 1983.

————. "Music and Lutheranism." In *The Cambridge Companion to Bach*, edited by John Butt, 35–45. Cambridge: Cambridge University Press, 1997.

Lehmann, Karl. "Er wurde für uns gekreuzigt." *Theologische Quartalschrift* 162 (1982) 298–317.

Lévinas, Emmanuel. "La trace de l'autre." In *En découvrant l'existence avec Husserl et Heidegger*, 261–82. Paris: Libraire philosophique J. Vrin, 2001.

———. "The Trace of the Other." In *Deconstruction in Context: Literature and Philosophy*, edited by Mark C. Taylor, 345–59. Chicago: University of Chicago Press, 1986.

Levine, Amy-Jill. "Second-Temple Judaism, Jesus, and Women: Yeast of Eden." In *A Feminist Companion to the Hebrew Bible in the New Testament*, edited by A. Brenner, 302–31. Sheffield, UK: Sheffield Academic, 1996.

Lewis, C. S. "Nice People or New Men." In *Mere Christianity*, 172–80. London: Collins, 1955.

Lietzmann, Hans. *An die Römer*. HzNT 8. Tübingen: J.C.B. Mohr (Paul Siebeck), 1971.

Lightfoot, J. B. *St. Paul's Epistle to the Colossians and Philemon*. 1875. Reprint, Peabody, MA: Hendrickson, 1993.

———. *St. Paul's Epistle to the Philippians*. 1868. Reprint, Peabody, MA: Hendrickson, 1993.

Loader, William. "Reading Romans 1 on Homosexuality in the Light of Biblical/Jewish and Greco-Roman Perspectives of Its Time." *Zeitschrift für die neutestamentliche Wissenschaft* 108.1 (2017) 119–49.

Lohse, Eduard. *Colossians and Philemon*. Translated by William R. Poehlmann and Robert J. Karris. Hermeneia. Philadelphia: Fortress, 1971.

Loy, David W. "Hegel's Critique of Greek Ethical Life." *Hegel Bulletin* 42.2 (2021) 157–79.

Luke, David, ed. and trans. *Goethe, Faust Part One*. World Classics. 1987. Reprint, Oxford: Oxford University Press, 1998.

———, ed. and trans. *Goethe, Faust Part Two*. World Classics. 1994. Reprint, Oxford: Oxford University Press, 1998.

Luther, Martin. "The Bondage of the Will." Translated by Philip S. Watson in collaboration with Bemjamin Drewery. *Luther's Works, Volume 33: Career of the Reformer III*, 3-295. Philadelphia: Fortress, 1972.

———. "Confession concerning Christ's Supper." Translated by Robert H Fischer. *Luther's Works, Volume 37: Word and Sacrament III*, 151-372. Philadelphia: Fortress, 1961.

———. "The Freedom of a Christian." Translated by W.A. Lambert. Revised by Harold J Grimm. *Luther's Works, Volume 31: Career of the Reformer I*, 327-77. Philadelphia: Fortress, 1957.

———. "Instructions for the Visitors of Parish Pastors in Electoral Saxony." Translated by Conrad Bergendoff. *Luther's Works, Volume 40: Church and Ministry II*, 263-320. Philadelphia: Fortress, 1958.

———. "Prefaces to the New Testament." Translated by Charles M. Jacobs and E. Theodore Bachmann. *Luther's Works, Volume 35: Word and Sacrament I*, 355-411. Philadelphia: Fortress, 1960.

———. "Temporal Authority: To what extent it should be obeyed." Translated by J.J. Schindel and Walther I. Brandt. *Luther's Works, Volume 45: Christian in Society II*, 75-129. Philadelphia: Fortress, 1962.

Luz, Ulrich. *Das Geschichtsverständnis des Paulus*. BEvTh 49. Munich: Kaiser, 1968.

McDermott, John M. "Ratzinger on Faith and Reason." *Angelicum* 86.3 (2009) 565–88.

McIntyre, John. *St. Anselm and His Critics*. Edinburgh: Oliver and Boyd, 1954.

McNeill, John T., ed. *Calvin: Institutes of the Christian Religion*. LCC 20–21. 2 vols. Philadelphia: Westminster, 1960.

Macquarrie, John. *Jesus Christ in Modern Thought*. London: SCM, 1990.

Magee, Bryan. *Confessions of a Philosopher*. London: Phoenix, 1998.

———. *One in Twenty: A Study of Homosexuality in Men and Women*. 1966. Reprint, London: Sacker and Warburg, 1968.

Martin, George. *Verdi: His Music, Life and Times*. New York: Limelight, 1992.

Martin, Ralph P. *Colossians and Philemon*. NCB. London: Oliphants, 1978.

Matlock, R. Barry, "Almost Cultural Studies? Reflections on the 'New Perspective' on Paul." In *Biblical Studies/Cultural Studies: The Third Sheffield Colloquium*, edited by J. C. Exum and S. D. Moore, 433–59. JSOTSup 266. Sheffield, UK: Sheffield Academic Press, 1998.

Meade, David G. *Pseudonymity and Canon: An Investigation into the Relationship and Authority in Jewish and Earliest Christian Tradition*. Grand Rapids: Eerdmans, 1986.

Mellers, Wilfred. *Bach and the Dance of God*. London: Faber and Faber, 1980.

Merklein, Helmut. *Der erste Brief an die Korinther, Kapitel 1–4*, ÖTzNT 7.1. Gütersloh: Gütersloher Verlagshaus Gerd Mohn/Würzburg: Echter, 1992.

Meyer, Gabriele E., and Egon Voss, eds. *Dokumente und Texte zu "Tristan und Isolde."* Sämtliche Werke 27. Mainz: Schott, 2008.

Miller, A. V., ed. *Hegel's Phenomenology of Spirit with an Analysis of the Text and Foreword by J. N. Findlay*. Oxford: Oxford University Press, 1977.

Moltmann, Jürgen. *The Crucified God: The Cross of Christ as the Foundation and Criticism of Christian Theology*. Translated by R. A. Wilson and John Bowden. London: SCM, 1974.

Moo, Douglas J. *The Epistle to the Romans*. NICNT. Grand Rapids: Eerdmans, 1996.

Moore, Arthur L. *The Parousia in the New Testament*. NovTSup 13. Leiden: Brill, 1966.

Morgan, Theresa. *Being 'in Christ' in the Letters of Paul: Saved through Christ and in His Hands*. WUNT 449. Tübingen: Mohr Siebeck, 2020.

———. *Roman Faith and Christian Faith: Pistis and Fides in the Early Roman Empire and Early Churches*. Oxford: Oxford University Press, 2015.

Nectoux, Jean-Michel. *Gabriel Fauré: A Musical Life*. Translated by Roger Nichols. Cambridge: Cambridge University Press, 1991.

Neusner, Jacob. "Mr. Sanders' Pharisees and Mine: A Response to E. P. Sanders' *Jewish Law from Jesus to the Mishnah*." *Scottish Journal of Theology* 44 (1991) 73–95.

Nicole, Roger. "Arminianism." In *Baker's Dictionary of Theology*, edited by Everett F. Harrison, 64. Grand Rapids: Baker, 1960.

O'Donnell, James J. *Augustine: A New Biography*. New York: HarperCollins, 2005.

Olson, Robert C. *The Gospel as the Revelation of God's Righteousness: Paul's Use of Isaiah in Romans 1:1—3:26*. WUNT 2.428. Tübingen: Mohr Siebeck, 2016.

Orledge, Robert. *Gabriel Fauré*. London: Eulenburg, 1979.

Packer, J. I. *Knowing God*. London: Hodder & Stoughton, 1973.

Pauck, Wilhelm, ed. *Martin Luther: Lectures on Romans*. LCC 15. Philadelphia: Westminster, 1961.

Pearson, Birger A. "1 Thessalonians 2:13–16: A Deutero-Pauline Interpolation." *Harvard Theological Review* 64 (1971) 79–94.

Pedersen, Johs. *Israel: Its Life and Culture, I-II*. Translated by Johs. Pedersen, Aslaug Møller, and H. Stewart Maclaren. Reprint, London: Cumberlege, 1946.

Philippi, Friedrich Adolph. *Commentar über den Brief Pauli an die Römer*. 2nd ed. Frankfurt am Main: Heyder & Zimmer, 1856.

Piper, John. *The Justification of God: An Exegetical and Theological Study of Romans 9:1–23*. Grand Rapids: Baker, 1983.

Pollock, John. *George Whitefield and the Great Awakening*. Tring, UK: Lion, 1972.

Porter, J. R. "The Case of Gerhard Kittel." *Theology* 50 (1947) 401–6.

Potter, Harry. *Hanging in Judgment: Religion and the Death Penalty in England*. London: SCM, 1993.

Pretsell, D. O., ed. *The Correspondence of Karl Heinrich Ulrichs, 1846–1894*. Cham, Switzerland: Palgrave Macmillan, 2020.

Rad, Gerhard von, Karl Georg Kuhn, Walter Gutbrod. "Ἰσραήλ κτλ." *TDNT* 3:356–91 (*ThWNT* 3:356–94).

Rajak, Tessa. "The Jewish Community and Its Boundaries." In *The Jews among Pagans and Christians in the Roman Empire*, edited by Judith Lieu, John North, and Tessa Rajak, 9–28. London: Routledge, 1992.

Ratzinger, Joseph. *Introduction to Christianity*. Translated by J. R. Foster. New York: Herder & Herder, 1969.

Ritschl, Albrecht. *The Christian Doctrine of Justification and Reconciliation [III]: The Positive Development of the Doctrine*. Translated by H. R. Macintosh and A. B. Macaulay. Reprint, Clifton, NJ: Reference Book, 1966.

———. *Die christliche Lehre von der Rechtfertigung und Versöhnung Band II: Der biblische Stoff der Lehre*. Bonn: Marcus, 1874.

Robinson, John A. T. *The Body: A Study in Pauline Theology*. Reprint, London: SCM, 1977.

Rose, Herbert J., and Jennifer R. March. "Agamemnon." *OCD*[3] 5–36.

Rowland, Christopher. "Eschatology." In *The Blackwell Encyclopedia of Modern Christian Thought*, edited by Alister E McGrath, 161–64. Oxford: Blackwell, 1995.

Ruether, Rosemary Radford, *Faith and Fratricide: The Theological Roots of Anti-Semitism*. New York: Seabury, 1974.

———. "The *Faith and Fratricide* Discussion: Old Problems and New Dimensions." In *Antisemitism and the Foundations of Christianity*, edited by A. T. Davies, 230–56. New York: Paulist, 1979.

Rüger, Hans Peter. "Aramäisch II." *TRE* 3:602–10.

Rupp, E. Gordon, and Philip S. Watson, eds. *Luther and Erasmus: Free Will and Salvation*. LCC 17. Philadelphia: Westminster, 1969.

Sabatier, A. *The Apostle Paul: A Sketch of the Development of His Doctrine*. Translated by A. M. Hellier; edited with an additional essay on the Pastoral Epistles by George G. Findlay. 4th ed. London: Hodder and Stoughton, 1899.

Sanders, E. P. *Paul and Palestinian Judaism: A Comparison of Patterns of Religion*. London: SCM, 1977.

Schiffman, Laurence H. *Who Was a Jew? Rabbinic and Halakhic Perspectives on the Jewish Christian Schism*. Hoboken, NJ: Ktav, 1985.

Schlatter, Adolf. *Gottes Gerechtigkeit: Ein Kommentar zum Römerbrief*. 5th ed. Stuttgart: Calwer, 1975.

Schlier, Heinrich. *Der Brief an die Galater*. KEK 7. 14th ed. Göttingen: Vandenhoeck & Ruprecht, 1971.

———. *Der Römerbrief*. HThKNT 6. 3rd ed. Freiburg: Herder, 1987.

Schmeller, Thomas. *Der zweite Brief an die Korinther (2Kor 1,1—7,4)*. Neukirchen-Vlyn: Neukirchener, 2010.

Schopenhauer, Arthur. *The World as Will and Representation*. 2 vols. Translated by E. F. J. Payne. Reprint, New York: Dover, 1966.

———. *Die Welt als Wille und Vorstellung*. 2 vols. ASSW 1–2. Darmstadt: Wissenschaftliche Buchgesellschaft, 2004.

Schrage, Wolfgang. *Der erste Brief an die Korinther*. KEK 7. 4 vols. Neukirchen-Vluyn: Neukirchener Verlag, 1991–2001.

———. *The Ethics of the New Testament*. Translated by David E. Green. Edinburgh: T. & T. Clark, 1988.

Schweitzer, Albert. *The Mysticism of Paul the Apostle*. Translated by William Montgomery. Preface by F. C. Burkitt. London: A. & C. Black, 1931.

Scott, James M. *Adoption as Sons of God: An Exegetical Investigation into the Background of ΥΙΟΘΕΣΙΑ in the Pauline Corpus*. WUNT 2.48. Tübingen: J.C.B. Mohr (Paul Siebeck), 1992.

Sellin, Gerhard. "Mythologeme und mythische Züge in der paulinischen Theologie." In *Mythos und Rationalität*, edited by Hans Heinrich Schmid, 209–23. Gütersloh: Gütersloher Verlagshaus Gerd Mohn, 1988.

Steele, David N., and Curtis C. Thomas. *Romans: An Interpretative Outline*. Phillipsburg, NJ: Presbyterian and Reformed, 1963.

Stendahl, Krister. "The Apostle Paul and the Introspective Conscience of the West." *Harvard Theological Review* 56 (1963) 199–215.

———. "Biblical Theology, Contemporary." In *IDB* 1:418–32.

———. *Paul among Jews and Gentiles and Other Essays*. London: SCM, 1976.

———. "Paulus och Samvetet." *Svensk Exegetisk Årsbok* 25 (1960) 62–77.

Stone, John. "Ultimate Beliefs." In *The Mozart Compendium*, edited by H. C. Robbins Landon, 146–47. London: Thames and Hudson, 1990.

Stonehouse, N. B. *Paul before the Areopagus and Other New Testament Studies*. London: Tyndale, 1957.

Stott, John. *The Authority and Relevance of the Bible in the Modern World*. Sydney: Bible Society of Australia, 1979.

———. *Issues facing Christians Today*. Basingstoke, UK: Marshall, Morgan & Scott, 1984.

———. *Romans: God's Good News for the World*. Leicester, UK: IVP, 1994.

Studer, Basil. *Trinity and Incarnation: The Faith of the Early Church*. Translated by Matthias Westerhoff; edited by Andrew Louth. Edinburgh: T. & T. Clark, 1993.

Stuhlmacher, Peter. *Biblical Theology of the New Testament*. Translated and edited by Daniel P. Bailey with the collaboration of Jostein Ådna. Grand Rapids: Eerdmans, 2018.

———. *Der Brief an Philemon*. EKK 18. 3rd ed. Neukirchen-Vluyn: Neukirchener, 1989.

———. "The Hermeneutical Significance of 1 Cor 2:6–16." In *Tradition and Interpretation in the New Testament: Essays in Honor of E. Earle Ellis*, edited by Gerald Hawthorne and Otto Betz, 328–47. Grand Rapids: Eerdmans, 1987.

———. "Zur neueren Exegese von Röm 3,24–26." In *Versöhnung, Gesetz und Gerechtigkeit: Aufsätze zur biblischen Theologie*, 117–35. Göttingen: Vandenhoeck & Ruprecht, 1981.

Tappert, Theodore G., ed. *The Book of Concord: The Confessions of the Evangelical Lutheran Church*. Philadelphia: Fortress, 1959.

———. ed. *Luther's Letters of Spiritual Counsel*. LCC 18. London: SCM, 1955.

Thiselton, Anthony C. *The First Epistle to the Corinthians*. NIGTC. Grand Rapids: Eerdmans, 2000.

———. "The Logical Role of the Liar Paradox in Titus 1:12, 13: A Dissent from the Commentaries in the Light of Philosophical and Logical Analysis." *Biblical Interpretation* 2.2 (1994) 207–23.

Thomasius, Gottfried. *Christi Person und Werk: Darstellung der evangelisch-lutherischen Dogmatik vom Mittelpunkt der Christologie aus*. 3 vols. Erlangen, 1852–56.

Thompson, Michael. *Clothed with Christ: The Example and Teaching of Jesus in Romans 12.1—15.13*. JSNTSup 59. Sheffield, UK: Sheffield Academic Press, 1991.

Thornton, L. S. *The Common Life in the Body of Christ*. 2nd ed. Westminster, UK: Dacre, 1944.

Traill, A. "Menander's 'Thais' and the Roman Poets." *Phoenix* 55 (2001) 284–303.

Twelftree, Graham. *Paul and the Miraculous: A Historical Reconstruction*. Grand Rapids: Baker, 2013.

Unger, Melvin P. *Handbook to Bach's Sacred Cantata Texts: An Interlinear Translations with Reference Guide to Biblical Quotations and Allusions*. Lanham, MD: Scarecrow, 1996.

Unnik, W. C. van. "Tarsus or Jerusalem: The City of Paul's Youth." In *Sparsa Collecta: The Collected Essays of W. C. van Unnik (Part One)*, 259–320. NovTSup 29. Leiden: Brill, 1973.

Valantasis, Richard. *The Gospel of Thomas*. New Testament Readings. London: Routledge, 1997.

Wallace, P. J. "Hodge, Charles." In *Biographical Dictionary of Evangelicals*, edited by Timothy Larson, 303–7. Leicester, UK: IVP, 2003.

Wanamaker, Charles A. "Philippians 2.6–11: Son of God or Adamic Christology?" *New Testament Studies* 33 (1987) 179–93.

Ward, Keith. *Holding Fast to God: A Reply to Don Cupitt*. London: SPCK, 1982.

Wasserman, Emma. "The Death of the Soul in Romans 7: Revisiting Paul's Anthropology in Light of Hellenistic Moral Psychology." *Journal of Biblical Literature* 126 (2007) 793–816.

Wedderburn, A. J. M. *Beyond Resurrection*. London: SCM, 1999.

Weiß, Bernhard. *Der Brief an die Römer*. KEK. 9th ed. Göttingen: Vandenhoeck & Ruprecht, 1899.

Weiß, Johannes. *Der erste Korintherbrief*. KEK 5. Reprint, Göttingen: Vandenhoeck & Ruprecht, 1977.

———. *Die Predigt Jesu von Reiche Gottes*. Göttingen: Vandenhoeck & Ruprecht, 1892.

———. *Jesus' Proclamation of the Kingdom of God*. Edited with an Introduction by Richard H. Hiers and David L. Holland. London: SCM, 1971.

West, Stephanie. "*Joseph and Asenath*: A Neglected Greek Romance." *Classical Quarterly* 24 (1974) 70–81.

Westphal, Kenneth R. "Hegel's Critique of Kant's Moral World View." *Philosophical Topics* 19.2 (1991) 133–76.

Wilckens, Ulrich. *Der Brief an die Römer*. EKK 6. 3 vols. Neukirchen-Vluyn: Neukirchener, 1978–82.

Williams, Bernard. "The Makropulos Case: Reflections on the Tedium of Immortality." In *Problems of the Self*, 82–100. Cambridge: Cambridge University Press, 1973.

Witherington, Ben. *Women in the Ministry of Jesus: A Study of Jesus' Attitudes to Women and their Roles as Reflected in His Earthly Life*. Cambridge: Cambridge University Press, 1984.

Wolff, Christoph. *Johann Sebastian Bach: The Learned Musician*. Oxford: Oxford University Press, 2001.

Wolter, Michael. *Der Brief an die Römer*. EKK 3. 2 vols. Neukirchen-Vluyn: Neukirchener, 2014–18.

———. *Paul: An Outline of His Theology*. Translated by Robert L. Brawley. Waco, TX. Baylor University Press, 2015.

Wrede, William, "Paulus." In *Das Paulusbild in der neueren deutschen Forschung*, edited by Karl Heinrich Rengstorf, 1–97. WdF 24. Darmstadt: Wissenschaftliche Buchgesellschaft, 1982.

Wright, N. T. "Jesus Christ Is Lord: Philippians 2.5–11." In *The Climax of the Covenant: Christ and the Law in Pauline Theology*, 56–98. Edinburgh: T. & T. Clark, 1991.

Yates, T. E. "Taylor, J. H." In *Biographical Dictionary of Evangelicals*, edited by Timothy Larsen, 657–60. Leicester, UK: IVP, 2003.

Zeki, Semir. *Splendors and Miseries of the Brain: Love, Creativity, and the Quest for Human Happiness*. Oxford: Wiley-Blackwell, 2009.

Ziesler, John. *Pauline Christianity*. OBS. Oxford: Oxford University Press, 1990.